The Nine Lives of Florida's Famous Key Marco Cat

UNIVERSITY PRESS OF FLORIDA

Florida A&M University, Tallahassee
Florida Atlantic University, Boca Raton
Florida Gulf Coast University, Ft. Myers
Florida International University, Miami
Florida State University, Tallahassee
New College of Florida, Sarasota
University of Central Florida, Orlando
University of Florida, Gainesville
University of North Florida, Jacksonville
University of South Florida, Tampa
University of West Florida, Pensacola

University Press of Florida
Gainesville
Tallahassee
Tampa
Boca Raton
Pensacola
Orlando
Miami
Jacksonville
Ft. Myers
Sarasota

The Nine Lives *of* Florida's Famous Key Marco Cat

AUSTIN J. BELL

26 25 24 23 22 21 6 5 4 3 2 1

Library of Congress Cataloging-in-Publication Data
Names: Bell, Austin J., author.
Title: The nine lives of Florida's famous Key Marco cat / by Austin J. Bell.
Description: Gainesville : University Press of Florida, 2021. | Includes bibliographical references and index. | Summary: "The story of an iconic artifact that has prevailed over impossibly long odds, this book explores the deep past of the Key Marco Cat, fascinating readers with the miracle and beauty of this rare example of pre-Columbian art"—Provided by publisher.
Identifiers: LCCN 2021007310 (print) | LCCN 2021007311 (ebook) | ISBN 9780813066998 (cloth) | ISBN 9780813072005 (epub)
Subjects: LCSH: Indian art—Florida—Marco Island (Island) | Figurines—Florida—Marco Island (Island)—History. | Cats in art. | Indians of North America—Florida—Marco Island (Island)—Antiquities. | Marco Island (Fla. : Island)—Antiquities | Marco Island Historical Society
Classification: LCC E98.A7 B45 2021 (print) | LCC E98.A7 (ebook) | DDC 704.9/432—dc23
LC record available at https://lccn.loc.gov/2021007310
LC ebook record available at https://lccn.loc.gov/2021007311

The University Press of Florida is the scholarly publishing agency for the State University System of Florida, comprising Florida A&M University, Florida Atlantic University, Florida Gulf Coast University, Florida International University, Florida State University, New College of Florida, University of Central Florida, University of Florida, University of North Florida, University of South Florida, and University of West Florida.

University Press of Florida
2046 NE Waldo Road
Suite 2100
Gainesville, FL 32609
http://upress.ufl.edu

for Florida

for Muspa

for Chloe

Contents

PREFACE: THAT DARN CAT ix
LIST OF ABBREVIATIONS xi

Introduction 1
1. Nature Made 9
2. Springing to Life 25
3. A Life with Purpose 42
4. Moment of Truth 59
5. Four Hundred Years of Solitude 77
6. Born Anew 91
7. Finding a Forever Home 112
8. Window to the World 133
9. National Treasure 158

ACKNOWLEDGMENTS 181
NOTES 185
BIBLIOGRAPHY 215
INDEX 229

Preface

That Darn Cat

The Key Marco Cat changed my life. No, I am not peddling pet products, nor am I introducing a 12-step program to beating cat meme addiction. That is simply the honest conclusion I have reached after spending the past eight years admiring, pursuing, studying, and writing about the Cat, a priceless archaeological wonder in the Smithsonian Institution's anthropology collections. While writing this book, I have also come to the realization that I am far from alone in my sentiment.

It has been one of the great joys of my life to be drawn into the orbit of the Key Marco Cat. The diminutive artifact, a six-inch-tall wooden carving, at times seems to have the gravitational pull of a celestial body. It was recovered from a waterlogged archaeological site on what is now Marco Island, Florida, in 1896, and has since ascended to pop-culture-icon status. The circumstances that led me to the Cat (because cats do not come to you) sometimes seem too convenient to be coincidental, too serendipitous to be a result of chance.

Regrettably, it took me twenty-one years living in Florida to learn of the Cat, and only then because I was volunteering in the Anthropology Division at the Florida Museum of Natural History, where a substantial portion of the Key Marco collection is housed. In 2009, after my volunteer gig had turned into a part-time job, I was asked by Elise LeCompte, William Marquardt, and Karen Walker to conduct an inventory of that very collection. At the time, all I knew was that the collection was incredibly fragile, important, and "cool," and I was humbled to be entrusted with the task.

Little did I know that while I was carefully examining each of the hundreds of items in the collection, construction was already under way on the Marco Island Historical Museum (MIHM), a new facility just three miles from the site where the objects originated. Four years, three internships, one master's degree, and a few gray hairs later, I was asked to be the curator of collections for the Marco Island Historical Society (MIHS), where I would spend the better part of the next decade in pursuit of the Cat. The Cat, it seemed, was one of the primary reasons for building a museum on Marco Island, in hopes of someday luring it "home" on loan from the Smithsonian. A form of museum "catnip," if you will.

In December 2018, after opening four new permanent exhibitions, raising hundreds of thousands of dollars, and completely overhauling the museum's collections and facilities, we watched the Cat—all seven ounces of it—unceremoniously settle into its new digs, pretending not to care (again, as cats do). It was the culmination of a twenty-five-year dream shared by the MIHS and Collier County Museums and, for me, the cherry on top of the already fulfilling experience of helping to transform what was once a largely empty museum into a community staple and popular tourist destination.

Still, the surreal experience of having the Cat on exhibit at the MIHM didn't fully sink in until a few months later, when I discovered that my nine-year-old nephew, Keaton Thimmer of Sebastian, Florida, had recently learned about it in his fourth-grade class. What a proud moment for him when he was able to casually tell his teacher that not only had he heard of the Cat, he had just seen it *in person* on a visit to Marco Island. Knowing that Florida public schools are now teaching kids like Keaton about Florida's Native American history and heritage—at an age twelve years younger than I was when I first learned about it—brings with it the satisfaction of realizing that progress has been made toward educating new generations of Floridians about the diverse peoples who lived, worked, and played here before them. I am hopeful that trend will continue, for there is still plenty more work to be done.

In compiling this object biography, I wholeheartedly acknowledge my own deficiencies in interpreting the Cat's original purpose. This book is intended as a summation of the already numerous interpretations applied to it, including some of my own. I am hopeful that some of the speculative threads I have laid out in the pages of this book will be pulled upon by future researchers, reducing many pages of theory into concise and provable scientific facts. Perhaps this book might also offer a model by which to engage the public with material culture studies. The reader will probably notice that I included quite a lot of information not pertaining *directly* to the Cat, but *indirectly* affecting its existence. Hopefully, after reading this book, the reader will be more well informed not just on the Cat, but also on the various contexts in which it partook.

Abbreviations

Many of the institutions mentioned frequently throughout this book have changed their names during the past century. Abbreviations, when employed, refer to the institutions below. Depending on the date referenced, the institution may have gone by a different name.

BAE	Bureau of Ethnology, Smithsonian Institution (1879–1894); Bureau of American Ethnology, Smithsonian Institution (1894–1970); Department of Anthropology, National Museum of Natural History, Washington, D.C. (1970–present)[1]
CCM	Collier County Museums, Naples, FL (1978–present)[2]
FLMNH	Florida State Museum (1917–1988); Florida Museum of Natural History, Gainesville, FL (1988–present)[3]
MIHM	Marco Island Historical Museum, Marco Island, FL (2010–present)[4]
MIHS	Collier County Historial Society, Marco Island Chapter (1994–1996); Marco Island Historical Society, Marco Island, FL (1996–present)[5]
NMAI	Museum of the American Indian, Heye Foundation (1916–1989); National Museum of the American Indian, Smithsonian Institution (1989–present)[6]
NMNH	United States National Museum, Smithsonian Institution (1846–1969);[7] National Museum of Natural History, Smithsonian Institution (1969–present)[8]
Penn Museum	Free Museum of Science and Art (1894–1913); the University Museum (1913–ca. 1990); University of Pennsylvania Museum of Archaeology and Anthropology (ca. 1990–2019); Penn Museum (2019–present)[9]

Introduction

A cat has nine lives. For three he plays,
for three he strays, and for the last three he stays.

–Proverb

Stuff Matters

A single object can change peoples' lives. In fact, *most* objects—at least those created by people, which archaeologists call artifacts—are made with the intent of *somehow* impacting the existence of *someone* at *some point*. Otherwise, why make it? An individual person might interact with dozens of objects over the regular course of an average day. Some objects are more impactful than others. Most objects, if intended to be impactful or useful, are not meant to be life changing. Fewer actually are.[1]

Utilitarian "objects," from toothbrushes to tourniquets, change lives every day. An object need not be large to be life changing. A syringe, depending on its contents, can save a human life just as quickly as it can end one. An ink pen might be responsible for the contents of a historical document. Objects can be significant not just for what they do, but also for what they represent. Yet, despite the seemingly significant roles such objects might play in the lives of people, they are largely disposable, due in part to their utilitarian nature, mass availability, and replaceability. They are largely disassociated from what artists or historians might consider a significant individual, moment, place, or movement, or lack affiliation with a communal history beyond the individual.

Rarer in human life are the objects that—regardless of their direct or indirect importance to an individual or group—are intentionally preserved beyond the extent of their normal life spans. Ironically, some objects that are unintentionally preserved by natural forces *become* worth preserving, particularly if enough time has elapsed since they were last seen by human eyes. This is frequently the case in archaeology, geology, and paleontology. In material culture terms, the very human practice of accumulation and preservation is called *collecting*, and has been conducted by individuals and groups for millennia.[2] During the past three centuries, specialized groups of people have coalesced around the idea of *professionally* collecting examples of particular object types for preservation. These groups—or now, more appropriately, organizations—are commonly regarded as *museums*.[3]

Not all objects are necessarily worth collecting, and not all objects worth collecting end up in museums. Many are held in private hands. Most of us have our own small collections of objects that we cherish or enjoy. Revered or sacred objects may be preserved or even actively used during religious ceremonies, such as in Roman Catholic churches or Native American communities. Just as not all revered or sacred objects are held by museums, not all objects held by museums are revered or sacred.

Whether collected in its natural condition, modified by humans, or synthesized by them, each object "lives a life" and has a different story to tell.[4] And in the end, each object will inevitably return to the earth, whether in a matter of seconds, perhaps destroyed by fire, or after many centuries, like the slow decomposition of synthetic plastic. Thus concludes the biography of an object that, even if an exact copy of a million other identical objects, will have lived a life all its own. Not every museum object's biography is inherently interesting or useful, but some objects, through sheer existence, tell a story far bigger than their own.

Rarer still than objects simply worth collecting and preserving are *iconic* objects—stars among the curated masses—that become so well known, so generally adulated, that they transcend their original times, places, and meanings to become, for all intents and purposes, entirely different objects. Examples of these types of objects include the Rosetta Stone at the British Museum and the *Mona Lisa* at the Louvre. Each is an individual item among millions at one of the world's most heavily trafficked museums. Each possesses an innate gravitas that attracts throngs to said museums. Objects like these can hold tremendous power, particularly over individuals, and can influence the world around them.

Extraordinarily powerful objects can even exert influence over entire institutions, often casting long shadows over the museums that house them. Their fame can be a boon to the less-heralded objects beside them through increased membership, notoriety, and visitation, which in turn can lead to greater funding for collections care initiatives. They can also prove problematic and destructive to a museum's reputation, such as with the contested Elgin marbles or Benin bronzes, which warrant demands of repatriation to their places of origin. Some have unexpected but relatable life histories, like the Hope diamond, which was *mailed* to the Smithsonian in a stamped envelope.[5] And some have a reach that extends far beyond the institution itself, such as the Shroud of Turin, a religious icon acknowledged by millions of Christian faithful as the cloth in which Jesus of Nazareth was buried. Whether they deliver exaltation, controversy, or both, these wildly different types of objects share a commonality in their statuses as "A-list" things—"celebrity objects," if you will.

In the realm of North American archaeology, few artifacts hold as much power and mystique as Florida's wooden "Key Marco Cat" statuette. Indeed, given the antiquity of North America's Native people, living on the continent for thousands of years prior to its invasion from Europe, and given that most material culture recovered from North American archaeological sites is refuse, relatively few such items of a truly transcendent nature have survived to present day. Sites are often more well known in America than the individual contents of their remains, and most materials recovered are derived from durable sources like clay, shell, and stone. When ephemeral or organic material is recovered from a Native American archaeological site, such as the Key Marco Cat, Northwest Coast basketry, or a dugout canoe washed up by a hurricane, the story often makes national news headlines.[6]

As museum objects go, few have had a more fascinating trajectory than Key Marco's Cat. The charismatic object, only six inches in height and likely carved from a native Florida hardwood, has resided at the Smithsonian's National Museum of Natural History (NMNH) for the past century. It is probably Florida's most famous archaeological artifact, excavated from a waterlogged site on what is now Marco Island, Florida, on March 5, 1896, by legendary anthropologist Frank Hamilton Cushing.[7] Since that fateful day, the object has taken on new meanings and new lives, while subtly revealing clues about its former ones. Partially for the sake of organizational humor, but truthfully because there are so many stories to tell, this book has been organized into nine different chapters, each representative of a different "life" in the feline object's history. The true number of "lives" lived is not necessarily so neatly fixed, nor so easily defined.

The continuum between this book's nine chapters is facilitated by a diverse sequence of human hands across history, from those that created the Cat, to those that uncovered it, to those which safeguard it today.[8] The mysteries surrounding it, the attention paid to it, and the seemingly endless coincidences and twists of fate that propelled it forward through time, far further than it was probably ever intended to go, have left me at times both awestruck and befuddled. This book tells the remarkable journey of a single life-changing object, an artifact made by one set of hands, passed through untold others, and gradually pushed so far forward through time that it has become an entirely different object altogether.

The Power of One

The Key Marco Cat has influenced countless human lives, from its unknown Glades or Calusa artisan to the members of the Pepper-Hearst Expedition who found it. As diverse as this centuries-old cast of characters may be, each has looked the Cat in its same two eyes. In fact, every person reading this book who has ever seen the Cat in person has that in common with everyone else who has ever seen it, from the Glades or Calusa villagers at Key Marco to the untold millions that saw it on exhibit at the NMNH. That is what is so special about seeing the "real thing" at museums: it is the chance to view with your own eyes what a Glades or Calusa person once saw with theirs.

The Cat is also a constant that "anchors" us in time. With so much uncertainty over the distant past, the Cat's "realness" is what tethers it to our reality, at least vaguely comprehensible if not fully understood. By tracking a single object across centuries, which this book attempts to do, we are in essence time-traveling tourists alongside it, peeking out at its surroundings and learning about the larger contexts of each before hurtling further forward through time.

The full story of the Cat continues right up to present day, with no shortage of adventure and intrigue since transitioning from an object of possible religious importance to one of "museum quality." For example, did you know that the Cat now belongs to the Smithsonian and not the Penn Museum only because a staff member, unaffiliated with the excavation, *really liked it*? Or, that it has traveled *12,000 miles* since it was recovered from Marco Island? Or, that it has been on exhibit for *seven decades*? The stories of what happens to artifacts after they are collected by museums are often just as fascinating as the original contexts from whence they came. The Cat, from its unique vantage point at the NMNH for more than century, also provides a unique window into the evolving histories of anthropology and museology.

Then and Now

The Key Marco Cat is an object that connects people through the ages, an "arc" between civilizations, so to speak, especially when you think about what has transpired since its creation. During the time that the Cat was preserved in the muck at Key Marco, it likely survived dozens of hurricanes, some of them major; a European invasion of the peninsula; politics and war between nations fighting for Florida; the birth of the United States of America, its growth, expansion, and the American Civil War; and for twenty-five years, American pioneer settlers living with it in their backyard without knowing it.

Since its excavation, the Cat has been on exhibit in Washington, D.C., during World War I; part of World War II; the Cuban Missile Crisis (during which Washington, D.C., was a likely target for Soviet nuclear warheads); and Apollo 11's voyage to the moon. Likely created in a time before European explorers first crossed the Atlantic Ocean, the Cat is now situated at a point in time where humanity's first voyage to the moon is "old news." The Cat sat in a drawer less than seven miles from Arlington, Virginia, on September 11, 2001, the day that American Airlines Flight 77 was intentionally flown into the Pentagon. Ten years later, a magnitude 5.8 earthquake struck the Piedmont region of Virginia, causing damage to the Museum Support Center in which the Key Marco Cat and millions of other priceless objects sat in storage.

During the 1918 flu pandemic, the Cat sat behind glass in a display case at the U.S. National Museum in Washington, D.C. At the time, famed anthropologist Aleš Hrdlička, now regarded as the "father of American physical anthropology," was coincidentally on Marco Island, following in Cushing's footsteps while noting the symptoms of the local ill.[9] In 2020, during the global coronavirus pandemic, the Cat sat in the dark behind glass while on loan to the Marco Island Historical Museum, which was forced to close to visitors for more than two months.[10] Of course, the Cat was likely carved before waves of disease were first introduced by Europeans to the Americas, decimating indigenous populations.

The object has seemingly achieved a level of immortality that would make Juan Ponce de León jealous, but with an obvious price: the loss of everything familiar. Its original surroundings have been stripped away by time, only some of its fellow artifacts remaining. Ponce de León is often associated with the myth of a "fountain of youth" in Florida. It seems that the Key Marco Cat might have bathed in it, for it outlasted not only the Spaniard, but also the Calusa that killed him. While Ponce de León and other Europeans were in search of gold and slaves, real treasures like the Cat were lying buried in sediment that Spanish explorers may well have seen or walked upon during their trips around the peninsula.

Today, the Key Marco Cat is practically a household name. Cushing's incredible discoveries sparked a century of archaeological discovery in Southwest Florida, which in turn led to both greater destruction (e.g., looting) and protection (e.g., preservation ordinances) of sites, as well as an overall increase in our collective knowledge and understanding of Florida's Native peoples. As famed American anthropologist Jesse Walter Fewkes put it, the Key Marco artifacts were "so radically different from any found elsewhere" that they "opened up a new chapter of archeological research in Florida."[11] That is still true today, as the finds have never been equaled, and the Key Marco Cat is now the unofficial ambassador for the entire collection, if not the state of Florida's archaeological history.

Transformational Powers

This book attempts to illustrate how a singular object, in this case the Key Marco Cat, can have its original intended power be transformed so significantly, yet simultaneously manage to transform so much—and so many—around it, simply by continuing to exist. Conversations between its admirers may always be changing with the times, but the Cat sits and listens to them all indiscriminately, inherently open to anything and everything. Through its material presence, it has stimulated countless discussions, ideas, stories, and thoughts over centuries, in both its original and current contexts. It is what some might call a *fetish*, "an object that, by virtue of its sheer material presence, affects the course of affairs."[12]

What became apparent in writing this book is that, even in discussing a single object, a multidisciplinary approach can bring to light new stories, new perspectives, and new ways of thinking about material culture. This microhistory of the Key Marco Cat—a "mixed method" research attempt—naturally incorporates archaeology, ethnography, and experimental anthropology, which all fall under the general umbrella of anthropology. But its story would be utterly incomplete without also incorporating art history, botany, biology, chemistry, cosmology, ecology, history, iconography, museology, philosophy, psychology, religion, and sociology—all of which are touched upon to varying degrees in this book.[13]

For an object believed by many to depict a being in a state of ritual transformation, the Cat has itself transformed, whether of its own agency, or of that applied to it by the numerous contexts in which it has found itself over the past millennium. As curator Joe D. Horse Capture puts it, "the physical tools and paraphernalia used in ceremonial life have emerged as objects of beauty. Whether their power and aesthetic quality derive from their physical properties or from their spiritual energy, such objects are imbued with their own stories. They are works of art, born from traditional life, that express the life-ways, philosophies, and worldviews of Native people."[14] The Cat is one of those objects. Its power continues to evolve and grow, now assuredly different than that of its Native maker's original intent, but still with stories to tell.

Figure 1. The Key Marco Cat. Catalog number A240915, Department of Anthropology, Smithsonian Institution.

1

Nature Made

Every object has an origin story. In museums—art museums in particular—the story of an object's life is generally referred to as its *provenance*. *Provenance* literally means "place of origin," but in museums it more commonly means "history of ownership," often researched through historical analysis.[1] Yet, very few museum object provenances start at the true beginning, where the raw materials that became the object first existed in their original forms. In order to best understand a museum object, one must begin there.

The Key Marco Cat, for all the fervor it now creates with its charismatic hand-carved face, began as a simple plant. The plant, likely a native species of tree or bush still found in Southwest Florida, grew slowly in its natural habitat for years or even decades, surviving constant environmental threats to its existence, including hurricanes, wildfires, and pests. At some point, whether through sheer coincidence or a deliberate search, a human being encountered this plant, or its remains, and decided that it would provide the perfect material from which to carve the now iconic figure.

The question of who exactly carved it, however, is largely unclear—and on numerous levels. Uncertainty surrounding its age, as well as a lack of documentation from the pre-Columbian Americas, make identifying an individual artist impossible. While the artist's European contemporaries were often credited individually in written records for their work, any knowledge of the Key Marco Cat's artist and his or her creations was likely transmitted verbally, until it was ultimately lost. The best attribution at this point is made to a larger cultural group, typically the Calusa of Southwest Florida. However, given the uncertainties over both the Cat's age and temporal distinctions between South Florida's Native cultural groups, even that designation is potentially problematic.[2]

This chapter explores the very first of the Key Marco Cat's "nine lives." From its patient emergence into Florida's pre-Columbian landscape, the

Cat's humble beginnings as a product of the natural environment eventually merged with the experienced hands of a skilled and motivated artist, setting the stage for its original intended use and sparking a fuse of intrigue that is still burning.

Flo-Grown

The Key Marco Cat's modern-day popularity is fueled in part by the many mysteries surrounding it. The object is an excellent secret keeper—at times frustratingly so—of even the simplest facts. One of the most fundamental known and observable facts about the object is that it was carved from a single piece of wood. Speculation over the species, however, continues to this day. It is also unknown if the plant was local to Marco Island, although it is generally assumed to at least be local to South Florida, as the verdant environment would have provided no shortage of options to the opportunistic harvester.

• • •

Marco Island is situated in the Gulf of Mexico, centered at N 25°56'13.5" and W 81°42'57", now part of Collier County, Florida. The region is considered subtropical, with defined dry and rainy seasons. Marco Island encompasses roughly 24 square miles, including 6 miles of beach and over 100 miles of modern waterways. It is part of what geologists consider the most morphologically diverse barrier-inlet system in the world. The island's unusual geological features, including aeolian (wind-generated) sand dunes soaring up to fifty-two feet—a mountain in South Florida—likely contributed to its attractiveness as one of the earliest known locations of long-term human settlement in South Florida.[3]

There are more than 300 native floral species growing wild on Marco Island. Botanists consider the island "unusual" in its plant diversity compared even to the nearby mainland. In its natural state, prior to its expansive development beginning in the 1960s, the island included seven primary types of habitats: mangrove swamps, saltwater marshes, freshwater marshes, pinelands, dense xeric scrub vegetation, tropical hammock, and unaltered shell mounds, as well as a dynamic sand beach. The modern-day vegetation of coastal Southwest Florida is assumed to have been in place for the past 5,000 years and therefore analogous to that encountered by the Calusa and their ancestors.[4]

Into the Woods

Wood was an important material to the person or people who created the Key Marco Cat. Likely an essential everyday material for all Southwest Florida people at the time, wood was also a popular medium of personal or societal expression. Wood, however, is generally underrepresented in the archaeological record due to its relatively rapid decomposition rate, particularly in South Florida's unforgiving climate. Ironically, if it were not for wood found in archaeological sites in South Florida, very little if anything would be known about its importance to Florida's pre-Columbian Native people.[5]

The most famous example of wood preservation in Florida comes from Key Marco, a spectacularly prolific waterlogged site on what is now Marco Island, excavated by Smithsonian anthropologist Frank Hamilton Cushing in 1896. The eponymous Key Marco Cat is so called because it was found at the site, just one of *hundreds* of ancient wooden artifacts preserved there in an oxygen-free environment. In reporting the finds, Cushing notes that "articles of wood far outnumbered all others" and attributes possible species identifications to several. Amongst his identifications are artifacts of buttonwood, cypress, ironwood, mangrove, and "spruce." His identification of spruce, a non-native tree, may be chalked up to improper nonlocal vernacular. All the wood and plant material recovered from the site is assumed to be indigenous to South Florida.[6]

At least two botanical studies of the Key Marco collection have been conducted during the past century.[7] Cypress and pine are the two most abundant genera of wood represented, both softwood conifers. Less prolific species described in artifacts at Key Marco include mangrove (whether black, red, or white is not denoted), buttonwood, gumbo-limbo, saffron plum, lignum vitae, mayten, stopper, black gum, Florida privet, and mahogany, all hardwood dicots. There are likely other presently unidentified plant species in the assemblage. Cushing also notes the presence of modified palmetto, the source of plant fiber netting found at the site.[8]

The thirteen species found at the Key Marco site generally align with those more thoroughly investigated at Pineland (a major Calusa site some fifty miles north in Lee County), which include cypress and pine in relative abundance, as well as black mangrove, red mangrove, gumbo-limbo, saltbush, wild lime, saffron plum, wax myrtle, wild coffee, and grape. Modified sea grape wood has not been identified at either site, but experimental artifact replication with shark-tooth tools demonstrates it as a possibility. Of the taxa described at Key Marco, all but one (lignum vitae) still occur naturally on Marco Island. Of the seven additional taxa described at Pineland (black mangrove, red mangrove, saltbush, wild lime, wax myrtle, wild coffee, and grape), all still grow wild on Marco Island, as does sea grape.[9]

The "ironwood" that Cushing describes is not found in either the Key Marco or Pineland assemblages. He uses the term interchangeably with *buttonwood* when describing timbers and pilings that he believed were "mooring posts" and part of "pile dwelling" structures, stating that "some of them were more than four inches in diameter, and were made of tough mangrove and buttonwood or ironwood." He also identifies a single-hole atlatl with a rabbit carving on one end as "ironwood," saying "it was made from fine, springy hard wood—like rose wood in appearance—probably the heart portion of the so-called ironwood of the region."[10] Florida's native black ironwood, or leadwood, has not been found in Southwest Florida archaeological contexts, but can grow a trunk between four and ten inches in diameter, making it another possible candidate for the Cat's source wood.[11]

Cushing describes the Cat as being "carved from an exceedingly hard knot, or gnarled block of fine, dark-brown wood." He similarly describes the wood of a shell tool handle from the same collection, calling its "hard, dark wood, like madeira [mahogany] in appearance," but stops short of providing an identification. Expedition artist Wells Moses Sawyer (1863–1960) supports Cushing's assertion about the Cat, calling it "very hard," but differing in his opinion about its coloration, calling it "light," revealing the inherent subjectivity of any analysis by coloration.[12] The object's hardness is thought to be a major contributor to its current state of preservation, which, in comparison to other objects from the same collection, is exceptional. The consensus of a hardwood likely rules out softer woods like cypress, of which many identified artifacts have since visibly deteriorated more significantly than the Cat.

Seeds of Hope, Seeds of Doubt

One of these twenty-two species of indigenous flora may well be the source of the wood used to carve the Key Marco Cat. Narrowing it down further, however, proves troublesome. In the case of Key Marco wood identifications performed at the FLMNH in 1988, small thin sections were taken from select artifacts—sections so small that one might hardly detect their absence.[13] This is a process that archaeologists and museum professionals consider *destructive analysis*, in which an object—or part of an object—is destroyed in order to gain new knowledge that could otherwise not be obtained. There is no guarantee that this would work on the Cat, though, as the formerly saturated object's cell walls might be compromised and therefore unidentifiable.[14] Given its fragility, rarity, and unusually high public profile, destructive analysis of the Cat at any level is unlikely, leaving more questions than answers about its floristic origins.

Assuming the Cat was carved from "head to toe" in parallel with its source branch or trunk, it might be possible for an expert to examine its cellular structure with a hand lens.[15] Until that happens, however, deductive reasoning using physical observations, comparative analyses, and experimental archaeology seem to be the only methods of further winnowing an identification. New methods of observation might include evaluating the Cat's coloration with a Munsell test, as has been performed on other wooden artifacts from Florida, or studying the Cat's density, particularly in comparison to other artifacts and equally sized wood samples of the species listed here.[16] Lignum vitae, for example, is so dense that it sinks when placed in water, as does South Florida's black ironwood, "the heaviest of all" native species and 30 percent heavier than water.[17]

Cushing speculated that the object was "either saturated with some kind of varnish, or more probably had been anointed with the fat of slain animals or victims." Either may have altered the original color or density of the wood, but likely contributed to the object's preservation. As Cushing reports, "it is still relatively heavier, harder, and less shrunken by drying, than any other specimen of like material in the collection." It should also be noted that the Cat likely underwent an undocumented treatment, possibly with preservative wax, in all likelihood making the object denser and heavier than it was in its found condition.[18]

While exceedingly rare, similar specimens suitable for comparative analysis *have* been found in Florida. Twelve of comparable dimensions and composition are known from Florida, eight of which are from South Florida—three alone from Key Marco. The Millar Figurine, a humanlike carving found near the shores of Lake Okeechobee, is thought to have been carved from lignum vitae, although other accounts identify the wood as black mangrove. The Millar figurine is depicted in a fashion similar to the Cat: a seated position with its hands resting on its knees. The famous Padgett Figurine, also from South Florida, is carved from pine roundwood and is similarly postured.[19] The geographical proximity of these sites to Key Marco brings to mind the possibility of a shared regional wisdom, harnessed and communicated across generations lived in South Florida. Perhaps it was common knowledge or practice that lignum vitae or other dense woods were used exclusively in the production of certain figures.

Experimental archaeology—the practice of experimenting, often through replication, "in order to provide data and insights that aid in the interpretation of the archaeological record"—might also offer clues to the Cat's secret identity.[20] Robin Brown has ably demonstrated the value in replicating shell and shark-tooth tool technology in his attempts to re-create artifacts similar to those found at Key Marco.[21] Brown's experimentation with woods such as cypress, basswood, gumbo-limbo, oak, hickory, and red mangrove offers valuable insight into the technology and skill required to create an artistic masterpiece such as the Key Marco Cat. Perhaps it is as simple as carving twenty-two replica Key Marco Cats out of the species listed here for direct comparison—although that is far easier said than done.

Of course, there is also the possibility that the wood used to carve the Cat is *not* amongst the twenty-two identified candidates, nor even indigenous to the region. For example, inkwood, a native species known for its density but not reported in any South Florida archaeological context, was found growing wild on Marco Island in 1966.[22] The prospect of imported wood, perhaps by long-distance trade or tribute, is tantalizingly posited at the Pineland site, where archaeologists have found possible evidence of spruce, a genus typically endemic to the Appalachian region. Perhaps Cushing's mention of "spruce" at Key Marco was, intentionally or not, correct after all. The notion that a known "special" wood, imported over a great distance, would be allocated toward the production of what may have been an item of spiritual significance seems reasonable. It is also possible that driftwood was the source of some carvings, as suggested by a figurine carved from non-native brazilwood found in northeastern Florida.[23]

In recent years, the Key Marco Cat has been prematurely, and perhaps erroneously, identified as buttonwood. This identification has not been verified but has spread rapidly through the proliferation of online digital media. Given that Cushing confidently identified several specimens as distinctly buttonwood, it is noteworthy that he did not even make the *suggestion* of such an identification regarding the Cat.[24]

For now, the Cat's wood type remains a mystery. Should a tiny piece of the object, perhaps from its base, ever be subjected to destructive analysis, a definitive identification might finally be made, also opening up the possibility for AMS radiocarbon dating, DNA sequencing, plant proteomics (the study of plant proteins), or strontium analysis, which could also potentially identify the wood's region of origin.[25]

The Archaic Ancestors

For as little as is known about the Cat's source wood, perhaps even less is known about the person or persons who transformed it into the object it is today. The Cat is most frequently associated with or attributed to the Calusa—a pre-Columbian Native American culture centered in what is now Southwest Florida. This attribution is far more tenuous than it appears on the surface, even if it is generally accepted by the public at face value. Just like the Cat's questionable identification as buttonwood, scratching at the surface of this question reveals more uncertainties than certainties.

To understand which Marco Island society is responsible for the production of the Key Marco Cat, one must first look beyond the Calusa in time to understand the local and regional contexts from which that culture emerged. There is archaeological evidence of people living on or near Marco Island for more than 5,000 years. The first humans to inhabit Florida more than 14,000 years ago (12,000 BCE) are known to archaeologists as *Paleoindians*, but there are less than 400 known Paleoindian sites in Florida, mostly in the northern half of the peninsula. There are three major Paleoindian sites within about 100 miles of Marco Island, all in sinkholes, but no known archaeological evidence of Paleoindians on Marco Island.[26]

Several archaeological sites on Marco Island and neighboring Horr's Island date to the ensuing Archaic Period. The term *Archaic* refers to Native American people who lived in North America after the Paleoindians, between roughly 7500 and 500 BCE. The Archaic Period began at the end of the Pleistocene, when climate changes contributed to the extinction of many animals, including megafauna, and brought wetter conditions to Florida. Rising sea levels dramatically reduced the peninsula's habitable surface area until about 3000 BCE, when South Florida's environmental conditions reached a relative stasis and began shaping the coastline, ecosystems, and natural processes known today.[27]

An Archaic village on Horr's Island reached its peak population between 2470 and 1615 BCE.[28] The site predates the known use of pottery in Florida by at least 500 years. Instead of pottery, the Archaic people on Horr's Island modified the shells of large lightning whelks to function as cooking and drinking vessels. A variety of other shell tools found at the site, crafted from the remains of robust marine bivalves and gastropods, offer some of the first evidence of a shell tool tradition that became essential to human life in the region for thousands of years. The evolution of these tools over time eventually played a role in the collection and initial shaping of the Cat's source wood.[29] Archaic sites on neighboring Marco Island contain traces of some of the oldest known fiber-tempered pottery in North America, dating to roughly 2000 BCE, or 500 years *after* the village at Horr's Island reached its peak population. Whether the Archaic people at Horr's Island and Marco Island are the direct ancestors of later cultural groups in the area—or are even related to each other—is unknown.[30]

The Glades and Caloosahatchee Cultures

The end of the Archaic Period is loosely defined by an increase in sedentism and, in South Florida, a transition from the use of fiber-tempered to sand-tempered pottery. People who lived on Marco Island after 500 BCE were part of a cultural area known to archaeologists as the "Glades" region, which is based largely on ceramic analysis. Marco Island lies within the northernmost boundary of the Glades region, just south of the Caloosahatchee region (map 1). The Caloosahatchee region is typically thought of as the heartland of the protohistoric Calusa. After 500 CE, Caloosahatchee pottery is mostly "plain" (undecorated) and increasingly crafted with clay commonly found near Lake Okeechobee.[31]

On Marco Island, however, much of the pottery after 500 CE is decorated with unique designs originating in the Glades region. Pottery types found in abundance on Marco Island, including Sanibel Incised, Key Largo Incised, Fort Drum Incised, and Gordon's Pass Incised, are generally found with less frequency at Caloosahatchee sites to the north. Glades Tooled is the only style of decorated pottery that occurs consistently in both Marco Island sites and known "Calusa" sites (e.g., Pineland). Aside from some early variations, it first appears in Caloosahatchee contexts after 1350 CE. After that date, Glades pottery begins to look much like Caloosahatchee pottery and is more widely distributed.[32]

Archaeologists believe that around 1350 CE, the increasingly powerful Calusa of the Caloosahatchee region may have absorbed, allied with, or entirely replaced the Glades people on what is now Marco Island. The Calusa expansion may have been in response to growing tensions with the Tocobaga to the north (of modern-day Tampa Bay), or in part influenced by environmental stressors, such as generally lower sea levels during a period of global cooling known as the Little Ice Age (1200–1700 CE). The Calusa may have united with—or perhaps coerced—their Glades neighbors to address these shared issues together.[33]

The Calusa exerted influence over all South Florida by the early 1500s.[34] Written records by Europeans describe a people led by "Carlos," an apparent mispronunciation of *Caalus*, and origin of the name "Calusa." The name of the

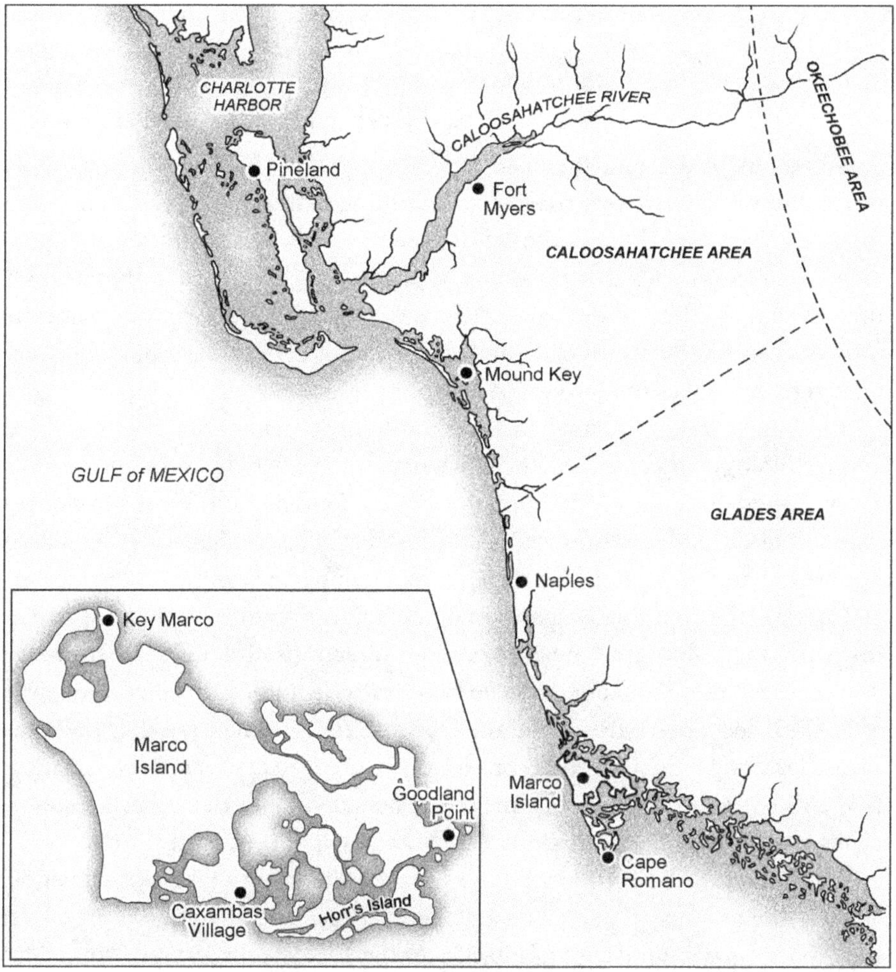

Map 1. Marco Island and its significant archaeological sites in relation to Southwest Florida's culture areas (boundaries approximated). Map by Merald Clark.

chief was attributed to his entire people, which according to the Spanish meant "fierce people" in the Calusa language. Thus, the people of Southwest Florida became known collectively as the Calusa, although it is unknown what they might have called themselves prior to European arrival, since their history was communicated orally rather than by the written word.[35] The Calusa capital was located at modern-day Mound Key in Estero Bay, about thirty miles north of Marco Island.[36] Many of the accounts written about in the ethnohistorical record occurred there.

The Calusa's prodigious prosperity—living sustainably in Southwest Florida without farming—is tied largely to their ingenious use of the area's abundant natural resources. The Calusa commonly ate land animals such as turtles and deer, but like their Archaic predecessors and Glades neighbors, their diet consisted mostly of fish and shellfish.[37] They likely kept small gardens of edible plants, but the Calusa were so effective at fishing that they simply had no need for large-scale agriculture. The leftover remains of these animals also provided the Calusa with raw materials to produce a sophisticated line of tools that served a variety of everyday purposes. Shell tools and ceramics are the most common varieties found in archaeological sites, but additional tools were crafted from bone, stone, wood, and plant fibers.[38]

The Calusa took advantage of their constantly regenerating source of food and technology for centuries. The efficiency of their fishing and hunting tools allowed them to dedicate less time to catching food and more time to art, religion, and leisure activities. This "comfortable" lifestyle led to an increased population and, in turn, the emergence of a complex society with distinct social classes. The continued expansion of the highly organized Calusa inevitably impacted their aboriginal neighbors in all directions. The Calusa became so powerful that they demanded tribute from Native American groups as far away as Lake Okeechobee, Miami, and the Florida Keys. For the Calusa, tribute was an "obligatory payment of goods or services in order to demonstrate allegiance" to their principal leader. Goods may have included food, rare objects, or even captive people, though the Calusa were not known to keep many slaves.[39]

Not limited to South Florida, the Calusa influenced other Native people as far away as Cape Canaveral—and likely exchanged materials far beyond the modern-day boundaries of Florida. Archaeologists discovered a fragment of galena (a mineral form of lead) dating to 1250 CE at Pineland. Sourced to southeastern Missouri, the galena traveled a distance of more than 1,000 miles to Southwest Florida.[40] Small amounts of pottery typical of Northwest and East Florida have been found on Marco Island, which means that the Glades and Calusa people there also participated in long-distance exchange.[41]

Spanish missionaries lived side by side with the Calusa during a failed mission attempt at Mound Key between 1567 CE and 1569 CE, producing some of the most valuable insights into Calusa lifestyles. Some of these records, including those by Father Juan Rogel, contribute the stories most frequently ascribed to the Key Marco artifacts, thus typically associating the Key Marco Cat with the Calusa.[42] Other records reference a Calusa town fitting the physical and geographical description of Marco Island: a place known as Muspa.[43]

Muspa

Early European maps and written accounts of a place called *Muspa* likely refer to the Marco Island area.[44] Consequently, Marco Island's longtime Glades residents are sometimes referred to as the "Muspa" or "Muspa Indians."[45] One of the earliest-known primary sources that mentions this place-name is the 1575 *Memoirs* of Hernando de Escalante Fontaneda, who was shipwrecked in 1549 (at the age of thirteen) off the coast of Florida. Fontaneda lived amongst the Calusa as their captive for seventeen years. According to Fontaneda, the town of Muspa was one of many under the Calusa domain, which he lists in geographic succession.[46]

The word continues to appear in Spanish documents as late as 1698, and many early maps of Florida place its location in the extreme southwestern portion of the peninsula.[47] The inaccuracies of these early maps make it difficult

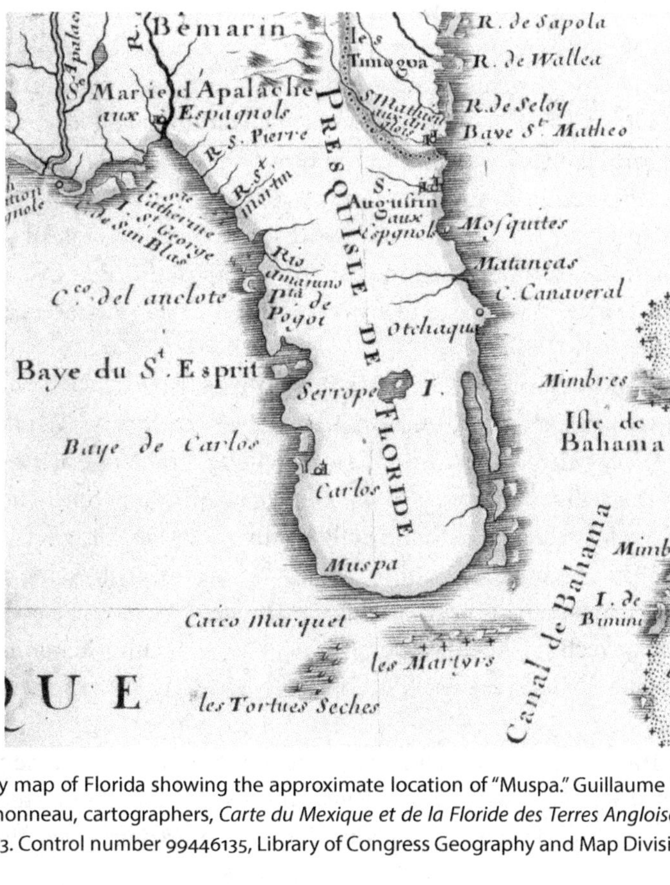

Map 2. Early map of Florida showing the approximate location of "Muspa." Guillaume De L'Isle and Charles Simonneau, cartographers, *Carte du Mexique et de la Floride des Terres Angloises et des Isles Antilles,* 1703. Control number 99446135, Library of Congress Geography and Map Division.

to know the exact location of Muspa, but historical records offer important clues. A 1575 report on the "geography and customs of Florida" by Juan López de Velasco, with modern-day interpretations in brackets, provides critical geographic details:

"From Carlos [Mound Key] to the point of Muspa, which would be at 25¾ degrees and would be about twelve or thirteen leagues [41 or 45 miles], the coast runs north-south and there are five creeks scattered along the coast that are outlets as it were of the ponds and swamps that are inland. . . . The aforesaid point of Muspa projects a shoal [Kice Island, Morgan Island, and Cape Romano] of a league [3.5 miles] toward the sea, between which and the mainland [Caxambas Pass] there is passage for the frigates. As distinguishing marks it has three little groves on top of it that are about half a league [1.7 miles] distant from one another."[48] The "three little groves" are likely the high sand dunes around Barfield Bay on Marco Island and Horr's Island, some of the tallest natural points in South Florida.

By the time Europeans arrived in Florida, Muspa fell under the domain of the Calusa.[49] Yet, its name, as interpreted by the Spanish, very well could have passed down through generations from the earlier Glades inhabitants of the area. Steve Howe, a friend of the Independent Traditional Seminole Nation of Florida, reports that the word means "mother" in the "old language" and apparently is still used in historical reference to all of South Florida and its "five tribes," including the Calusa.[50] Some have asserted that remnants of the Muspa lived in Charlotte Harbor as late the early 1900s, part of the so-called Spanish Indians whose ancestry instead likely consisted of Creek, Yamasee, and Spanish heritage.[51]

Dating the Key Marco artifacts has proven problematic, with postulations ranging anywhere between 50 CE and 1675 CE.[52] Interpretations of the Cat's specific age vary between institutions as well, the general range being 500–1500 CE. Given the regional identity of the Glades or Muspa people prior to 1350 CE, it may be incorrect to automatically assume the Cat is a strictly "Calusa" creation.[53] While Spanish accounts of Calusa behavior remain some of the best clues to its purpose, the object's seemingly de facto use as an icon of Calusa culture may be technically improper. It is possible that cultural memory of the Key Marco site at Muspa persisted in Calusa society long after its abandonment or destruction.

Since 2014 at the Marco Island Historical Museum, a permanent exhibition, *Paradise Found: 6,000 Years of People on Marco Island*, interprets the Key Marco Cat as created by either a Calusa or Muspa artisan, given the general uncertainty over its age. The museum also applies the blanket term *Muspa Indians* to the Native American populations on Marco Island between 500 BCE and 1350 CE.[54] Regardless of who is to credit, the Cat in all likelihood came from a place that at one time was known as Muspa, whether it was in active use or lying underground in Muspa territory. Perhaps it should be known as the Muspa Cat.

Key Marco

Muspa may have referred generally to the Marco Island area, or to a specific site, like Key Marco. Other major sites in the Marco Island area include Caxambas, Goodland Point, Horr's Island, Blue Hill, and Dismal Key.[55] The Key Marco site, on the north end of Marco Island, where the Gulf of Mexico mixes with the deepwater Marco River, is perhaps one of the most famous archaeological sites in North America. Roughly eighteen hectares—or forty-four acres—in size, the prominent shellwork site on the Southwest Florida coast was likely a location of major spiritual and strategic importance.[56] The site's fame is due not necessarily to its size or any distinct features, but to the unique finds Cushing made there in 1895 and 1896.

At Key Marco, hundreds of centuries-old articles of wood and plant fiber were preserved like new in a putrid but largely undisturbed 7,114-square-foot "water court."[57] Cushing dubbed this sodden section of Key Marco the "Court of Pile Dwellers," believing its occupants once built their homes along its shores and on top of its shell mounds and ridges.[58] As Aleš Hrdlička later put it, Key Marco was thought to be "undoubtedly an important and extensive Indian site, though as learned later on by no means the most important of the western coast, except for Cushing's discoveries."[59] The water court that Cushing excavated—a highly saturated low-lying area situated between shell "benches" and mounds—was a common feature of other sites in Southwest Florida and may have been used as a "fish trap" or "fish storage area."[60] No other water courts have yielded as prolific an archaeological assemblage as that unearthed at Key Marco.

Among the treasures Cushing unearthed were painted wooden face masks, carved animal figureheads, and other extraordinary works of art—the types of ephemeral materials so tragically underrepresented in the North American archaeological record. The Key Marco Cat was chief among these and has since been interpreted and exhibited in myriad ways. For many, the discovery of these types of artifacts meant that the site carried major political and religious

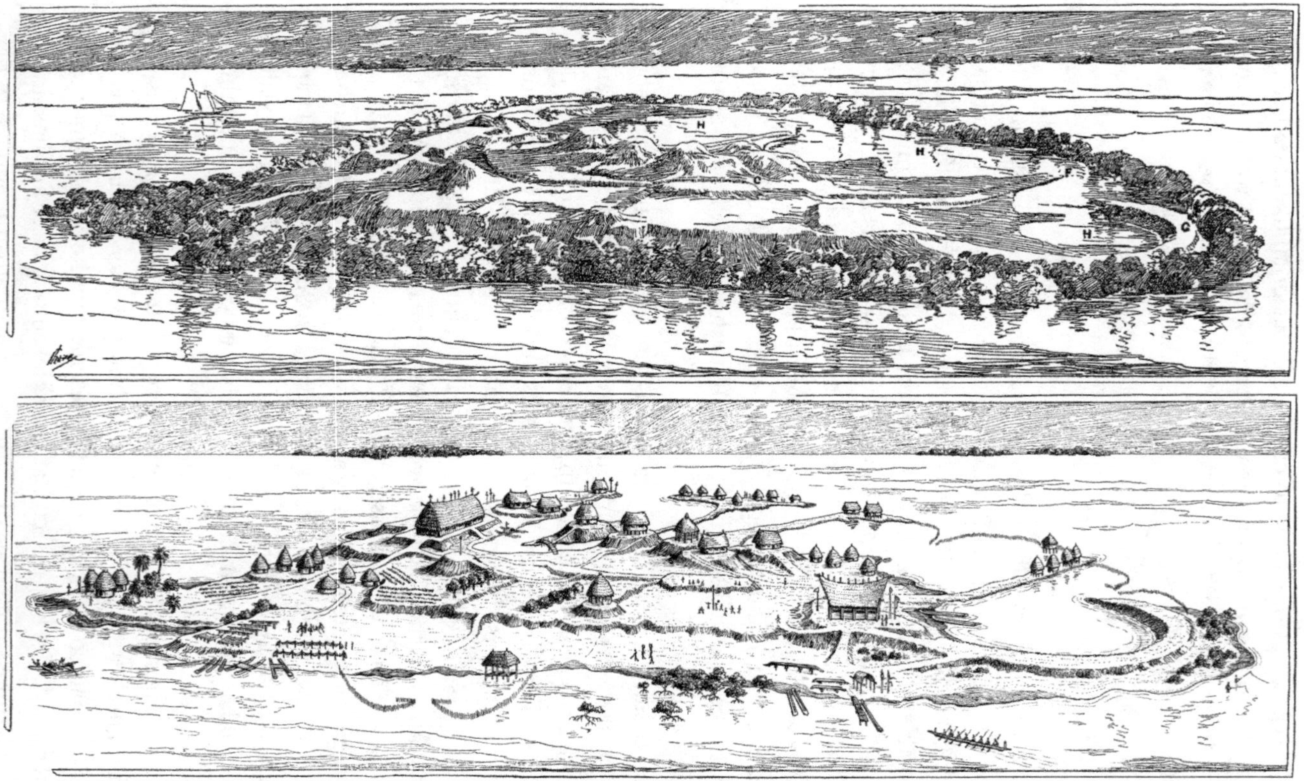

Figure 2. *Above:* View of the Key Marco site in 1896, with prominent features, mounds, and shellworks likely exaggerated for emphasis and modern structures removed. "Hand-built Island, or Shell City of the Ancient Sea Dwellers of Florida," after sketches by Frank Hamilton Cushing [artist unknown], *The Journal,* June 21, 1896. *Below:* Artist's rendering of the Key Marco site during its occupation. Artwork by Merald Clark.

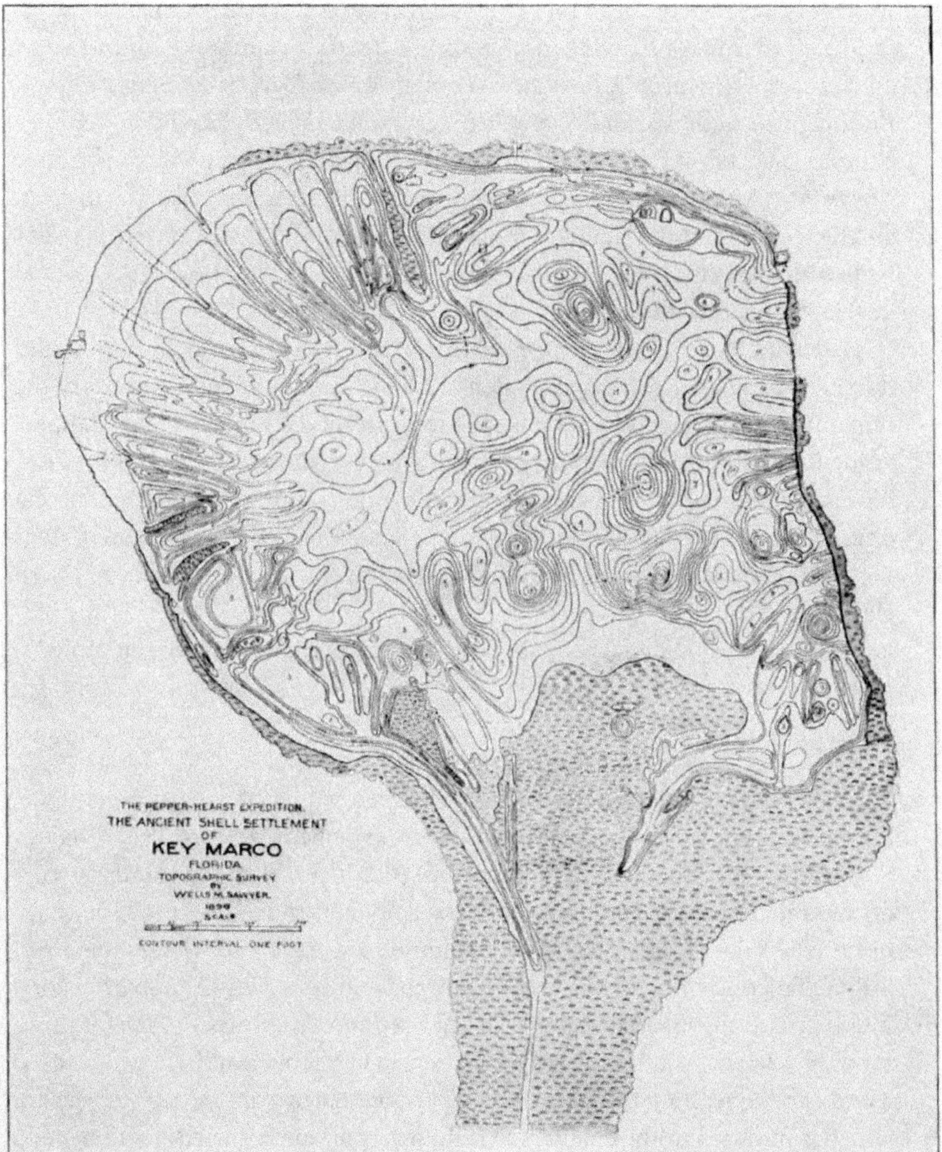

Map 3. Topographical map of the Key Marco site. This area is now known as "Old Marco" on Marco Island. The triangular *Court of the Pile Dwellers* is in the southwest portion of the site. Map by Wells Sawyer, 1896. By permission of the American Philosophical Society.

significance.[61] However, it is also possible that the Key Marco site was "just another site," as Hrdlička alludes, remarkable only in that it preserved what would ordinarily have been found at other sites all over the peninsula.

The entire site consisted of marine shell. All sixty-one mounds and 240,000 cubic meters of it would have been enough to fill the United States Capitol Building's rotunda six and one-half times. Archaeologist Randolph Widmer believes that the site was capable of supporting a village of up to 500 people, suggesting that it was divided into three unique districts: a ceremonial district, an elite residential district, and a non-elite residential district.[62] Strong site-wide empirical evidence is lacking, however, due largely to the area's continual development since the early 1900s.

Had the site remained as Cushing first found it in 1895, much more would doubtless be known about it via systematic excavations and further study of the remains in its courts and middens. The well-preserved Pineland Site Complex at the Randell Research center, thoroughly investigated by University of Florida archaeologists for the past three decades and counting, offers a tantalizing example of what might have been at Key Marco.[63] Today, the Key Marco site is flat across—most of it under buildings and private properties—bulldozed to an elevation of about seven feet above mean sea level.[64] It is still periodically surveyed by professional archaeologists during small-scale development projects.

Time Sensitive

The Key Marco Cat may have sprung to life in a matter of days or even hours, but its addition to the world was hardly an expedient process. It first had to grow from the earth, find the right person, and then rely on thousands of years of cultural knowledge and tradition, passed down through the ages to be channeled into a raw block of wood. The cultural landscape into which it emerged is simultaneously one of the great triumphs and tragedies in human history. The ancestral culture that created the Cat lived sustainably in the area for thousands of years without farming, only to be wiped out by invading Europeans in a matter of generations. That the Cat survived to have eight more lives, each of which is outlined in the chapters that follow, is to our knowledge and benefit. The Cat is an important testament to the remarkable artistry and complexity of South Florida's Native people.

2

Springing to Life

It takes just one look at the Key Marco Cat to tell that it was created with remarkable precision, thought, and attention to detail. It holds a charisma and sophistication that speaks to the talent of the person or people that created it. It has variously been described as "heroic," "masterly," "extraordinary," a "gem," "captivating," "exquisite," "magnificent," and "compelling."[1] It has graced the covers of books, magazines, and postage stamps, its status rising to that of a popular culture icon.[2] Only after a fortuitous encounter with humanity, would its life—at least as we now know it—truly begin, one that would see it harvested from the environment and set down a path of creation resulting in what it is today.

What's My Motivation?

The process by which the Key Marco Cat was produced was labor intensive and very well could have been a collaborative effort. For instance, one person with specialized knowledge or skills may have collected the wood, another may have prepared it, and another may have performed the detailed carving work. Or one person could have done it all. The Calusa were, after all, a stratified society that produced enough surplus to allow for leisure time, and likely with it, individual pursuits.[3] That person could have been local or perhaps even a traveling "professional" artisan.[4]

There is no way of knowing the circumstances under which the Key Marco Cat was made. One can, however, look to other cultures for comparison. In the 1500s, the Yucatan Maya commissioned specialists to produce wooden idols by way of a ritualized process, after which they received compensation.[5] Perhaps the person or people responsible for the Cat were somehow rewarded for their work. They might also or instead have been commanded, frightened, or threatened into doing so by a higher authority (socially, politically, or spiritually). Or perhaps they just felt inspired one day. While it is impossible to know who specifically made the Cat or their precise motivations, attempting to reconstruct the process by which it was made lends greater appreciation to the likely arduous efforts that resulted in its existence.

The Bare Necessities

In order to understand *how* the Cat was made, one must first examine the physical attributes that make up its material being. The Key Marco Cat, by my own estimation, stands just a whisker under 6 inches in height, with a maximum width of 1.75 inches and a depth at its base of 2.75 inches.[6] Its weight, at less than one-half pound (197.5 g), is approximately equivalent to that of a half-empty 12-ounce aluminum beverage can.[7] Given its size and material composition, I would describe the Cat as "heavier than it looks." Still, the frailty of the object is palpable during physical handling, its diminutive size belying its outsized personality and reputation.

Of all the known pre-Columbian wooden figurines from South Florida, the Key Marco Cat is by far the most finely polished, at least in its current condition. The figure is almost entirely symmetrical across a central vertical plane from head to base, with only minor inconsistencies that might be partially attributable to degradation. For instance, its proper left ear is not as round and is less substantial than its proper right ear. Condition reports partially chalk this malformity up to "loss," although photos showing the artifact in 1896 at the excavation site indicate that its ears were always somewhat asymmetrical.[8]

The figure is skillfully carved from a dense unknown wood and depicts a crouching or seated human-feline form.[9] It is considered anthropomorphic, meaning it exhibits both animal and "human attributes."[10] Cushing describes it as "a manlike being in the guise of a panther," likely in a general manner referencing all of humanity as opposed to gender.[11] While generally accepted as an anthropomorphic object, it might also or instead be zoomorphized, meaning it was made to "conceive of or symbolize or represent (a deity or supernatural being) as an animal" in "stylized" form.[12] Archaeologist Robert S. Carr explicitly describes the Cat as a "zoomorphic" representation of a panther.[13]

Its most conspicuous humanlike characteristic is the way it is crouching or seated, which, if applied literally, would be physically impossible for most

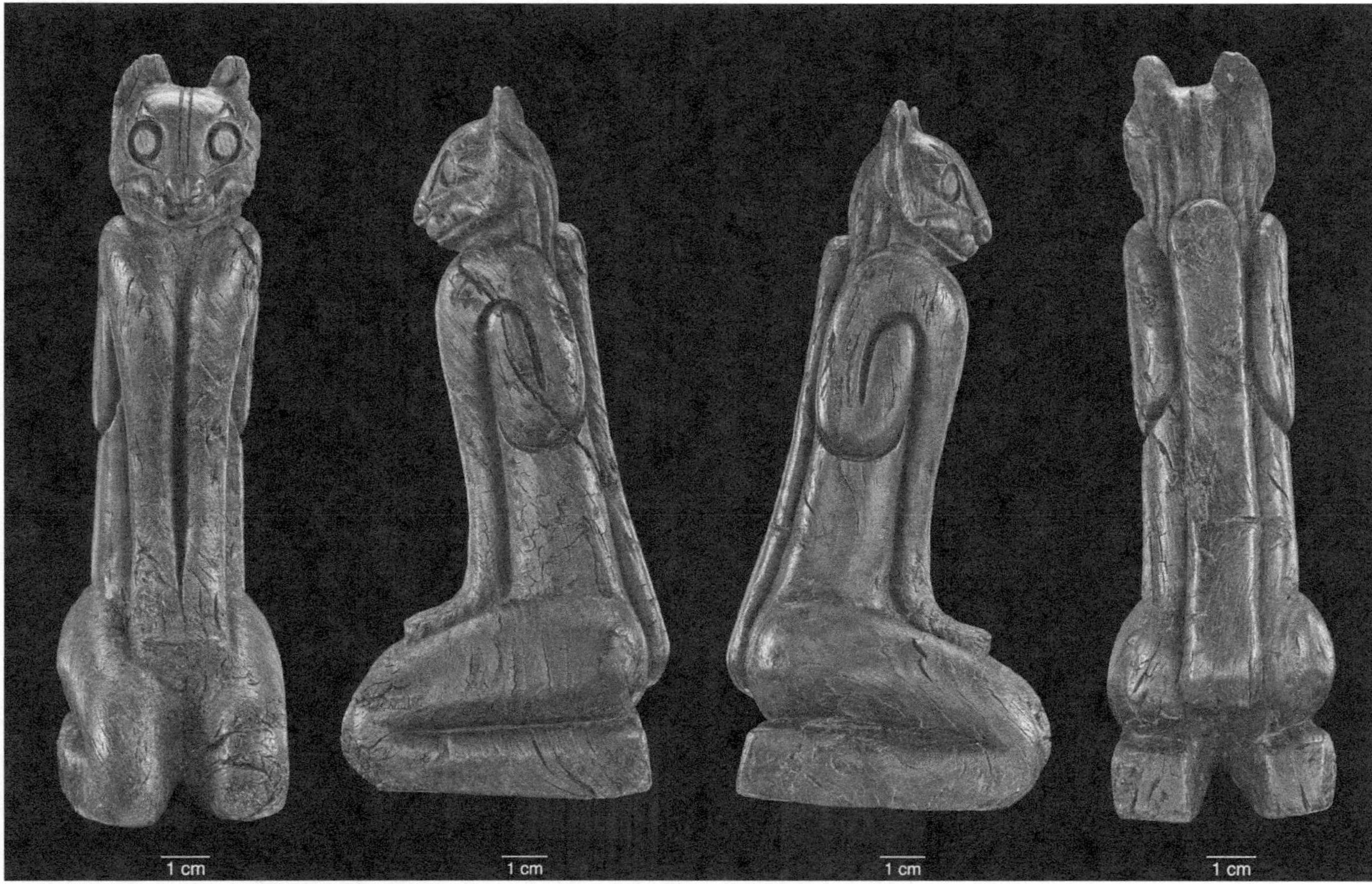

Figure 3. Catalog number A240915, Department of Anthropology, Smithsonian Institution. Photo by Lucia R. M. Martino.

Figure 4. One of the first photographs of the Key Marco Cat, probably taken in the field at Key Marco. Photo by Wells Sawyer, 1896. National Anthropological Archives, Smithsonian Institution (NPC096565.00).

Figure 5. Artist's rendering of (*left to right*) a Florida panther, the Key Marco Cat, and a costumed "panther man" at Key Marco. Artwork by Merald Clark.

cats. By contrast, the pose is very similar to the Virasana (or "Hero Pose"), an ancient Asana posture in yoga, which modern human beings regularly participate in for a variety of reasons.[14] Ironically, Cushing described the object as "heroic" in his preliminary report on Key Marco: "Although it is barely six inches in height, its dignity of pose may fairly be termed 'heroic,' and its conventional lines are to the last degree masterly."[15]

The crouching or seated position is not unique to the Key Marco Cat. At least four similarly postured wooden carvings—with forelimbs resting on the ground, lower limbs, or lap—have been discovered in Florida.[16] These carvings are now known as the Padgett Figurine, the Millar Figurine, the Mahoney Figurine, and the Rollins Figurine, or Rollins Cat.[17] The Rollins Cat's slender forelimbs are broken off and are suggestive of having once extended to the carving's base. Archaeologist Barbara A. Purdy notes that the Mahoney figurine in particular "is interesting because it is kneeling in a manner similar to the famous feline figure from Key Marco."[18] The seated posture evokes patience and reverence.

The human-feline figure is resting on its knees with its posterior seated directly on top of its lower limbs. Its forelimbs and paws are resting side by side in its lap, slightly to the inside of its upper thighs. Its upper forelimbs spiral back into abstractly depicted shoulders on either side, perhaps suggestive of musculature or scapulae. A long tail sweeps upward along the back of the figure. Its facial features are distinctly feline, with pointed ears on top of its head, two large circular forward-facing eyes, a clearly delineated muzzle and nose with nostrils, and realistic catlike mouth with a subtle curvature that creates an almost mischievous smile. Cushing describes the Cat's pupils as "concave . . . hollowed and polished," believing the artist carved them that way to "increase their gleam."[19] A "tri-forked design" around the eyes, perhaps indicating "stylized eyelashes," is thought by some to have a larger cultural significance.[20]

The figure's extremities also drew Cushing's attention: "While the head and features—ears, eyes, nostrils and mouth—are most realistically treated, it is observable that not only the legs and feet, but also even the paws, which rest so stoutly upon the thighs or knees of the sitting or squatting figure, are cutoff, unfinished; bereft, as it were, of their talons."[21] Cushing believed the squared-off appendages to be intentional and an important indicator of the object's spiritual importance. At least two incisions are visible on the top of each of the front paws, indicating three toes per paw—two less than a real panther.[22] Interestingly, no apparent effort was given to delineate toes on the rear paws, likely because they rest on the underside of the figure, where they were not meant to be seen. This lends credence to the idea that the Cat was constructed to rest upon something.

Making a Masterpiece

The Key Marco Cat's precise lines, smoothness, and symmetry are oft-heralded examples of the finest-known woodworking from its time and place. It is presented as a shining example of what can be achieved using the tool types found generally at pre-Columbian sites throughout South Florida, including Key Marco. The tool most cited as instrumental to its aesthetic is a hafted shark-tooth knife.[23] However, in all likelihood, a number of tools and materials were used in the production of the Key Marco Cat.

The Glades and Calusa cultures were prolific shell tool manufacturers, as evidenced by the abundant material remains found at Southwest Florida archaeological sites.[24] While wood was likely just as instrumental a material in daily life, if not more so, shell tools are durable, multifunctional, reusable, and survive far better in the archaeological record.[25] The relative absence of natural stone as a toolmaking resource in South Florida undoubtedly contributed to the continuous use of shell tools over thousands of years, a tradition established in the Archaic Period.[26]

Archaeologists believe that the Glades and Calusa cultures had special workshop sites where shell tool production was the primary focus.[27] Armed with a cadre of shell tools from one of these sites, the Cat's source wood collector might have set out in search of a particular type of wood, or just in search of wood generally. A modern shopper might mill about in the lumber section of the local hardware store, but to the Glades or Calusa wood collector, the "store" was an entire wilderness. If based out of Key Marco, he or she might have traveled by foot if the lumber sought was available on the island. Depending on local availability, however, they may have had to leave the island, very likely in a dugout canoe.

The collector might have been on the lookout for wood that required less investment of physical labor, such as from a naturally fallen or fragmented tree. More likely, however, "cost" was of little importance when it came to making the Cat. Perhaps the collector selected a living tree, maybe even one known locally for its association with panthers or a sacred landscape, to reinforce life or otherworldly qualities in the Cat. For example, the Iroquois carve false face masks from living trees, believing it reinforces life in the masks. Other cultures will only carve ceremonial objects from trees in certain areas.[28]

There is similar precedent for lumber selection in the ethnohistoric record. In the nearby Caribbean, the Taíno, as observed in 1498 by Spanish friar Ramón Pané, engaged in a *dialogue* with trees being considered for the production of wooden religious items called *zemis*. In fact, the tree itself, embodied by a spiritual entity, made the final decision, able to "articulate [its] desire to be carved" to the shaman, who would ask it: "'Tell me who you are, and what you are doing here, and what you wish from me, and why you have had me summoned. Tell me if you want to be cut down, or if you want to come with me, and how you want to be carried, for I will build you a house with land.' Then that tree or *zemi*, turned into an idol or devil, answers him, telling him the manner in which he wants it to be done. And he cuts it and fashions it in the manner he has been ordered."[29] In this case, the tree finds the collector rather than the collector finding the tree.

Once the wood source was decided, the collector most likely turned to a robust cutting-edged shell tool (sometimes also referred to as a pick or adze) to separate it from the source plant.[30] In the Glades region of Southwest Florida, the most common tool of this type was a large gastropod, typically either lightning whelk or, less commonly, horse conch. Either would have been hafted to wooden handles with lashing, "probably a rawhide thong or a stout cord."[31] A "stout cord" might have been comprised of animal sinew or strong plant fibers, such as those from the century plant, which could be manipulated into cord or rope.[32] Cushing found evidence of lashing at Key Marco, as well as wooden handle remnants still attached to shell tools, providing the still only known concrete evidence of how these composite tools were assembled and functioned.[33] Brown, in experimental archaeology on shell tools, reports "an ax made from a large whelk fitted with a 3-foot-long handle chopped wood surprisingly well."[34]

Archaeologist William H. Marquardt, in identifying fifty-two shell artifact types from Southwest Florida, speculates that a particular type of hafted cutting-edged tool, in which a portion of the shell's outer whorl has been removed, might have made for easier "chopping out a channel or groove, or in deepening a cut against a vertical plane."[35] This could well have been a method employed while collecting wood to carve the Cat. While impossible to know the original wood-harvesting context, an apparent plethora of choices suggests that the collector may have used a *specialized* shell tool to collect it, depending on the situation presented by the source plant. Much the way a modern contractor might assess a situation before selecting a Phillips or flathead screwdriver, the Glades or Calusa wood collector may have selected a certain type of shell tool to acquire it. Other shell tools that might have contributed to its collection, and should not be ruled out, include handheld columella cutting-edge tools, shouldered gastropod adzes, gastropod adze/celts, bivalve adze/celts, and quahog clam choppers.[36]

It is possible, although far less likely, that a chert tool (or hafted chert tool) was used to collect the source wood. Although high-quality chert outcrops occur only as far south as the Tampa Bay area, chert bifaces, microliths, hammerstones, and cores have been found at other South Florida sites such as Pineland.[37] Microliths are stone tools that "occur in a variety of forms" and "were multifunctional tools used for tasks as diverse as scraping, graving, and shredding as well as drilling and perforating."[38] Chert has also been found at Key Marco and neighboring Horr's Island.[39] Given the source wood's supposed density, it is not unreasonable to suppose that it required a special processing tool like chert, which would have been the hardest material available—a sort of "master key" tool when chopping and shaping particularly tough wood.[40]

It is also possible that *no tools* were used to collect the block of source wood, be it made available through natural processes or other forces, perhaps even the brute strength of human hands and muscles (individual or collective). But the ingenuity of the Glades and Calusa people, as well as the ubiquitous nature of shell tools in the area, make it highly likely that shell tools were, at the very least, cursorily involved in the collection process, if not extensively.

Straight from the Source

The source wood for the Cat, if collected away from "Key Marco" proper, was likely transported either by foot or dugout canoe, perhaps bundled with other wood or foraged materials, or even carried in a basket or ceramic vessel. It seems more likely that detail work on the figure would not begin at the collection site, but rather at home or a "workshop" location, perhaps one specifically designated for woodworking. The further away from home the source wood was collected, the more labor was required to collect it, thereby making it increasingly likely to involve some level of participation by the wider Key Marco community.[41]

The source wood was likely stripped of its bark (if any), possibly with a bivalve scraper or quahog clam "spokeshave," and further reduced from its original size until it was no less than six-by-three-by-two inches.[42] In considering the figure's final size, it is interesting to think about *why* it was sized that way. Was it a product of limitations, say due to the size of the (possibly rare) available source wood? Was it designed for a specific location, say to rest on a piece of furniture? Was it designed to be handheld, or used as a toy like a modern-day "action figure?" Cushing found miniature wooden "toy" canoes at Key Marco.[43] Perhaps it was designed to fit within one of these canoes, part of a larger symbolic representation of its ritualistic passage between worlds. Any number of practical, personal, or spiritual considerations could have influenced its size.

Any further reduction of the wood's size may have been performed with the introduction of fire. As Robin Brown discovers during replicative experimental archaeology, "shell gouges and scrapers [perform] slowly, but satisfactorily, to shape soft wood. When a lot of wood had to be removed as in making a bowl, unwanted areas were burned and shell scrapers used to clean away the charred wood." This could be done by creating hot coals using a durable fuelwood like oak, placing them on the surface to be shaped, and blowing through a hollow stem blowpipe to control direction of the burn.[44] The Cat's wood, given its density and description as a "hard" wood, may have necessitated the use of

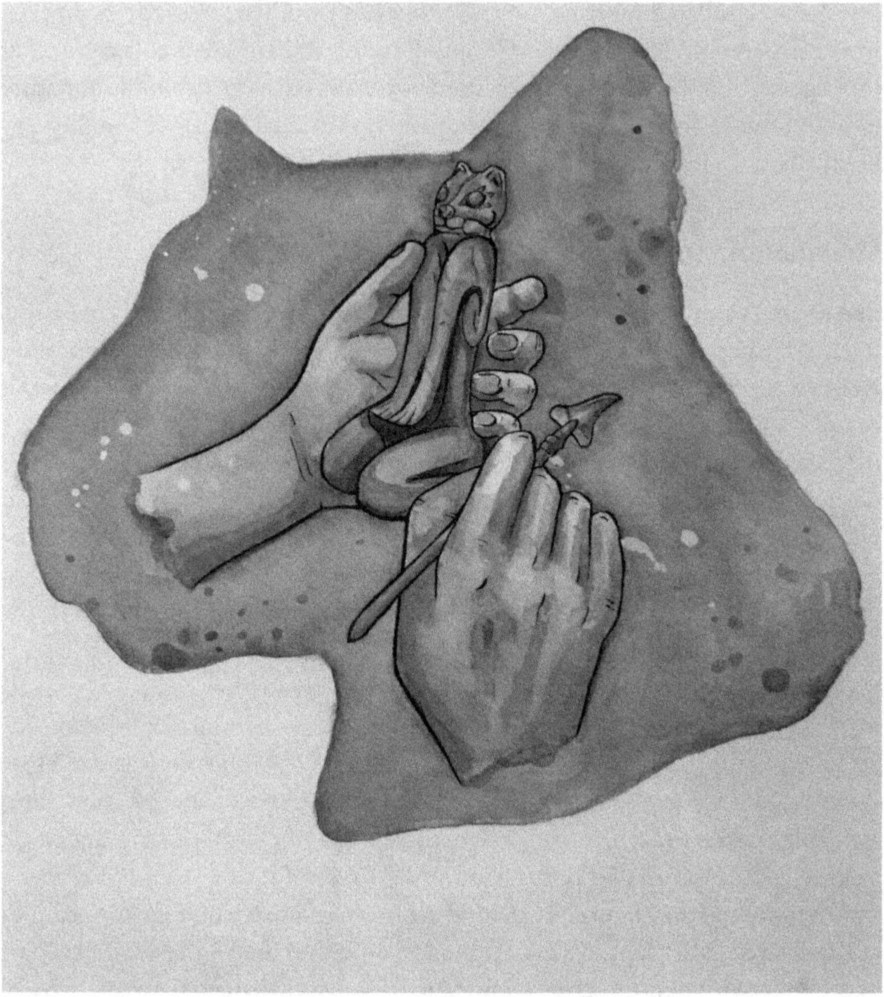

Figure 6. Artist's rendering of the Key Marco Cat being carved with a shark-tooth tool. Artwork by Amanda Wagner-Pelkey.

fire.[45] If the figure were entirely made from heartwood, fire would have been useful in removing the source wood's softer outer layers. Brown notes that the "burning could be controlled and directed with astonishing accuracy," perhaps allowing the Cat's maker to not only reduce its size, but also begin shaping the figure itself.[46]

Wood could be smoothed and finished with sand, grass, local limestone, or shell tools, but more economically and liberally with the rough-but-flexible sandpaper-like texture of wet sharkskin.[47] Sharkskin, known also as *shagreen*, is rough due to the presence of dermal denticles.[48] When dry, sharkskin acts more as a rigid "file," but would be especially useful for smoothing flat surfaces.[49] Cushing found "a few strips of carefully rolled-up shark skin" at Key Marco, further pointing to its possible use as a smoothing agent on the Cat.[50]

With the basic wood block prepared, the artist might have switched to a more specialized tool arsenal for greater accuracy and control. Shell tools that may have aided in shaping the Cat's basic figure include the aforementioned cutting and chopping tools, as well as the handheld columella cutting-edge tool ("chisel") or columella perforator ("awl"), either of which could be struck by gastropod hammers to improve effectiveness.[51] Controlled wood burning may have been utilized to make the process go faster. Other materials that may have aided in this work include large shark teeth (including fossilized Megalodon), limestone, and chert. Specialized composite bone tools like antler-socketed adzes and sawfish-tooth adzes may have also been useful in shaping wood.[52] Hafted barracuda jaws found at Key Marco are thought by some to have been wood finishing tools, possibly as "saws," but would likely have been too large and clumsy to effectively work the Cat.[53]

Fine Lines

Once the source wood was collected, transported, shaped, and ready for carving, the person or persons who created the Key Marco Cat likely used a shark-tooth tool for the fine detail work.[54] Cushing leaves no room for ambiguity, saying "the spaces between the legs, still show the characteristic marks of the fine-edged shark-tooth-blade with which the figure was carved."[55] Shark remains are found in large quantities in Florida archaeological sites, particularly in South Florida.[56] A single shark might provide up to 400 teeth, each ready for immediate use, with no need for sharpening.[57] Shark teeth are useful not only for shaping wood, but also engraving bone, working shell, and drilling holes in other shark teeth.[58] Since sharks are primarily cartilaginous, the only other remains they typically leave behind are centra (vertebrae), of which there are typically 150 to 200 per live shark.[59]

Given the amount of woodworking apparently done at the Key Marco site, where "cutting and carving knives of shark's teeth . . . were found by the hundreds," it seems probable that a shark tooth was more common than chert as a tool of precision in carving the details and contours like those seen on the Key Marco Cat.[60] As Wells Sawyer describes, "The cutting edge of flint flakes

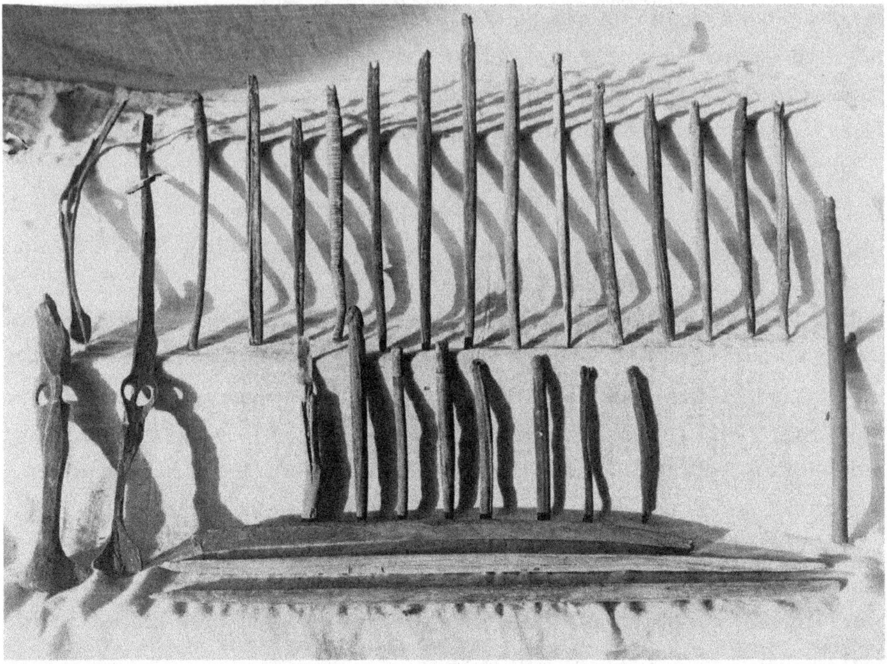

Figure 7. Wooden artifacts recovered from Key Marco, including atlatls and shark-tooth tool handles. Photo by Wells Sawyer, 1896. National Anthropological Archives, Smithsonian Institution (NPC096778.00).

compared with this tooth are but rude knives compared to fine rasors [*sic*]. Then too the line which the tooth cuts is long, clean and continuous, either as a straight line or as a curve and the line which can be rubbed by the flint is rough, irregular and broken. So the tool which the Floridian used was to an extent an explanation of his superior workmanship."[61] Several other wooden artifacts found at the site exhibit serrations that indicate the "obvious" use of shark-tooth tools.[62] Archaeologist Marion Gilliland, like Cushing, is decidedly unambiguous about the matter: "Decorated incision was done with shark tooth knives. These were likely extensively employed in three-dimensional carving as well."[63]

As Cushing observed, there were two classes of shark-tooth tools:

> The greater number of them consisted of shafts from five to seven inches in length by not more than half or three-quarters of an inch in diameter at their thickest portions. Some were slightly curved, others straight, some pointed, others squared at the smaller ends. All were fur-

> nished with nocks at the lower ends—which were also a little tapered—for the reception of the hollow bases of the tooth-blades that had been lashed to them and cemented with black gum. Not a few of these doubly-tapered little handles were marvels of finish, highly polished, and some of them were carved or incised with involuted circlets or kwa-like decorations, or else with straight or spiral-rayed rosettes and concentric circles, at the upper ends, as though these had been used as stamps in the finishing of certain kinds of work. The other class of handles was much more various, and was designed for receiving one or more of the shark-tooth blades, not at the extremities, but at the sides of the ends, some transversely, others laterally. They were nearly all carved; a few of them most elaborately; and they ranged in length from the width of the palm of the hand to five or six inches, being adapted for use not only as carvers, but also, probably—such as had single crossblades—as finishing adzes.[64]

The notion of "involuted circlets or . . . decorations" on the handles of some shark-tooth tools is intriguing, as perhaps each decorated tool was ascribed to an individual artist or designated purpose. Or, perhaps the decorations served other broader functions, acting as regional or territorial identifiers, as suggested by wood paddle-stamped pottery in North Florida.[65] Cushing was so impressed by the shark-tooth tools at Key Marco that he immediately began replicating them at the site. In evaluating their effectiveness, he proclaimed them "by far the most effective primitive carving tools I had ever learned of, and therein perceived one of the principal causes of the preeminence of the ancient key dwellers in the wood carver's art, so constantly evidenced in our collection."[66] Sawyer too, as an artist, was impressed with the usefulness of the tools, saying "for very delicate carving the tooth of the leopard shark offered a cutting edge which surpassed any primitive implement employed by the American Indian."[67]

The sharks that provided teeth for tool use were more than likely hunted, as opposed to washing up on the shore. Many were probably hunted in nearshore and inshore waters, although offshore longline fishing has been hypothesized as a nighttime industry.[68] Shark remains typical to South Florida archaeological sites include the Atlantic sharpnose shark, bonnethead shark, blacknose shark, blacktip shark, dusky shark, lemon shark, great white shark, sand tiger shark, tiger shark, scalloped hammerhead, great hammerhead, and bull shark, although zooarchaeologist Laura Kozuch notes that tiger and bull shark teeth were probably the most commonly sought for use as tools.[69] Kozuch documents thirty-one South Florida archaeological sites known to contain shark remains,[70] including Key Marco and Horr's Island.[71]

Shark-tooth tool handles varied in size and may have been used for different levels of detail, much the way a painter would select a narrow or broad paintbrush depending on the level of work being done. At Key Marco, seventeen handles ranged in size from four to eleven inches in length, also varying correspondingly in diameter.[72] Similarly, artistic preferences may have merited certain species of shark teeth for certain tasks. Brown reports that the pointy teeth of lemon, sand, bull, dusky, and blacktip sharks make for natural use as awls and drills, while the sharp edges of mako shark teeth make excellent shaving knives. The large saw-edged great white shark's tooth and serrated tiger shark's tooth also make exceptionally sharp scrapers, slicers, and cutters.[73]

Logically then, when examining the Cat with this in mind, it seems the "pointier" awl and drill-like teeth might have been better for making deep incisions, such as those that form the outlines of the Cat's facial features and limbs. Variance in the depth and width of the facial feature incisions (for example, the circular eye vs. the vertical lines down the center of the face to the top of the nose) indicate that different sizes of the same type could have been used as well. To the artisan, the broader but sharper teeth would have been useful in refining the overall shape, smoothing it out, and making it generally symmetrical.

Alternatives (or complements) to sharks' teeth that could have been used in the final stages of creating the Key Marco Cat, which previously have not been given much consideration, include sawfish teeth and carved bone points.[74] Sawfish teeth, which typically line the rostrum on the animal's exterior, are not particularly sharp, but dense enough to have been used to make incisions. The same could be said for a particularly sharp bone point, of which Cushing found several at Key Marco.[75] There are at least eleven known types of bone points that occur in the Glades area, including socketed bone points, stemmed bone points, and bone daggers, although most are thought to be fishing paraphernalia.[76]

Finishing Touches

Soon after his excavation at Key Marco, Cushing speculated that the Key Marco Cat's excellent condition might in part be owed to its original preparator(s). "[It] had either been saturated with some kind of varnish, or more probably

Figure 8. Artist's rendering of a woman and child anointing the Key Marco Cat after its fabrication. Artwork by Merald Clark.

had been frequently anointed with the fat of slain animals or victims. To this, doubtless, its remarkable preservation is due; for it is still relatively heavier, harder, and less shrunken by drying, than any other specimen of like material in the collection."[77] There is ethnographic precedent for the ritualistic care and "feeding" of feline fetishes in the American Southwest (where hunters and warriors carried them as good luck charms), usually with the blood of slain animals.[78] If Cushing's suspicion was correct, it likely represented one of the final steps in the Cat's preparation. Yet, Cushing presents no ethnographic or scientific rationale for making his assertion, nor does he explicitly identify any "specimen of like material."

Many ethnographic museum objects have been treated or coated with oils and fats, some even for the distinct purpose of preservation. This can alter the appearance of the object, such as in the case of wooden sculptures from Mali in West Africa, which exhibited a whitish surface bloom after being treated with local shea nut fat. A combination of gas chromatography and infrared spectrometry confirmed the bloom as fat and helped identify a portion of a restored sculpture as being non-original carnauba wax.[79] This approach might be useful to an examination of the Key Marco Cat. Condition reports at the NMNH indicate the presence of a "white residue" and "tinted wax" in the cracks and recesses of the object.[80] Through gas chromatography or infrared spectrometry, a sample of these substances might be identified as fatty—as Cushing theorized—or the result of a modern "undocumented [conservation] treatment," as is currently assumed.[81]

Nondestructive X-ray fluorescence (XRF) spectroscopy, performed on the Cat in 2018, revealed the presence of elements such as iron, a transition metal found in almost all plants and animals. Yet, whether the iron is from plant or animal matter is undetermined, only that the "major" amounts detected are attributable to "clay materials from the surrounding excavated ground."[82] Perhaps technological advances in elemental analysis will allow scientists to search specifically for traces of animal remains on artifacts. Or, perhaps after centuries in the wet soil, the elemental composition of the artifact at this point more closely resembles that of its surrounding environment than its "anointed" condition, making it a lost cause.

Many of the other animal carvings found at Key Marco show traces of paint pigments, also assumed to be derived from native plant and animal life. The Calusa were well known for their use of body paint and doubtlessly used it prolifically on material culture as well.[83] Brown has successfully replicated possible Calusa pigments, mixing the sap of a strangler fig with naturally occurring ingredients, including charcoal, powdered shell, clays, and purple marlberries, to make a variety of different paint colors.[84] Dolomite, red ocher, and galena—possible coloring agents—have been found in archaeological deposits in Southwest Florida.[85] As a result, some visitors to the Marco Island Historical Museum ask if the Cat was once painted like the other animal artifacts, but there is no evidence for that. However, a promising new study shows the potential in using XRF technology to determine if wooden artifacts were once painted, even if paint is no longer visible.[86] Comparing XRF readings from known painted Key Marco artifacts to the Cat's might definitively indicate whether or not the Cat was ever painted.

Forever Linked

The process of transforming a piece of raw wood into the Key Marco Cat was complicated and intensive. It could have involved the direct or indirect labor of multiple people and clearly was finished by a skilled artisan. It started with raw ingredients, possibly the very same ones that still surround us in Southwest Florida, and ended with a timeless masterpiece. Any number of instruments were utilized during its creation, evidence not only of a culture's technological ingenuity and proficiency, but also of its artistic prowess. Suddenly, a new appreciation for the inordinately abundant and seemingly mundane shell tool emerges, its potential to create such striking beauty held in the charismatic six-inch statuette it helped shape. So too for the shark-tooth tools and other utilitarian items, for what purpose did they serve if not to create?

The Key Marco Cat is a fine example of the artistic potential that lies all around us every day—in the trees, the water, the earth. To any artist, it is an inspiration of the highest order. Whoever made the Cat literally "made something out of nothing" for reasons we will never know with certainty. I think the most special thing about the Cat's material composition is that it came from the natural environment—and more likely than not, Florida's natural environment. For as far away and as long as the Cat strays from "home," its corpus—the wood that it was chiseled from, its essential *being*—is a permanent reminder of its (literal) Florida roots. The wood is the Cat's direct link to place, a local identifier for an otherwise worldly (and world-famous) artifact. Even if *we* do not know where exactly "home" was, the Cat certainly remembers. The location is hidden deep within its cell walls, a secret that may one day be revealed by science.

3

A Life with Purpose

The Cat's third life truly began upon its completion, which someone had to evaluate and consciously decide during their artistic process. It was at this point that the Cat was instilled with *agency*, making it more than just an everyday human-made object. By definition, it became "a . . . thing through which power is exerted or an end is achieved," a power that would grow, change, and evolve over the coming centuries.[1] More simply put, it was at this point that it first meant something to someone.

The Key Marco Cat's fabrication, however performed, was a remarkable feat of artistry and technological prowess. Ironically, even less is known about *why* the Cat was made because ideas and individual motivations typically do not leave tangible clues on objects the way that hands and tools do. Yet in studying this artifact, this example of material culture, one can also try to understand something about the broader culture that produced and used it.[2] Material culture studies not only elucidate *how* people lived and survived in the distant past, but also, more abstractly, *why* they lived—or to put it another way, *what they lived for*. Museums are repositories of material culture dating back centuries, and in some ways now serve as "field sites" for modern anthropologists seeking answers to such questions.[3]

Material culture can include anything produced by human beings "for the satisfaction of their needs," including survival purposes or to facilitate "social intercourse, delight our fancy, and symbolize meaning."[4] Artifacts can fall on either end of that material culture spectrum. For example, a tchotchke purchased on a family trip to Disney World may not be essential to survival, but it was purchased for a reason, and its presence on a bookshelf is a part of its owner's identity, both individually and culturally.

Of course, to some, a Han Solo action figure may not be as important as, say, a religious heirloom passed down through familial generations, but both objects have inherent meaning. Say a person dies and is buried with both their favorite Star Wars toy and a religious heirloom. If of the two objects, Han Solo survives the centuries while the religious item decomposes, a future anthropologist analyzing the burial out of context might suppose Mr. Solo was the important religious token.[5] Therein lies the difficulty of interpreting intent, abstractions, ideas, and symbolism. It is inherently biased and problematic, but still attempted because there is only so much that hard science can tell us about an object like the Cat.

This chapter will examine the Key Marco Cat's original purpose, or "reason for being." If chapter 2 outlined *how* the Cat was made, chapter 3 explores *why* it was made. In doing so, I fully acknowledge my own interpretive limitations, particularly as a non-Native researcher. The Cat may well be a "Han Solo action figure" of its time, misinterpreted by practitioners of a European worldview, including my own, since its excavation. However, by examining the Cat's physical attributes, as well as the possible motivations behind them, I aim to at least scratch the surface (or in this case, the sofa leg) of the object's greater meaning.

Here Kitty, Kitty

The most elementary interpretation of the Key Marco Cat lies right in its name. At this point, it is largely assumed to represent—at least partially—a feline. Yet, there was no identifying "artist's statement" uncovered with the Cat, nor a set of skeletal remains in its interior. In fact, there is no irrefutable proof that it is a Cat at all. It is a basic interpretive assumption made through examination of its physical characteristics. But if the Cat is indeed a cat, what species does it represent? For now, let us set aside its anthropomorphic physiognomies and approach it strictly from a biological perspective.

Since its initial discovery, the Key Marco Cat has been variously referred to as a panther, lion, mountain lion, and—more generally and most commonly—feline.[6] In North America, all of these species fall under the *Puma* genus and more or less represent the same identification, which also includes the cougar and puma, depending on local vernacular. Few have offered alternative identifications, but artist and anthropologist Merald Clark explicitly identifies the animal as "panther or bobcat," leaving open the possibility of a different felid.[7] Archaeologist Ryan J. Wheeler identifies it as a "panther (or similar cat)," stopping short of identifying any specific alternatives.[8]

In identifying the species of animal represented by the figure, one must consider the native fauna present in pre-Columbian Florida. This approach assumes, of course, the creature depicted is not completely a product of the imagination, but at the very least a compilation of characteristics inspired by native wildlife, if not a single species. It is important to note that "many animals depicted in Floridian and Southeastern art may be composites or mythological beings."[9]

The species most associated with the Key Marco Cat is the now-endangered Florida panther, which is the last surviving Puma subspecies in the eastern United States.[10] It once roamed a large part of the Southeast but is currently limited to just 5 percent of its original territory. This reduced territory is located in South Florida and extends to Marco Island, where the Key Marco Cat was found, making the modern-day visual connection even more immediate. In fact, there are "panther crossing" signs on Collier Boulevard (State Road 951) just north of the island. The species has become an icon of Florida's native wildlife and a symbol for ecological preservation.[11]

The Florida panther, now limited to a population of about 200 individuals, was more prevalent during the centuries prior to European colonization.[12] In fact, the animal is thought to be depicted in several other pre-Columbian Floridian artifacts.[13] It was certainly an animal known to the Calusa and their ancestors, if not more abstractly thought of, or possibly even revered. The isola-

Figure 9. Artwork by Russell Beans.

tion of the Florida panther subspecies is thought to have occurred during the past two centuries, making precontact panthers from Florida the same species as other large cats in North America (cougar, mountain lion, etc.).[14]

I believe the artist intended to represent a Florida panther, but in the interest of transparency, cannot entirely rule out other felines, or even other mammals for that matter. Some visitors to the Marco Island Historical Museum have suggested, partially in jest, that the carving looks more like a squirrel than a cat. While easy to laugh off, it is worth noting that the other animal carvings found at Key Marco are generally larger and more in scale with the physical size of creatures they supposedly represent.[15]

The size and stature of the Key Marco Cat, however, are more in keeping with those of the eastern gray squirrel or fox squirrel, both native species of eastern North America, than they are with any native felid. The Cat's long upward sweeping tail, small rounded ears, and upright posture resemble behaviors and characteristics commonly seen in squirrels. Cushing does generally describe the Key Marco animal carvings as "somewhat smaller than the heads of the creatures they represented," but aside from the Cat, a wooden blue crab is the only other intact carving that represents the animal's *entire body* rather than just a body part.[16]

This is not to suggest, however, that the carving ought to be renamed the Key Marco Squirrel. It is simply to point out that, while now widely accepted as feline, the truth is that the artist's true intent will never be known with 100 percent certainty. But from a literal, strictly visual assessment of the creature's likeness, it does appear to be feline, and likely a panther. Other inferences, however, can be made through comparisons with other cultures and their material culture, past and present.

Panthers in Florida's Archaeological Record

Despite their once-prolific populations across the Southeast, actual panther faunal remains are rare in Florida's archaeological record, so far turning up in only five South Florida sites. The primary reasons for their paucity could have to do with the panther's status as a major predator, coupled with a possible spiritual veneration—or simply being known to "not taste good"—making it unlikely to be hunted or eaten as food. Most of the known panther bones in Florida are not thought to be associated with human burials nor other special features that would indicate reverence.[17]

Panther remains are documented at Key Marco by archaeologist Marion

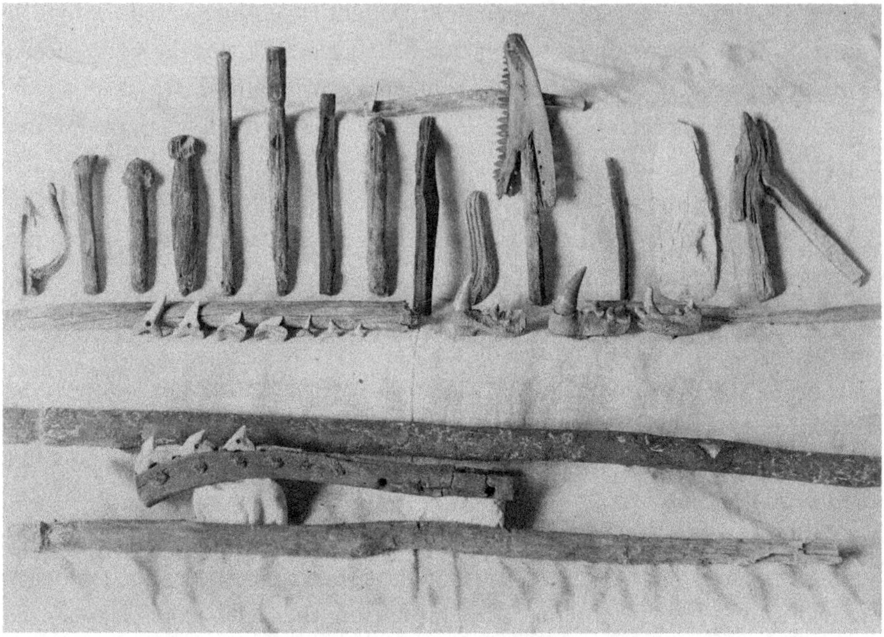

Figure 10. Artifacts recovered from the Key Marco site, including (*center*) modified panther jaws. Photo by Wells Sawyer, 1896. National Anthropological Archives, Smithsonian Institution (NPC096786.00).

Gilliland in her 1965 master's thesis.[18] She reports three modified "cougar jaws" in the faunal assemblage, two at the Penn Museum and one at the NMNH. Yet, these specimens do not appear in more recent inventories of archaeological panther remains from Florida.[19] So, in August 2019, I visited the Penn Museum to examine two of them firsthand. The bones are obviously modified, as Gilliland describes, and were identified through comparative analysis (figure 11) as almost certainly from a single large feline, probably a Florida panther.[20]

The presence of modified panther bones at Key Marco has potential interpretive ramifications for the Key Marco Cat. As Gilliland points out, the jaw bones likely had a "ceremonial purpose" due to their apparent modification, comparing them to "those found at Ocmulgee," almost certainly a reference to the famous copper-covered panther jaws found in Georgia.[21] Could the panther jaws have been used in direct association with the Cat? At the very least, they are evidence that the people at Key Marco interacted with literal panthers in a deliberate fashion, if not ceremonially.[22]

Rarer still than literal panther remains in Florida's archaeological record are

Figure 11. Dr. Katherine Moore analyzes modified panther jawbone (object no. 40703) at the Penn Museum. Photo by the author, August 26, 2019. By permission of Dr. Moore and the Penn Museum.

artistic representations of panthers. At Key Marco, in addition to the Cat, Cushing also found a wooden mask designed to resemble a feline, probably a bobcat.[23] Cushing described some of the figureheads as having physical counterparts or being bundled with matching masks.[24] Cushing's pairings were "based on their respective physical proximities when found and on similarities in their painted markings," meaning that if the Cat and the "bobcat" mask were a pair, as Clark posits, they might actually represent the same species of feline.[25]

A small eroded wooden panther carving at Rollins College in Winter Park, Florida, is depicted in a similar crouching position as the Key Marco Cat, but has less provenance than the Key Marco artifacts.[26] Like the Cat, it is distinctly feline in appearance. At the other end of the spectrum of anthropomorphic felines, in which the figures are decidedly more human than catlike, are the Mahoney Figurine (also known as the Riddle Statue) and the Padgett Figurine, both humanlike wooden carvings from the Lake Okeechobee area in southern Florida. Both figures are in crouching postures similar to the Key Marco and Rollins College cats, and both are possibly meant to depict a human wearing a face mask or headdress with catlike ears.[27] At Fort Center, another well-known waterlogged site in southern Florida near Lake Okeechobee, wooden carvings discovered in a mortuary pond include several depictions of large mammals, including cats, which date to between 200 and 800 CE.[28]

The panther may also be depicted in nonwooden objects, including bone and pottery. A small portion, or *adorno*, of a Weeden Island vessel from the Tucker site in Franklin County, Florida, appears to represent the face of a bobcat or panther.[29] A recent find at the Hutchinson site in Palm Beach County, Florida, presents a possible panther cub carving in bone. The fragment, just 3.4 cm wide and 2.7 cm tall, was likely a personal item rather than an object of communal worship. Archaeologist Christian Davenport goes so far as to suggest the bone may be *from* a panther, perhaps if its maker removed it from a panther carcass. This could have been done for supernatural reasons, perhaps to retain the animal's "bone soul."[30] If so, this would add another Florida site to the inventory of those with panther remains.

A 10-cm-long bone pin found near Kendall (Miami) in South Florida may represent a spotted feline, but others have suggested it may be an opossum. Its finder, startled upon reassembling the fragmented object, commented that the pieces "fit together and appear to depict a cat very similar to the Key Marco Cat discovered by Frank H. Cushing." He goes on to point out similarities in the tails, paws, noses, and eyes of the bone carving and the Key Marco Cat in justifying his identification. Davenport believes the figure, if indeed a feline, more closely resembles a bobcat than a panther.[31]

Cats Rule the World

Assuming the Key Marco Cat does, indeed, represent a "cat," what does it mean? Did the creature have a greater significance to the individual artist, their community, or broader culture? Was it the product of a personal hobby, one in a series of carvings of native wildlife by the same artist? Was the artist just enamored with wild cats at the time, much the way many people on the internet are today? Again, the answer will never be known for sure. But that has not stopped anthropologists from formulating theories. As one ventures further away from the objective end of the observable spectrum and closer toward the subjective, the answer becomes less clear, if not more interesting.

In a global context, cats have been the subject of countless works of art, culture, and religious paraphernalia. The first artistic representations of felines appeared at least 30,000 years ago in European cave art, as well as a remarkable ivory carving, the *Löwenmensch* ("lion-human") figurine, carved from a mammoth's tusk and now at the Museum Ulm in Germany.[32] In ancient Egypt, big cats and domestic cats alike were worshipped as deities. Since as early as 3100 BCE, cats have been included in vast cat cemeteries, paintings, and "statuettes" similar in form to the Key Marco Cat.[33] Perhaps the most famous cat figurine in the world is the bronze Gayer-Anderson Cat, in possession of the British Museum in London since 1939. The cat, in a posture reminiscent of Key

Figure 12. The Gayer-Anderson Cat. © The Trustees of the British Museum.

Marco's, dates to Egypt's Late Period (644–332 BCE), predating the earliest suggested date at Key Marco by about 1,000 years.[34]

In other parts of the world, cats have long been associated with divinity as well. Ancient Neolithic sites in Turkey, Sumer, Crete, Greece, and India have all yielded material culture indicating the importance of cats in society—particularly, big cats. Some attribute this to an inherent divine femininity, noting that "the cat, especially the great cats, appear to have been regarded as having a special affinity with female divinity, particularly those ancient, great Mother figures, creator and protector of the natural world, strong, autonomous goddesses whose characters were regarded as emulating those regal, powerful, beautiful and mysterious creatures, the great felines."[35]

It is perhaps unsurprising, then, that Cushing immediately drew comparisons to ancient Egyptian and Middle Eastern material culture. In his words, "nothing thus far found in America so vividly calls to mind the best art of the ancient Egyptians or Assyrians, as does this little statuette of the Lion-God."[36] However, despite the aforementioned list of works from Florida, known examples of ancient feline art are far more rare in the Americas than other parts of the world. Plus, interpretations of European feline art are not necessarily directly applicable to pre-Columbian Amerindian societies. In the Americas, particularly Central and South America, jaguars are the most frequently depicted felines.[37]

In North America, one of the best-known feline depictions—aside from the Key Marco Cat—is a steatite panther effigy "great pipe" from Indiana, associ-

Figure 13. Panther Effigy Pipe (Woodland Period). Black Steatite, 2 3/8 × 6 5/16 × 1 9/16 in. (6 × 16 × 4 cm). Anonymous loan, courtesy of the Brooklyn Museum L49.5.

ated with the Allison/Copena culture and dating to 100–500 CE.[38] Ironically, this beautiful artifact was displayed in the same exhibition as the Cat *twice*, in 1985's *Ancient Art of the American Woodland Indians* and *Hero, Hawk, and Open Hand: American Indian Art of the Ancient Midwest and South* from 2004 to 2005.[39]

Cat Person

Perhaps the most important physical attributes of the Key Marco Cat in determining its purpose or role in society are those considered by most to be "anthropomorphic."[40] Indeed, many of its traits, from its posture to its extremities, do exhibit humanlike qualities, as expressed by the expert woodcarver who created it.[41] These traits seem to indicate a possible extra level of importance to its maker and end users. Just *how* humanlike it really is seems to be up for discussion. Some have suggested that the figure may represent a more literal depiction of a masked or costumed performer.[42] Others believe it to be in a state of transformation, somewhere between human and panther, but not fully either.[43]

These two notions on their own inherently discount a third: that the object might be an abstract, if biologically inaccurate, representation of the panther in its purest form, much the way an artist might create artwork depicting a favorite wild animal or pet with only partial realism, sometimes dependent on skill. While the notion of a tamed Florida panther living in or near the village may seem farfetched, and probably is, the presence of a modified panther at the site does not preclude unique circumstances that could have produced such a scenario, at least on an individual basis. Some suggest that the Fort Center panther carvings could have "practical symbolism" as biological symbols of hunting prowess.[44] Felines, after all, have been the Americas' apex predator since before humans arrived on the scene.[45]

The Key Marco Cat also exhibits human characteristics that could be described as both feminine and masculine. Archaeologist Nancy White described the Cat as feminine, particularly in the buttocks and hips, after seeing it in person.[46] Its demureness and poise are traditionally feminine, in keeping with cultural theories of the divine femininity inherent in large cats. However, it cannot go without mentioning the object's decidedly masculine phallic shape, particularly when viewed in profile from the side. While not mentioned to date in any scholarly description of the item, it is an opinion that I have routinely and unavoidably encountered—usually accompanied by giggling—via museum visitors, generally younger ones seeing it for the first time. The object's size, at just under six inches in length, does it no favors in this regard, and some have gone so far as to inquire whether it was utilized in sexual activity.

There could be some inherent truth to what is an obvious and immediate visual interpretation. If it is truly a work of art, which it is frequently and unfailingly cited as, could it not have multiple meanings, themes, or purposes? Perhaps it is intentionally both masculine *and* feminine, making it a more representative, all-encompassing, and universally appealing work of art. Or perhaps it was intentionally phallic in shape, an ode to the masculinity of the presumably male hunter or warrior it was supposed to represent.

Panthers in the Ethnohistoric Record

Ethnohistoric accounts—contemporaneous records from eyewitnesses, in this case from colonial Europeans in Southwest Florida—are rare in themselves, let alone in relation to specific artifacts. The Calusa and their ancestors did not keep written records, so the only firsthand accounts from their time were written by Europeans, who were clearly prejudiced, with their own agendas for describing the "savages" they met in Florida. While biased, these records, many of which are now housed in the *Archivo General de Indias* (General Archive of the Indies) in Seville, Spain, are the best-known eyewitness accounts of the Calusa, particularly when it comes to abstract or allusive observations not possible in the archaeological record.

The most frequently cited ethnohistoric account associated with the Cat and other Key Marco artifacts, including painted human face masks, comes from translations of a Spanish missionary's recollections of interactions at Calos (now Mound Key), the Calusa capital, in 1567.[47] Father Juan Rogel describes a "temple of idols there, which were some very ugly masks, which some Indians donned, delegated by it. And they went out into the village with them. And the wretches performed their worship and adored them, with the women singing certain canticles." The Key Marco Cat may have been a type of "idol," making it an item of possible religious or spiritual importance.[48] In use, it may have been handheld, mounted to another object, or functioned simply as a "piece of shrine furniture."[49]

The Calusa were also known to practice human sacrifice. Sacrifices made to "idols," presumably like the ones Rogel describes, included severed heads that might placate the idols' appetites for human eyes. The sacrificial heads were carried in dances or ceremonies, but most of those observed by the Span-

Figure 14. Artist's rendering of a religious procession at Muspa. Artwork by Merald Clark.

ish were of captive fellow Spaniards.[50] Cushing found only two human skulls at Key Marco, which according to Gilliland, showed no "deformation of any type."[51] Interestingly, at Tarpon Springs, which he excavated during the same expedition as Key Marco, Cushing describes finding "one skull artificially flattened and broadened in the frontal and coronal regions, evidently in order to heighten its resemblance to the characteristic form of the head of the mountain lion or puma, since it was found associated with the fragments of a sacrificial bowl on which the symbols of the puma were prominently and dually depicted."[52] While this individual was not necessarily a human sacrifice, they apparently sacrificed their corporeal body (if Cushing's observations are taken at face value) to appease their idol. These cases present limited but compelling evidence that people very may well have permanently altered their appearances or even died to "please" the Cat.

Another important note about these ethnohistoric accounts, aside from their obvious biases, is that they were written *after* contact with the Calusa, which is when some argue that the Calusa achieved peak complexity, transforming from a "complex chiefdom" to a "hegemonic state."[53] If the Key Marco artifacts date to precontact times, which archaeological evidence suggests that they do, the ethnohistoric accounts cannot automatically be literally applied to the distant past, which may span hundreds of years. Things changed quite a bit when Europeans arrived, and while the Calusa stood fast to their cultural traditions, which presumably were carried on for generations prior to contact, there is not necessarily a direct lineal descent from the practices at Key Marco to what happened at Mound Key in the sixteenth century.

Panthers in the Ethnographic Record

Finally, anthropologists can look to the ethnographic record—observations learned from living cultures—for clues to the importance of the panther in modern Native American societies. Ethnography, like archaeology a subfield of anthropology, has been practiced (if informally) in the Americas since the eighteenth and nineteenth centuries, often descriptive of tribes still deeply rooted in the traditions of their Mississippian predecessors.[54]

Generally, in Southeastern tribes, the panther (sometimes also referred to as the "tiger") is portrayed as a dangerous creature in myths relating to hunting or warfare. These myths indicate that panthers hold special powers or knowledge that can sometimes be transmitted to humans. Cushing's initial instincts about the Cat fall in line with this idea. He cites the proximity of other artifacts of warfare as evidence to the Cat's purpose: "Not far away were found, a large stool, a decayed mask, portions of a short wooden stave, and of symbolic ear-buttons; a sheaf of about two dozen throwing arrows, and other remains of warrior-and hunter-paraphernalia and accoutrements. This affords convincing evidence that the statuette was a fetish or god of war or the hunt, like its clumsier stone analogues in Zuni land."[55]

To the Ucita people of Tampa Bay, during the sixteenth century, it was generally considered "miraculous" to kill a panther and anyone who did so was afterward venerated. Perhaps someone captured or killed a panther at Key Marco and was honored by the creation of the Key Marco Cat in their likeness as a sign of respect. There is a 1591 illustration of a panther skin being worn by a principal Timucuan leader in Florida, thereby also assigning possible social status with the panther, contrary to prevailing theory on the correlation between panther symbolism and social rank.[56] This illustration, however, has proven to be problematic if not outright fraudulent.[57] Panther skin robes, however, are well known to have been worn in the American Southwest and are sometimes the sources of panther remains (usually paw bones) in the archaeological record.[58]

Creek migration legends tell of a panther that was threatening the group's ancestral people. After hunting, capturing, and killing the creature, the Creeks preserved its bones, offering a potential explanation for the ceremonial treatment of the famous Ocmulgee copper-covered panther jaws and others.[59] The Florida Seminoles, who at one time may have lived alongside the Calusa in Florida and have traditions rooted in Creek, also feature the panther prominently in their creation story.[60] The panther is thought to have special powers being the Breathmaker's (creator's) favorite and the first to walk the earth, giving it special powers such as the ability to heal and give wise counsel in making laws.[61]

Perhaps the Key Marco Cat represented an eponymous kinship group at Key Marco. Often, in Southeastern tribes, special offices or duties are held by members of certain clans.[62] The head medicine man of the Seminole always belongs to the Panther clan, for example.[63] If the Cat represented a family group, perhaps it was an identifying symbol somewhere on or inside their dwelling, likely also in their names, with other families in the community delineated by other animal symbols. Some have suggested that the wood carvings at nearby Fort Center, which included felines, were clan totems.[64] Certain houses at Key Marco may have represented specific lineages (e.g., a "Panther clan"), gaining prestige and status over considerable periods of time through a "commitment to place."[65] Or, perhaps the Cat symbolized a season—or seasonal residents. Some Woodland cultures likely associated felines and their fur with the earth and winter, perhaps coupling cyclical communal responsibilities to the individuals associated with them.[66] In the American Southwest, mountain lions are also sometimes associated with the cardinal direction north, with tokens and fetishes arranged accordingly in shrines.[67]

Throughout the Mississippian Southeast, temple shrines built on the tops of mounds were dedicated to the worship of ancestors and acted as "the consecrated repositories of the tribe's sacred forces."[68] These ceremonial structures would have been the most important ones in the community and the storage location of "cult paraphernalia" when not in use. "A basic furnishing of the shrine house was the ancestor cult figure. Sculpted in wood or stone, these images were evidently representations of the founding ancestor."[69] At Key Marco, the Cat may have represented a "founding ancestor," stored in a temple shrine analogous to the "temple of idols" referenced by Rogel. Perhaps the shrine was a location of principal importance in the Calusa domain, maybe even a capital, as Marquardt theorizes that "the traditional currency of chiefly authority was not the possession of or ability to distribute resources and products. Instead, it was the possession of and manipulation of esoteric knowledge and control of a limited number of *sacra*—representational art objects, artifacts, and icons charged with supernatural meaning." The Cat's physical presence at Key Marco might therefore also indicate the former presence of a very important individual, possibly even a paramount leader.[70]

In many Native stories, panthers are the progenitors—or original ancestors—of tribal clans and could travel between worlds, transforming between human and panther, often associated with warfare and sometimes seen as protectors or guardian figures. This is consistent with a theory about the Key Marco Cat first posited by Cushing, and frequently perpetuated thereafter, likely informed by his ethnographic work with the Zuni of the Southwest. Cushing also suggests that the figure perhaps represents a person in a state of ritual transformation. Wheeler expands on that idea, suggesting the Key Marco Cat "might be a person in a panther disguise, a mythological creature, or a shaman partly transformed into a panther." These creatures that alternate between animal and human form are found in Cherokee, Creek, and Oklahoma Seminole stories.[71]

Anthropomorphic animal figures like the Key Marco Cat are often thought to be evidence of shamanism. Shamanism is a religion "characterized by the belief that the unseen world of gods, demons, and ancestral spirits is responsive only to the spirits" and is typified by "the use of mediumistic trance." According to some, shamanism features prominently in Hopewell art found in the archaeological record. In the ethnographic accounts of the Southern tribes, these figures and their supernatural abilities are "almost exclusively linked to witchcraft." The Cochiti of the American Southwest use mountain lion parts and imagery to cure "individuals whose illness was caused by witches." Cushing believed the Cat's squared-off appendages to be intentional, rendering safe the feline spirit's most "harmful or destructive members." He interpreted the masks and figureheads to be shamanistic, writing that the objects were "the means of becoming actually incarnated with the spirits of ancestors, mythic beings, and animals, or totem god."[72]

A modern ethnographic analog of the potential shamanism practiced at Key Marco might lie in South America with the Olmec, a culture with practicing were-jaguar shamans often outfitted with jaguar skins, artwork, stories, and supernatural transformational abilities. Here, the shamans practice nagualism, which describes the relationship between shaman and his or her animal alter ego in shapeshifting and sorcery, reminiscent of the Southeast's Underwater Panther. "The Olmec jaguar is, almost without exception, always depicted as an anthropomorphic creature combining both human and jaguar features."[73]

Finally, we need look no further than western popular culture for examples of masked characters utilized in fictional stories for entertainment purposes. Clark likens the Mighty Morphin Power Rangers to the Key Marco "characters" represented by the masks and figureheads found by Cushing. In a lecture to the MIHS and its members, Clark posited the idea of a Key Marco "Cat Man," utilizing imagery from the 2018 blockbuster movie *Black Panther* as a modern analog. Clark also suggests the masks and figureheads could have been used in a variety of ways, perhaps encompassing all or none of the possibilities described previously. It is also possible that beliefs, uses, and traditions could have changed or been modified over time. Depending on the age of the objects prior to their deposition, which is unknown, it is possible that the Key Marco Cat was used in a variety of ways, perhaps even in a variety of locations.[74]

Cat's Got Our Tongues

Interpretations of the Key Marco Cat's true meaning range from the mundane to the mystical. Making empirical sense of the ambiguous differences and relationships between animals, humans, and monsters, particularly in ancient Native American culture stories, can prove difficult even to the cultures that create them—and maybe that is the whole point. Ambiguity is reflected in the physical manifestations of those beliefs, such as the Key Marco Cat, which is neither fully feline nor human, neither fully feminine nor masculine, neither fully earthbound nor otherworldly.

While the Cat's true purpose is probably the single most important bit of information to know about the object, it is also the most frustratingly elusive, almost certainly impossible to ever truly discern. Even if archival researchers were to find a new written account of sixteenth century European explorers in Southwest Florida—even if specifically written about Muspa and the Key Marco artifacts—it would inherently be biased and diluted without the direct written input of the Cat's makers, users, practitioners, or spiritual partners. Perhaps these mysteries are in part what makes the object so fascinating. In the meantime, new archaeological discoveries and evolving ethnographic inferences will continue to inform us about the expanding possibilities of the diminutive object's intended purpose.

4

Moment of Truth

A defining moment in the Key Marco Cat's life was probably also an unexpected one: that moment when it was suddenly deposited into the muck that wound up preserving it for centuries. Its deposition may have been the result of accidental or even tragic circumstances. Hurricanes, enemy invaders, or general "hard times" are a few of the potential culprits. As if the cause were not mysterious enough on its own, even less is known about the *time* itself. Was it 500 years ago, or 1,500, or somewhere in between? Did the Cat go into the muck on the same day—or at the same moment—as every other artifact? Or was it deposited individually, perhaps even intentionally?

They say that "age is just a number," but for the Key Marco Cat, there are at least a thousand possibilities. Just how does one go about determining the Cat's true age? As archaeological and material culture studies have evolved over the past century, so too have the techniques and technologies available to them. A blend of hard science, nuanced inference, and abstract analysis has produced a blanket chronological range for the entire site, which is in turn typically applied to individual objects like the Cat, unless more specific information can be extrapolated on case-by-case bases.

This chapter outlines the various means and methods through which archaeologists have attempted to ascribe an age to the Key Marco artifacts, as well as the possible causes of their deposition. Associated context, ceramic chronologies, radiocarbon dating, and stylistic analyses have produced a dizzying array of results that seem to only widen the chronological possibilities with time. The depositional event, whether part of a gradual accumulation or an unexpected phenomenon, became the world's gain after Cushing's excavation. To this day, Key Marco represents the most comprehensive and spectacular assemblage of pre-Columbian Native American material culture ever discovered in Florida.

Archaeology 101

In archaeological sites, the age of a given artifact is often approximated based upon the presence (or absence) of diagnostic artifacts or features nearby. Ideally, these features are from the same slice of the site's stratigraphy—that is, the same level in the soil. The law of superposition, routinely employed by archaeologists and a basic lesson of Archaeology 101, says that objects found in layers closer to the surface are generally "younger" than those found at lower strata, although this is not always the case.

Much of modern archaeological practice is built upon these ideas, evolving necessarily over the past century and a half to incorporate meticulous documentation of contextual observations in the field. New technologies, such as digital photography and three-dimensional mapping, have made this increasingly thorough in recent years. However, these practices, as common as they now may be, were not utilized during Cushing's excavation at Key Marco. Technology, and archaeology as a discipline, just were not there yet.

Cushing, for his part, was on the cutting edge of 1896 archaeology, even employing the use of a grid system at Key Marco. However, a full-scale systematic excavation of a waterlogged site in Florida had never been attempted. Cushing, although able to visualize the stratigraphic layering of sites he encountered, made few attempts to document it, opting instead to describe it in retrospect using his trademark flowery language.[1]

Rather than open square test units with carefully maintained walls, Cushing's crew scoured the entirety of the muck pit by feel, collecting with their bare hands and garden tools as they moved from one 10' x 10' "unit" to another. Most of the artifacts came from what Cushing described as a single layer of "gray peaty marl," demonstrating an overall lack of stratification (or "layering") and making many (if not most) of the items theoretically contemporaneous. Only about 20 of more than 1,000 artifacts were denoted within his grid system, inexcusable by today's standards, but generous at the time.[2]

To Pre- or Not to Pre-

Despite the shortcomings of 1896 archaeology, there is still something to be learned about the site's chronology not only from the finds, but also from the conspicuous absences. Most notably, no European goods were found in Cushing's excavation of the site. This seems to indicate that the site is pre-Columbian, or in other words, dates prior to European contact.[3]

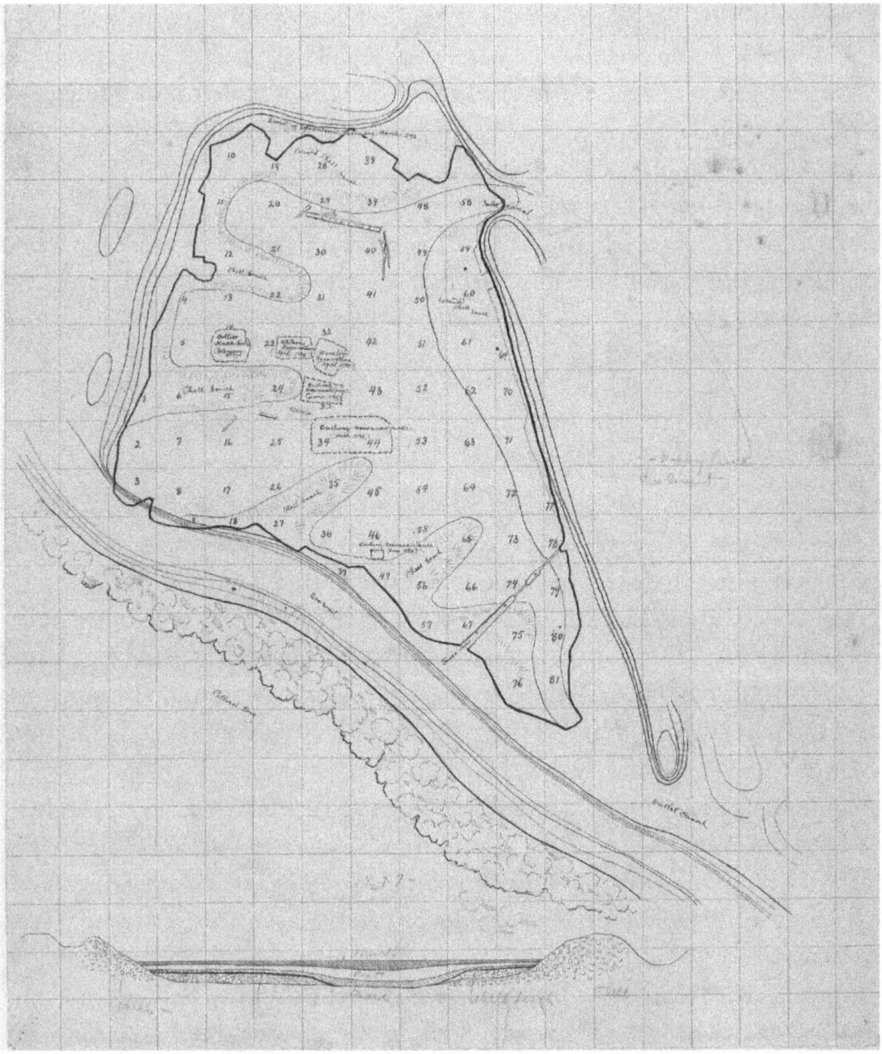

Figure 15. Map of the *Court of the Pile Dwellers* by Frank Hamilton Cushing, 1896. Brooklyn Museum Archives, Culin Archival Collection. Cushing Collection (6.3.026): A143.

Archaeologist Marion S. Gilliland writes that "there are absolutely no European materials present and contact was early in this area," noting that Juan Ponce de León first visited the region in 1513 CE and "others followed frequently thereafter." Gilliland, assuming that Key Marco was a site of political or religious importance, argues that if the site were post-1513, there would almost be certainly be gold due to the stratified society observed at the time of European contact.[4]

While at least one Spanish artifact *has* been recovered from the larger Key Marco site in more recent excavations—a Middle Style olive jar (1560–1800 CE) excavated in 2004—it is not indicative of a timestamp for the contents of the *Court of the Pile Dwellers*, nor necessarily even Key Marco "proper."[5] Cushing too found ceramics at the site—just not Spanish ones. He found at least 143 pieces of sand-tempered pottery, seven (later reconstructed) partial vessels, and one unbroken vessel.[6] If Cushing did find European ceramics, he makes no mention of them. Thus, the terminal date for the age of the Key Marco Cat—the most recent possible date that it was deposited into the muck—is likely 1513 CE, more than 500 years ago.

Just My Typology

For most of the past century, ceramic analysis has been the primary determinant of regional and temporal boundaries in South Florida archaeology. Each culture area (e.g., Glades) has its own corresponding chronologies based on pottery decorations and wares, but there is often less variation in other material culture (e.g., shell tools) to further delineate between regions.[7] Decorated pottery can be diagnostic, with a chronology that has been studied and refined over the past century. John M. Goggin, a curator at the Florida State Museum (now the FLMNH), largely established the Glades area and ceramic typology still in use by archaeologists today.[8]

Most of Cushing's Key Marco ceramic bowls and potsherds are Glades Plain, a pottery type found ubiquitously throughout time and space in Southwest Florida. However, his collection also includes certain types of decorated pottery, such as Glades Tooled, St. Johns Check Stamped, and Surfside Incised, that tend to indicate a later (1200–1513 CE) date at Key Marco's *Court of the Pile Dwellers*.[9] In a May 12, 1946, letter to Harriet Newell Wardle, curator at the Penn Museum, Goggin, then curator at the Yale Peabody Museum of Natural History, writes:

"You may be interested in the fact that I have been able to date the Key Marco site, that is, the 'court.' It fits into my Glades IIIb period. This period dates from just before to just after the time of historic contact. Since any evidence of historic contact is lacking at Key Marco, I would assign it to pre-contact times. An estimated date would be the latter part of the 15th century as contact was early in this area. Ceramics form the basis for the dating. The vessel with the pie crust rim (Glades Tooled) is a late type whose position is well known."[10]

Since Goggin's attribution, thousands of new Key Marco ceramics have added considerable time depth to the overall site, if not necessarily to the *Court* artifacts specifically. In 1965, the Van Becks excavated more than 2,000 potsherds from Key Marco at a midden about 195 meters northeast of Cushing's *Court*. Although some of the decorated sherds were initially misidentified (or unidentified), the Van Becks found a variety of early Glades types, pointing to a much broader occupation at Key Marco, beginning at roughly 500 CE.[11] Subsequent archaeologists have found similarly early ceramics in more recent excavations, many of which are now curated at the Marco Island Historical Museum (MIHM).[12]

In 2014, Ann Cordell, ceramic technologist at the FLMNH, reconstructed three nearly complete ceramic vessels from a 2004 excavation led by archaeologist Robert Carr. Cordell was able to collect samples of charred food residue from each of the vessels in the process.[13] The samples, when submitted for radiocarbon analysis, yielded consistent results, all landing between 640 and 775 CE.[14] These early dates are consistent with those indicated (500–1513 CE) by the presence of certain types of decorated Glades potsherds.

Figure 16. This Key Largo Incised vessel from Key Marco is more than 1,300 years old. Catalog number 2014-12-7-9, Marco Island Historical Society. Photo by Pat Payne.

Clearly, there is cause for confusion with Key Marco's ceramic chronology. Based on pottery decorations found at Cushing's *Court* alone, one might conservatively ascribe a later date between 1200 and 1513 CE to the Key Marco artifacts—including the Cat. However, in weighing the totality of the site, along with the hundreds of decorated sherds that it has produced since 1965, as well as recent radiocarbon data, the range more than triples to between at least 500 and 1513 CE.

Radiocarbon Dating

Radiocarbon dating is a method of measuring the amount of carbon 14, a carbon isotope, in organic materials to determine their age. Carbon is present in all living organisms and consequently, any objects created from living organisms, including the Key Marco Cat. All organic materials are part of what is known as the carbon cycle. When an organism dies, it is cut off from that cycle, thereby beginning a process of decay. By measuring the rate of decay, or half-life, of carbon 14 in organic materials, scientists can provide a range of dates in which that decay first began—also known as an approximate age. Radiocarbon dating became a staple of archaeological and geological studies after its introduction by Willard F. Libby in 1946.[15]

In 1968, James A. Ford, curator at the Florida State Museum (now the FLMNH), submitted a sample of Key Marco plant fiber—cordage from a bundle of netting—for testing at the University of Michigan.[16] Ford's rationale for submitting the material was the relative lack of diagnostic ceramics in the Key Marco collection: "Decorative motifs in preserved wood specimens suggest relationships to Middle Mississippi and imply 'Southern Cult.' No European trade goods were found. Date in 16th or 17th century is not unlikely."[17] The resulting radiocarbon date of 1670 CE seemingly confirmed Ford's suspicion.

In 1974, Barbara Purdy, curator at the FLMNH, met with the inventor of radiocarbon dating himself, Nobel Prize winner Libby. Libby was reportedly "fascinated" by the Key Marco artifacts and "offered to date a few of them." Purdy submitted six samples to Libby's laboratory at the University of California Los Angeles for radiocarbon dating. While only five of the samples produced results, they were strikingly different from the sample performed in 1968. Four of the five dates, taken from wooden fragments (including the famous painted woodpecker board), fall between approximately 600 and 900 CE. A fifth date, taken from part of a wooden canoe paddle, is even older, dating to approximately 55 CE.[18]

These results came back by March 1975, just in time to be published in Gilliland's *The Material Culture of Key Marco, Florida*. Upon receiving the results, Gilliland writes that they "lend great support to the author's thesis that this site was occupied over an extended period and demonstrate the presence of sophisticated art forms in Florida at a very early date."[19] Gilliland clearly accepted the dates at face value. Aside from the varying results between the 1968 sample and the 1974 samples, it is worth mentioning that the material types sampled were also different (cordage in 1968 and wood in 1974) and six years had passed in the refinement of what was still an emerging technology.

Three years after Gilliland's book, Jerald Milanich, curator at the FLMNH, challenged the radiocarbon dates, calling them "greatly in error." He attributes the error to the contamination of the artifacts while in storage at the FLMNH, most likely from petroleum-based pesticides applied monthly, "or any of the compounds frequently sprayed, painted, or otherwise emitted in the Museum storage area." Most compellingly, Milanich cites the early date of the canoe paddle, which Cushing found in the "uppermost portion" of the relic-bearing stratum at Key Marco, as an indicator of their error.[20] Cushing reports finding the paddle "slantingly and deeply embedded in the mud, while its long handle reached obliquely up nearly to the surface of the muck, and was there . . . burned off slantingly on a line that must have corresponded to the original level of the water."[21] Following the law of superposition and assuming the site was undisturbed, the paddle should logically date to the most recent occupation of the site. Yet, its date of 55 CE is more than 600 years older than the other four artifacts.

Purdy believes Milanich's concerns are overblown, citing research on the effects of contaminants on much older organic Holocene materials. In her opinion, any contaminants would "not be sufficient to alter the indicated age of the sample by an amount in excess of the statistical variance attached to the age estimate. It would be rare that samples, such as those from Key Marco, would yield dates 600–800 years older than anticipated." Purdy makes the point that it seems reasonable to demand specific evidence of contamination when making such a claim.[22] Milanich does not contest the seventeenth century date yielded by the 1968 test, stating only that it "was obtained shortly after the Key Marco collection arrived" at the FLMNH from the Penn Museum, where the collection had been in storage for decades. Thus, Milanich perhaps implies that pesticides were applied to objects at the FLMNH sometime between 1968 and 1974, but they were likely applied to objects while at the Penn Museum as well.[23] Randolph Widmer, archaeologist at the University of Houston, supports

Purdy's stance, stating after his 1995 excavation at the site that "there is nothing out of place with respect to the existing radiocarbon dates on the Cushing collection."[24]

In 2018, I initiated a request of an X-ray fluorescence (XRF) analysis of the Key Marco Cat prior to its loan to the MIHM. XRF scans can identify the presence or absence of elements in a sample, particularly metals. The results of that analysis may have some practical applicability to this ongoing debate. It detected "small amounts of bromine, lead, and possibly mercury most likely residues from previous pesticides treatments."[25] The results are not directly applicable to the controversial radiocarbon dates, as the Cat has a different postexcavation history than the tested Key Marco artifacts, having never been stored at the FLMNH or radiocarbon dated. However, the analysis does confirm that the object was likely treated with pesticides at one time, a common practice, especially in early twentieth-century museums. If pesticide residues appear on the Cat, they very likely also appear on the objects radiocarbon dated in 1968 and 1974, which also "lived" in Philadelphia long before they lived in Gainesville. An XRF analysis of the original radiocarbon-dated specimens might confirm the presence and nature of any potential contaminants on the objects, providing the geochemical signatures that Purdy seeks from Milanich.

A Matter of Style

Across the Southeast, archaeologists have ascribed broad cultural affiliations to large swaths of the region, encompassing multiple cultures living in different landscapes and ecosystems. These affiliations are based more on known chronology and lifestyle similarities—and less on ceramics—than the South Florida cultures. Examples include the Hopewell, Ortona, and Yent cultures, which rather than being assigned individual chronologies, are lumped into eras known as the Archaic (8000–1000 BCE), Woodland (1000 BCE–1000 CE), and Mississippian Periods (1000–1500 CE). Some Mississippian cultures are thought to be part of Southeastern Ceremonial Complex (SECC), "an assemblage of artifacts and art styles widespread in time and space" dating conservatively to between 1200 and 1400 CE.[26]

Of these, only the Archaic Period is commonly prescribed to chronologically correspondent sites in South Florida. The succeeding Caloosahatchee and Glades cultures are in some regards thought to be on their "own time," not ordinarily lumped into larger categories or complexes like other Native southeastern groups. One of the primary reasons that Florida groups tend to stand on their own is their lack of reliance on agriculture, which is a defining and uniting characteristic of many cultural groups in the SECC.[27] Additionally, "Florida . . . has been somewhat marginalized . . . as Cushing's finds at Key Marco have largely been viewed as a phenomenon in some ways related to but peripheral to late prehistoric artistic developments to the north."[28] Only recently have South Florida's cultural groups been thought of in broader terms relating to the Woodland and Mississippian Periods.[29] Confusingly, archaeologists have associated symbolism from Key Marco with *both* periods.[30]

Woodland Key Marco

The Woodland Period in the American Southeast spans from roughly 1000 BCE to 1000 CE. It is divided into three subperiods, Early, Middle, and Late, which respectively denote "the first widespread use of pottery across the Southeast, the rise and then decline of a vast panregional ceremonially based interaction network, and, finally, a period of political fragmentation, increasing agricultural intensification, and population growth in many areas, out of which the complex agricultural chiefdoms that characterize the ensuing Mississippian era arose."[31] Generally speaking, populations became larger, more sedentary, and increasingly complex. The aforementioned "interaction network" is known more generally as the Hopewell Tradition, which connected different populations across North America during the Middle Woodland Period. But was Key Marco part of that network?

While there is little evidence of Hopewellian exchange "away from major centers" like Cahokia, Moundville, or Poverty Point, there are some indicators of its possible influence at Key Marco. For example, the Middle Woodland saw the rise of social organization in clans, which claimed "descent from common or mythic ancestors," which the Cat might represent. However, while animal-based iconography like that at Key Marco gave way largely to solar and warfare iconography in the Late Woodland, archaeologists believe this was due to the dramatically increasing importance of agriculture (maize) in food production.[32] Of course, the Glades or Calusa cultures at Key Marco did not rely on agriculture, so it does not necessarily make sense for their cosmological worldview to change concurrently with those of the rest of the Southeast. Hopewellian artistic portrayals are also generally more naturalistic than later Mississippian imagery.[33] However, there is a lack of consensus over whether the Key Marco Cat is "naturalistic" or not.[34]

In comparison to the Key Marco artifacts, Penn Museum curator Megan

Kassabaum notes the "striking" similarities of naturalistic wooden carvings—several of which are thought to represent felines—at Fort Center, a known-Woodland site in South Florida.[35] Widmer also points to Fort Center, as well as the "Miami Circle," as evidence of trade "throughout the Woodland period in south Florida," noting Hopewellian monitor pipes and ground stone celts respectively at the sites.[36] Kassabaum also notes that flat-topped, or platform, mounds are thought to be a later development in the long history of mound-building, but there is increasing acceptance of platform mounds during the Woodland Period.[37] In reference to Widmer's 1995 excavation at Key Marco, she points out that the presence of a platform mound, would, in the past, have been presumed Mississippian, but now cannot necessarily be ruled out as Woodland.[38]

Mississippian Key Marco

The Mississippian Period, which follows the Woodland Period from 1000 to 1500 CE, refers in southeastern archaeology to a time during which chiefdom-level cultures generally "practiced a maize-based agriculture, constructed (generally) platform mounds for elite residences and various corporate and public functions, and shared, to a considerable extent, a common suite of artifact types and styles, particularly in the realm of pottery (usually shell-tempered) and certain symbolic or prestige related artifacts."[39] Woodland animal-focused religion gave way to cosmologies centered around "solar and warfare iconography."[40]

The Key Marco artifacts are commonly associated with known Mississippian designs and motifs. In the mid-twentieth century, they were important in defining the "Buzzard Cult" or "Southern Cult," an early precursor of the SECC.[41] Archaeological sites thought to be emblematic of the Buzzard Cult included such major cultural centers as Etowah, Spiro, and Moundville, and at least according to archaeologist John Griffin, Key Marco. Griffin compares two artifacts from Key Marco, one wood and one stone, with six others from Florida, all of which bear spider designs.[42] Milanich too cites evidence of the spider motif—which is also carved into materials of European origin—as evidence of Key Marco's placement within the Southern Cult and a post-1250 CE date.[43] Circular shell gorgets, carved into cross symbols out of lightning whelks, are also possible Mississippian indicators at Key Marco.[44]

Feline deities also appear as imagery in the Mississippian SECC—particularly in the form of *piasas*, or "Underwater Panthers." Examples of these "monstrous" creatures, usually composites of felines, birds, reptiles, and humans, are found in engraved bone and shell artifacts in Arkansas, Mississippi, Oklahoma, and Tennessee.[45] Generally, the Underwater Panther is believed to preside over the Underworld and is frequently associated with shamanism and witchcraft. A "metaphorical creature" and symbol of fertility, a *piasa* has the ability to travel between realms—the Underworld, Middle World, and Overworld.[46] Clearly, the Cat must at least be considered a *piasa* candidate due to its composite human and feline features, although its "heroic" and (debatably) naturalistic depiction seemingly subvert the monstrosities ordinarily depicted in Mississippian artwork.[47] The forked eye and scroll, a variation of which appears on the Cat, is also a common SECC decorative motif representing the Underworld.[48]

Yet, some archaeologists have pointed out that "the [Key Marco] designs bear only partial similarities to those associated with the SECC" and have either placed them into a category all their own or acknowledged the possibility of an earlier—possibly even Woodland—date.[49] Archaeologists William Marquardt and Karen Walker argue that the Calusa were never fully "Missisippianized," given that they never adopted the three practices considered essential to Mississippian culture: "maize agriculture, special-purpose nonmortuary earthworks, and the manufacture of shell-tempered pottery."[50] Perhaps then, Key Marco's mysterious artwork is best explained as a Woodland/Mississippian hybrid: "Woodland-esque" motifs on Mississippian-aged artifacts, in part chalked up to Calusa isolationism.

Clearly, there are quite a few differences in thought when determining an age or cultural affiliation for the Key Marco artifacts. Collectively, their unique designs and motifs cannot even be definitively pinpointed to either the Woodland or Mississippian Periods. This only adds to the confusion produced by the divergent radiocarbon dates, contradictory pottery types, and other factors, resulting in a stubbornly uncertain age for all of Cushing's artifacts, including the Key Marco Cat. So, while the exact age of the Cat itself remains unknown, it is at least 500 years old—and possibly up to 1,000 years older. Whether all of the Key Marco artifacts are the same age depends on whether the bulk of them were deposited in a single event or accumulated sporadically over a long period of time.

A Date with Destiny

One of the major unknowns in the Key Marco Cat age conundrum is just how it wound up in the muck that preserved it. This mystery, like so many others surrounding the site, is oft debated. There are four primary theories: 1) hurricane (or storm), 2) fire, 3) fleeing invasion, or 4) facing invasion. These theories all have one thing in common: eventual abandonment of the site by its residents. As Gilliland points out, "the wealth, variety, and conditions of the artifacts are evidence that abandonment was sudden and involuntary." Most of the artifacts seemed to still be in functional or aesthetically pristine condition when found, leaving one to question why they would be left behind. Gilliland points to a lack of intact full-size canoes at the site as further evidence of its abandonment, as its residents likely used the canoes in their journey or escape.[51] However, the presence of a single canoe paddle, along with two canoe fragments, does confirm canoe usage at the site.

The Storm Theory

Hurricanes have been a part of life in Southwest Florida for as long as humans have lived there. In the past century plus, the Marco Island area has suffered direct landfalls from several major hurricanes, including the 1910 Cuba Hurricane, Hurricane Donna (1960), Hurricane Wilma (2015), and Hurricane Irma (2017). It has also been impacted by east-coast landfalling hurricanes that traversed the narrow peninsula, such as the 1926 Miami Hurricane, the 1929 Bahamas Hurricane, the 1935 Labor Day Hurricane, and Hurricane Andrew (1992)—all deadly storms known primarily for the catastrophic destruction and fatalities they caused elsewhere. Over a chronological window of more than fifteen centuries, the Key Marco location has likely been impacted by dozens of major hurricanes.

Southwest Florida's archaeological record can indicate the presence of hurricanes.[52] At the Wightman site on Sanibel Island, for example, archaeologists uncovered possible evidence of major storms associated with sea-level rise between 400 and 600 CE.[53] The presence of certain species of deeper-water marine animals, such as surf clams, pen shells, and sea urchins (not ordinarily food sources), can suggest a storm surge, especially if they are found en masse in a single layer.[54]

When Cushing excavated Key Marco in 1896, he and his crew found important objects like masks and figureheads, many in perfect condition, scattered across more than 8,000 square feet. What's more, they were found in a "somewhat thicker stratum of brownish gray peaty marl, soft, tremulous, exceedingly foul-smelling, and rich in the best preserved relics we discovered."[55] In a visit to nearby Everglades City shortly after Hurricane Irma in 2017, I observed a thick layer of foul-smelling gray "slime" uniformly coating much of the area.

Figure 17. Artist's rendering of the aftermath of a major storm at Key Marco. Artwork by Merald Clark.

It was particularly heavy at the inlet of the Barron River, which is where the brunt of the storm surge entered the city. Could this be an explanation for the thick sublevel of "peaty marl" unearthed by Cushing? Perhaps a dramatic storm surge enveloped the large shellwork site, depositing all the objects at once into a low-lying cavity and sealing them in for centuries. Some experts think that is exactly what happened.

Cushing was the first to postulate that the items had been deposited into the muck by a hurricane, doing so in his 1896 *Report:* "For at this point other charred specimens occurred, as though here fire had added its destructiveness to the storm that demolished the buildings or scaffolds from which all these things seemed to have fallen."[56] Cushing also apparently suspected that Key Marco's residents were accustomed to frequent storms, suggesting that they used engineering to combat their ill effects: "A number of long, straight and narrow canals . . . stretched in from the western side, the lower end of which was enclosed and extended by a massive, level-topped sea-wall . . . reaching nearly a quarter of a mile into the mangrove swamps, and indicating that when it was built, this had been the stormward side, which it had therefore been necessary to protect."[57]

Furthering Cushing's belief that the items were deposited by storm were his observations of the placement of objects. "By far the greater number of objects were, however, promiscuously scattered—although, as I have said, more abundant between and around the ends or along the edges of the low, submerged benches I have described, than elsewhere. Not a few of them—and this was especially the case with long and originally more or less fragile articles like spear-shafts and stays—appeared to have been broken in falling. Occasionally we found fragments separated by considerable distance which, when brought together, fitted perfectly. . . . From the fact that many of the objects lay suspended, as it were, in the mud above the bottom, I judged that when these remains were thrown down into the little water court, the spaces between the house-benches and around the borders of the quays at least, must have been already choked up somewhat with debris or refuse and slime or mud; for out in the middle of the court where the deep open space occurred throughout the channel between the two canals, little was found in the way of art remains, except such as lay directly upon, or very near to, the bottom."[58]

In the years since Cushing's report, others have supported his theory that the items were deposited in a single storm event. C. B. Moore also postulates that a hurricane deposited the artifacts. "We believe Mr. Cushing's discoveries at Marco were an isolated case, and in fact, Mr. Cushing has so expressed himself to us. Perhaps a hurricane crushed in, at that spot, a group of dwellings, including a temple or sacerdotal house."[59] The hurricane hypothesis continued into later decades, likely influenced by Cushing's and Moore's assertions. In 1951, Harriet Wardle writes, "In all that cleared court of the Pile Dwellers, no trace was found of the coming of the Spaniards; yet, in the light of the modern science of pot-sherd dating, scarcely half a millennium has passed since the Key Marco people fled their falling homes before the fury of the hurricane."[60]

Milanich points to Cushing's description of the single layer of "gray peaty marl" in which the artifacts were found as evidence that the materials "at least partially, accumulated during occupation."[61] An accumulation, by definition, has greater time depth than a single event deposition (such as a hurricane), but Milanich still believes the window to be relatively restricted to the fifteenth century. William E. McGoun also recognizes the site as "of a single component," but it is unclear if he believes they were deposited in a single event or accumulated gradually over a relatively brief period of time.[62] Neither specifically mentions a hurricane as the causal event.

In more recent years, Widmer has supported the hurricane theory, even going so far as to argue that routine interactions with hurricanes helped shape the culture's complexity: "Hurricanes are important factors that disrupted the cultural adaptations in south Florida, and so political systems were needed to mitigate their adverse effects. Hierarchical chiefdoms provide a mechanism for dealing with the adversity caused by hurricane disruption to existing and future food supplies, and the destruction of houses and necessary economic resources, such as nets, boats, and other fishing gear. We have ample evidence of this loss at the 'Court of the Pile Dwellers' where utilitarian articles of wood were found buried in a submerged peat bog."[63]

Other Theories

Gilliland is the first to describe alternative scenarios, casting some doubt on the idea of a hurricane as the sole causal event.[64] Evidently, there was significant fire damage to many artifacts found at the site, as described by both Cushing and Sawyer.[65] In suggesting that a hurricane demolished the site, Cushing also notes evidence of fire: "For at this point other charred specimens occurred, as though here fire had added its destructiveness to the storm that demolished the buildings or scaffolds from which all these things seemed to have fallen."[66] Sawyer also writes, "The general conclusion that this 'Court of the Pile Dwellers' was wrecked at some time, possibly from certain evidences destroyed by fire; that the objects fell into the mud at the bottom of the shell paved lagoon and had been left here for ages until they had almost ceased to be wood."[67] As an example, the canoe paddle found at the site was standing upright, its handle burnt off at the water's surface level.[68]

However, as Gilliland points out, the torrential rains and storm surges that accompany hurricanes are not generally conducive to fire. The extreme heat generated from lightning strikes, of course, cannot be ruled out, nor can a more concentrated type of storm, such as a tornado, waterspout, or severe frontal boundary. Or perhaps the items were deposited by a hurricane only to be burned later in a "clean-up" effort by displaced residents. It might seem plausible that a fire at the site days or weeks after a storm could have burnt off what remained near the surface. However, there is some evidence that the fire started *before* their deposition, such as charring on the *lower* end of the canoe paddle (the end farthest from the surface).[69] The notion of a solely fire event, say from a lightning strike, accident, or intentional torching, is unlikely due to the large quantities of wood and plant fiber that survived uncharred.

Gilliland also points out that the objects would likely have to have been pushed down into the muck by something larger and heavier, such as a collapsing roof or building framework. Otherwise, she reasons, many of the wooden objects would have had a tendency to float on the watery surface, while those objects of denser materials, such as ceramic, shell, and stone, would have naturally sunk to the bottom. She references the apparent tendency of "many [Southeastern Native] peoples living in thatched dwellings . . . to store articles not in use up under the thatch roof."[70] Gilliland also notes that the site may have given up only a small fraction of what was originally destroyed in the event, which would have been strewn about elsewhere and faced rapid deterioration in the Florida sun.

Cushing's description of the site as he found it meshes well with Gilliland's observations and seems to rule out an intentional deposition. To Cushing, the artifacts "did not present the appearance of deliberate deposition. They looked as though they had fallen and sunken where we found them—some being upside down—as though they had been hanging, or else lying, tucked away in the houses or on the scaffolds above, and had been washed out . . . into the water alongside and below, had become water-logged and had gradually been covered by mud."[71] He too envisioned the site's original residents living "side by side all around the court, [in] comparatively long, narrow, and low, thatched and latticed houses."[72]

The most likely alternative to a natural storm-induced deposition is one caused by human activity, possibly even hostile or tragic in nature. Again, Gilliland offers several scenarios. Perhaps the community faced an invasion from a hostile agent, maybe a warring tribe or European invaders, and fled the location, burning their village behind them. Or, perhaps the invaders themselves burned the empty village to the ground. Gilliland speculates that if the village's men were away in their canoes, leaving only women and children vulnerable to a surprise attack at the site, it could explain the absence of canoe remains.[73] Indulging this theory further, perhaps the men set the fire after returning to find they had lost everything, with no further desire to live at the site.

The absence of European goods at the site does not necessarily preclude European involvement in the village's destruction. As is known from Father Juan Rogel's interactions with the Calusa at Mound Key in 1567, he "repeatedly pushed for the destruction of the 'temple of idols.'"[74] While he was unsuccessful at Mound Key, perhaps some of his likeminded compatriots got their wish at Key Marco.

Cushing did recover two human skulls from Key Marco, along with some long bones of possible ceremonial importance. The Calusa were known to dance with the heads of human sacrifices, which could account for the skulls. Two of the human long bones, both fibulae, were fashioned into daggers, meaning that they were not the result of a sudden burial. Based on this evidence, if the site were invaded, and victims claimed on location, there is little evidence for it, especially at a village with an estimated 500 residents.[75] However, in Gilliland's inventory of human remains from the site, she lists ten whole human femurs, five fragments of human femurs, and one fragment of a child's femur. This indicates a minimum of at least seven individuals found at the site, five from the ten whole femurs, one from the child, and at least another one from the femur fragments. Closer study of these remains might reveal new information about the individuals themselves, which could in turn provide new information about the site.[76]

New Theories

I venture to offer several additional theories, which to my knowledge have not been put forward. Perhaps the Key Marco villagers, likely well aware of Juan Ponce de León and the Spanish before their first excursion to the Southwest Florida coast in 1513, preemptively abandoned the site in order to avoid contact with the foreign invaders.[77] They may have destroyed the village themselves to cover their own tracks, or, perhaps upon discovering what they perceived to be an abandoned site full of sacrilegious articles, the Europeans destroyed it with prejudice and in support of their own religious beliefs. Perhaps the villagers even deposited the items with the hope of someday returning to collect them, as others have suggested.[78] Maybe the site's abandonment was a reaction to European-borne diseases, which would have been taking a noticeable toll on the population. The only logical course of action in dealing with the spread of disease might have been to destroy the site and abandon what might have been perceived as "spoiled" or ineffective goods while retreating to a less sickly location.

Or perhaps the site's destruction had nothing to do with Europeans. Instead, it may have been a form of punishment handed down from the Calusa capital at Mound Key for perceived disobedience or switching allegiances. As mentioned in chapter 1, archaeologists believe the area known as Muspa fell under Calusa control sometime around 1350 CE.[79] Perhaps the destruction of this site was a direct result of whatever political or social realignments were happening in the area at the time. There is precedent for this in the ethnohistorical record, as on October 2, 1568, Jesuit Juan Rogel witnessed the Calusa king dancing with the heads of four slain town chiefs for switching allegiances after he assumed the throne.[80] Or, if the sixteenth century dates for the Key Marco site are correct, perhaps this account even describes the *literal* events at Key Marco, disowned and abandoned during a period of European-induced political turmoil.

The theory of gradual accumulation over many centuries would require remarkable cultural memory over dozens of generations, granted it may have been a place of major spiritual importance. However, the general consistency of the artistic styles seen on decorated pieces does not seem to indicate gradual deposition, nor does the generally inefficient and apparently random placement of artifacts from an otherwise complex and organized society. This theory also assumes a stasis in the environment over many centuries, when in fact Key Marco's people may have left and resettled several times over in response to changes in climate and sea level, as has been demonstrated at Pineland.[81]

This raises a final hypothesis, that perhaps the residents at Key Marco were simply responding to local environmental factors outside of sudden and short-term storm events. Perhaps certain preferred food supplies were being overharvested, or a severe and prolonged red-tide episode made the location undesirable or uninhabitable. Overharvesting of fish and shellfish might have materialized in the archaeological record if the site had been properly excavated and recorded. Given the site's irreversibly altered condition, that level of detail is now virtually impossible to extrapolate. One can only speculate as to whether the *Court of the Pile Dwellers* was the sad result of its Native population reaching a breaking point, waving a "white flag" before relocating in hopes of finding a more prosperous situation elsewhere.

More or Less

Clearly, the age of the Key Marco Cat is still up for debate. Paradoxically, it seems that sometimes the more is learned, the less is known with certainty. During more than a century of study, the Cat's acceptable date range has expanded from a single century to more than ten. Yet, as promising new technologies continue to emerge and the artifacts continue to be preserved, there will be new opportunities to add to our collective understanding of the site's chronology. Hopefully, any new clues will narrow the timeframe for once, rather than expanding it further.

5

Four Hundred Years of Solitude

When Ponce de León first reached the Gulf coast of Florida near the mouth of the Caloosahatchee River on May 23, 1513, the Key Marco Cat likely sat beneath the surface at what is now Marco Island. It would continue to sit there for *at least* another 382 years, until its recovery in March 1896.[1] That's more than five times the average modern global life span, and likely closer to ten times that of the Key Marco residents.[2] Generations of people came, lived upon, and left Marco's shores during those intervening years, all of which the Cat silently survived.

On the day the Cat was entombed in Marco's muck, a Glades or Calusa cacique likely governed the region, their culture still holding sovereignty over its native land. When it was extricated on March 5, 1896, Henry Laurens Mitchell governed the state of Florida, by then a territory of the United States of America.[3] In between, the Cat, unbeknownst to it, changed metaphorical "hands" *five* times, technically belonging to *four* different governments.

This chapter examines the more than 382 "lost" years between the Cat's deposition and its rediscovery, examining the occurrences (and nonoccurrences) happening just a whisker away, all of which would subtly influence its life's ultimate trajectory. It explores not only what was occurring above the surface, both culturally and politically, but also underneath the surface, examining the unique chemistry and geology that prevented it from deteriorating.

Above the Surface (1513–1896)

Calusa Persistence (1513–1711)

It is important not to necessarily connotate the original "loss" of the Key Marco artifacts with a singular event marking the decline of Calusa society. It is generally accepted that the artifacts were deposited into the water "court" prior to contact with Europeans. So, even while the artifacts sat beneath the surface, Calusa people continued to traverse the shell mounds and sandhills of Muspa for another two centuries. Several generations of locals may have been relatively unaffected by, at least on a direct individual day-to-day level, the larger peninsular incursions happening farther north. The deposition of the Key Marco Cat and other artifacts may have foreshadowed the eventual demise of Calusa society, but it did not define it.

The Calusa resisted European colonization for more than 200 years. By the mid-eighteenth century, however, the combination of disease, warfare, slavery, and displacement proved too much to overcome. The Calusa had no guns to repel enemy invaders and even the most formidable weapons could not defend against disease. Smallpox, measles, typhus, and other deadly illnesses dramatically reduced the number of Calusa in Southwest Florida. Further complicating matters for the Calusa, displaced Native American groups to the north, such as the Creek and Yamassee, began moving into Florida during the late seventeenth century. Between 1704 and 1711, these groups routinely raided and captured the Calusa as slaves, trading them to the English in exchange for muskets and ammunition.

In 1711, a Calusa cacique guided 270 Native Floridians to Cuba to escape persecution. More than 200 died of disease shortly thereafter, including the cacique of Muspa. In 1760, the last of South Florida's Native people—about sixty people in total—fled to Cuba after a brutal Creek raid at Key West. Spain surrendered Florida to England in 1763 and those that remained at Spanish missions also withdrew to Cuba, the last known exodus of Florida's Native people. It is possible that some Calusa descendants survived in Cuba. It is also conceivable that some Calusa remained in Florida, eventually living alongside the Seminoles, whose ancestors moved into South Florida in the 1800s. However, because there is no living speaker of the Calusa language, nor is there a place to go and meet Calusa people, anthropologists consider the Calusa "extinct" as a culture.[4]

Marco under Five Flags (1760–1870)

More than a century passed between the last Calusa exodus from Florida and the arrival of W. T. Collier, Marco Island's first pioneer settler, in 1870.[5] On the surface, it appears that "not much" happened on Marco Island during those 110 years, especially when compared to the generations of human activity that occurred during the preceding 6,000 years. Yet, historical accounts describe Marco Island during an age of conflict and expansion. On a local level, the island carried on its function as an important navigational landmark and haven for farmers and fisherfolk. On a national level, it played an important role in Florida's Seminole Wars and the American Civil War. Though "dormant" by comparison to the periods it was sandwiched between, Marco Island's "forgotten century" was fundamental to its transition from a prominent Calusa town to an industrious pioneer settlement on the edge of the American frontier. Its development ultimately resulted in the discovery of the Key Marco Cat.

Viewing this period in Marco Island's history from a macroperspective reveals a fascinating microstudy in global geopolitical history. The Key Marco Cat is now thought of as a "national treasure" of the United States of America. Appropriately, it is preserved in perpetuity by the Smithsonian Institution, the U.S. federal government's official repository of objects, works of art, and scientific specimens.[6] Yet, since its loss at Key Marco, it sat encased in muck that at various times technically "belonged" to several other foreign entities. Aside from falling under the jurisdiction of *at least* one Native American culture prior to its deposition, the Key Marco muck changed proverbial "hands" five different times between four different governments since 1760. Marco Island has metaphorically "flown the flag" of Spain (1760–1763; 1783–1821), Great Britain (1763–1783), the Confederate States (1861–1865), and the United States of America (1821–1861; 1865–present).[7]

Even after the United States officially staked its claim to Florida, the boundaries around Key Marco continued to change. Key Marco was technically within the boundaries of three Florida counties prior to 1896, including St. Johns (1821–1823), Monroe (1823–1887), and Lee (1887–1923) counties.[8] Florida's Seminoles also had legitimate claim to the Marco Island area for about two months in 1839, after negotiating a peace with Gen. Alexander Macomb and the United States government during the Second Seminole War. However, that agreement was nullified after an attack on a Southwest Florida trading post.[9] When the artifacts were collected by Cushing in 1896, Marco was still part of Lee County. Marco Island has been part of Collier County since its formation out of Lee County in 1923.[10] This sometimes leads to confusion in dated museum records, which still describe present-day Collier County artifacts as being from Lee County.

Marco's Pioneer Settlers (1870–1896)

One important factor in the Key Marco Cat's preservation, often mentioned only in obligatory passing, is the landowner's willingness to allow an archaeologist to not only exhume materials from his Florida land, but also to receive all of the accolades, credit, and fame for their discoveries. William David Collier (1852–1934) was the owner of the parcel at Marco that would yield the famous treasures, and in fact, was their first discoverer.[11] The objects that Collier found, sometime in early 1895, consisted of "curious old rope, fragments of wood and a neatly finished shell cup, made from a conch."[12]

When Collier first settled the island with his family in 1870, one of W. T. and Barbara Collier's nine children, he was about eighteen years old. As a young man, he transported goods, produce, and livestock by sailboat along the Gulf coast between New Orleans and Key West, earning his common moniker, "Captain Bill." In Cedar Key, north of Tampa, he met his first wife Margaret "Maggie" Eliza McIlvaine (1858–1896), where the two were married in 1880. Collier moved back to Marco with Maggie in 1882 when he learned of his father's poor health and quickly became its most influential resident. He built, owned, and operated a general store, post office, shipyard, lumberyard, and hotel at Marco, transforming the remote point of land into an essential stopover on any journey along the Southwest Florida coast. Collier was also a successful farmer, growing large vegetable crops, fruit trees, and thousands of scenic coconut-bearing palms.[13]

Clearly, Collier was a man of ambition and forethought, carving out a niche for himself in the Florida wilderness while consistently pulling up the rest of his community with him. Enter Frank Hamilton Cushing in 1896, a Victorian-era academic elite from the nation's capital, with a grandiose vision of Collier's land and bold claims about its significance. What was a valuable source of vegetable fertilizer to Collier was a priceless treasure box to Cushing. Collier more typically engaged with people from the remote—and often dangerous—Everglades and Ten Thousand Island regions of Florida, including the infamous murderer Edgar J. Watson of nearby Chatham Bend and the legendary John Gomez of Panther Key.[14]

Yet, Collier also had an appreciation for adventure, culture, and nature, having traveled from Florida to the Centennial International Exposition of 1876 in Philadelphia—the first World's Fair—at age twenty-four. There, he presented such curiosities as "birds, bird's eggs, peculiar fish, and strange shells," collected during his travels around the Florida peninsula.[15] In a remarkable coincidence, a nineteen-year-old Frank Hamilton Cushing was also at the expo as curator of an exhibition for the Smithsonian Institution, as was a thirteen-year-old Wells Sawyer, who was just beginning to discover the interests that would drive him to become a career artist.[16] Their paths likely never crossed at the time, but when the trio was brought together at Marco twenty years later, they unknowingly had something in common.[17]

When Cushing arrived at Collier's place for the first time—likely without prior warning—at around five o'clock in the evening on June 3, 1895, Cushing described him as "very civil (but bursting with irreligion)."[18] Some have taken this to mean that he constantly swore, which might have offended the polite Cushing, but Collier's father was an ardent atheist, so Cushing's description could also have been literal.[19] Regardless, Cushing describes being "most courteously received" by Collier. He continues by describing artifacts that Collier showed him, noting that he was "very willing for digging; probably keen, but most civil and interested beyond question." The next day, Collier showed Cushing around the entirety of the Key Marco site, by which Cushing was impressed and inspired. In his journal, he again noted Collier's cordiality, writing, "Collier very courteous and invites me to dine with them tonight. Has also several men and offers to take me out to numerous sand mounds." Cushing, before heading back to Washington, D.C., secured permission from Collier to return the following year.[20]

When Cushing returned to Marco on February 26, 1896, he made note in his journal of Collier's "fine new hotel," which had opened since his previous visit.[21] Collier wasn't there when initially called upon, but thankfully Cushing found Maggie Collier, who "was very cordial and said digging would be free to us & welcome." Cushing did later find Collier, who once again was "most affable."[22] As I know firsthand from performing archaeological surveys across rural Florida, each requiring advanced permissions from private landowners, not everyone is excited to see strangers with shovels on their property—expected or not. Collier not only permitted the excavations to occur, but also contributed directly to their success, pitching in materials such as the wood and "gutter" used to drain water from the site, and a shack for storage.[23] The Colliers also offered their hotel parlor for the drying and photography of specimens.[24]

Always the entrepreneur, perhaps Collier's intentions were not entirely altruistic, as his wife's diary indicates that he was "very proud of the muck Mr. Cushing has thrown out for us, thinks it worth $500."[25] Cushing's entire excavation was a source of fertilizer for Collier's various enterprises, although neither the scope of the project nor the amount of fertilizer produced could have been known from the outset. He likely saw it as an added bonus to what he was already going to allow on his property.[26] However, had Collier known what they would find, perhaps he would have reconsidered his written agreement, which Cushing seems to have gotten the better end of:

Figure 18. Profiles of (*left to right*) Frank Hamilton Cushing, Emily Cushing, and Wells Sawyer. Artist's rendering of their arrival at Marco aboard the *Silver Spray* in 1896. Artwork by Merald Clark.

"Immediately on arriving at Key Marco, I made arrangements with Captain Collier whereby, in return for saving such muck as we should turn over in our excavations, I would be permitted to retain all objects discovered, and if desirable, to exploit the little triangular 'Court of the Pile Dwellers' from border to border."[27]

"The beauty of our finds is such that even the crude natives here are interested. They are moved to excavate for themselves as soon as I shall have gone; but fortunately I made a written contract with Captain Collier that for the privilege of working undisturbed to the end I would save for him all the surface muck removed. I have reason to think even he is now beginning to regret the exclusive right he gave me."[28]

Perhaps Collier's enthusiasm over the muck's value was self-inflated in order to mask his own regret, but in the end, he must have taken some solace in knowing that finds from his land would be appreciated for generations to come. As Pulitzer Prize–winning author Jack E. Davis puts it, Collier's "lack of greed" demonstrates that he "was acting in the interest of historical research."[29] Considering the circumstances before him, Collier's unselfishness, even if borne partially out of ulterior motives, was laudable. The Antiquities Act of 1906, created out of concern over rampant looting of archaeological sites, would not be ratified for another ten years. Historic preservation was not a major obstacle in the development of the United States' hinterlands, and there were no regulations protecting archaeological sites like there are today. Yet Collier was willing to give away, free of charge, all archaeological findings at the site. The spirit of most American homesteaders at the time was to acquire as much land as possible as cheaply as possible, often to turn a profit. While Collier certainly turned a profit out of his forty-plus acres at Marco, he never saw the archaeological discoveries as an opportunity to "make a buck," treating Cushing hospitably in both 1895 and 1896, promising him the finds, and not reneging when they turned out to be astonishing.

In fact, Cushing was not the only archaeologist that Collier allowed to collect from his property. Amateur explorer and retired British military officer Charles Day Durnford (1846–1908), who in 1895 brought his discoveries to Philadelphia and wound up attracting Cushing to Marco, donated items from Collier's property into the British Museum's collections.[30] Notable anthropologists C. B. Moore, Aleš Hrdlička, and Matthew Stirling visited Collier's property in Cushing's wake, all with diminished results, but each collecting at will.[31] Collier himself is even credited as a donor of a large "unusually fine" lightning whelk shell tool presently at the NMAI. It was apparently rejected by Cushing during his 1896 field excavation but held on to by Collier and presented as a gift to the Museum of the American Indian, Heye Foundation (now the NMAI), via C. B. Moore around 1924.[32]

Despite his generosity, the years following the Pepper-Hearst Expedition were especially cruel to Collier. His wife Maggie, whose diary serves as a valuable third-party chronicle of Cushing's time at Marco, died during childbirth only months later, in October 1896.[33] Just two years later, in March 1898, three of the Colliers' young sons were killed in a tragic boating accident (which Collier himself survived) that made national news headlines.[34] Maggie and the boys, George, Thomas, and Wilmer, are buried beneath marked headstones at the Marco Island Cemetery.[35] Given the timing of the deaths, Cushing's similar early demise, and the general public's fascination with the morbid and mysterious storytellers sometimes speak of a "Calusa curse" on Marco Island.[36]

A second notable Marco property owner, George Elliott Cuthbert, was pe-

Figure 19. A building, likely Collier's or Cuthbert's, atop the shell mounds at Key Marco. Photo by Wells Sawyer, 1896. National Anthropological Archives, Smithsonian Institution (NPC096546.00).

ripherally involved in the dig and lent support to the excavation. Cuthbert was a plume trader based out of Marco who made the "score" of a lifetime in 1889—slaughtering so many birds for their feathers that he was able to purchase four parcels of land from the Collier family that same year.[37] Although the water court was not on his direct property, portions of the larger Key Marco site were. On June 4, 1895, Cushing recounts, he "went about with Captain Collier seeing great shell settlement on his own and Capt Cuthberts place."[38] In reporting his permissions to explore the site, Cushing notes that Cuthbert, in addition to Collier, "gave me entire freedom to explore wheresoever I would, and in whatsoever manner."[39] Cuthbert also allowed Cushing and crew to use his packing house for storage during the 1896 excavation and it was on Capt. Cuthbert's wharf that Maggie Collier describes seeing the famous woodpecker tablet and three painted masks for the first time.[40]

Beneath the Surface (1513–1896)

While wars raged, boundaries changed, storms wrought havoc on coastlines, and the peninsula dramatically depopulated (then repopulated), the Key Marco Cat and its artifactual "cohort" sat virtually undisturbed in an anaerobic environment for nearly 400 years. Thus, the finds themselves seem miraculous—and in a sense, they are. They are principally derived from perishable materials such as wood, plant fiber, gourd, and natural pigments that decay more rapidly than the bone, ceramic, shell, and stone artifacts typically found in South Florida archaeological sites. But, despite their predominance in the archaeological record, the "usual suspects" likely represent only 10 percent of the overall material culture.[41] The other 90 percent is rarely (if ever) found, making Key Marco a remarkable anomaly in the Florida archaeological record and one of the most comprehensive assemblages of material culture known from pre-Columbian North America.[42] Yet, miraculous as they may seem, well-known scientific properties resulted in their preservation.

Perhaps the biggest "miracle" is that the Key Marco artifacts were recognized as artifacts in the first place. Archaeological wet sites, like the one Collier discovered on his property at Marco, are rare and often found by accident, usually because of human development or activity. The environment that safely entombs them also makes them visually unremarkable and virtually "invisible," especially to the untrained eye.[43] Collier was not an archaeologist but probably harvested garden fertilizer routinely from his surroundings. His familiarity with the local land, combined with his recent experiences at the World's Fair, probably made it easy for him to detect abnormalities that would turn out to be products of human invention. His recognition of the atypical—or out of place—is a skill that archaeologists hone over many years of visual training in their oft-specialized regions.

Cushing, in his 1896 report, provides an idea of what Collier saw at the Key Marco muck pit:

> The surface deposit throughout the entire court consisted of a stratum of spongy black or dark brown muck, permeated by both rotting and living rootlets. It was . . . thin at the margins, but eighteen or twenty inches thick throughout the middle. Below this was a somewhat thicker stratum of brownish gray peaty marl, soft, tremulous, exceedingly foul-smelling, and rich in the best preserved relics we discovered. This stratum directly overlaid and surrounded the benches I have described. Finally underneath it, between the benches and throughout the middle of the court, was a less well-defined layer of less peaty marl, intermixed with shells and other debris, and also with abundant ancient remains—which, indeed, we continued to encounter even in the underlying, comparatively firm shell and clay-marl bottom. This, however, although nearly a foot and a half thick, we could not venture to excavate, since the slightest opening made through it into the sandy reef below let in a steady stream of water from the sea.[44]

Wells Sawyer, with his vivid artistic insights, paints an even more unseemly picture:

> I shall never forget the first impressions of the muck hole in Marco, which, under the same magic touch, became the famous Court of the Pile Dwellers; the little shoots of mangroves coming up here and there, many curious weeds growing not more than twelve or sixteen inches high, all underlaid by foul-smelling black muck into which a few trenches had been dug. These were filled with water, and indeed, the whole place was like a thick sponge saturated with water holding a great quantity of salt and a large variety of smells. We had brought a crew of workmen from up the coast, but almost to a man they looked with absolute revolt upon the unpromising hole. Each face showed the feelings of its owner, and in the group of faces only one [Cushing's] was lighted by enthusiasm as we stood on the edge of the Court of the Pile Dwellers.[45]

Cushing's documentation of the site's stratigraphy is extremely limited by today's standards, but descriptive by his own time's. The details in his report, paired with a profile drawing at the bottom of Sawyer's grid system illustration, give a general idea of the site's overall composition, describing five different strata.[46] His account of an "exceedingly foul-smelling" level is consistent with the presence of hydrogen sulfide, which can only exist in the absence of oxygen and is often a telltale indicator of a waterlogged, or "wet," site. Rotting organic material gradually depletes the layer's oxygen, prohibiting bacterial growth and enabling the formation of hydrogen sulfide.[47] The gas is poisonous when breathed in large quantities, and one wonders if it affected the health of the excavators, especially Cushing, who frequently complained of headaches. The formation of an oxygen-free—or anaerobic—environment is the single most important condition of several that preserved the Key Marco artifacts, inhibiting the bacteria that ordinarily cause decay.

The term *muck* is frequently and liberally applied as a general descriptor of the *Court of the Pile Dwellers*, but may have greater significance. Cushing variously uses the distinct terms *muck*, *marl*, and *peat* to describe portions of the site's stratigraphy, but the terms are clearly not meant to be interchangeable. If Cushing used them correctly, the terms may indicate chemical properties at the site. Peats and mucks are both organic soils differentiated by the percentage of organic matter they hold. Peats form through the decomposition of vegetation and typically contain more than 75 percent organic matter. Mucks are typically comprised of between 25 percent and 75 percent organic matter in a dry state. Peats also tend to be fibrous in comparison to mucks, which are typically nonfibrous. Marls, which are also called calcitic muds, usually develop in the presence of limestone and are generally located in areas where a long dry period alternates with a brief wet period.[48]

Cushing's site descriptions are potentially useful in reconstructing past environments and depositional processes at Key Marco, although they may not mesh with modern scientific understandings of the terms. For example, he describes the surface level "muck" as "permeated by . . . rootlets" making it decidedly fibrous in nature in comparison to the "peaty marl" beneath it, which contradicts the definitions just established. He also does *not* describe the peat as fibrous, which might indicate a level of oxidization that would otherwise make the preservation of artifacts unlikely. However, his assertions cannot necessarily be dismissed as inaccurate, as it is possible for artifacts to be deposited into an already stabilized stratum, such as during a catastrophic event.[49]

It is also almost certain that, given their incredible preservation, once the items at Key Marco became saturated with water, they stayed that way until 1896. Artifacts at waterlogged sites are usually found in permanently saturated

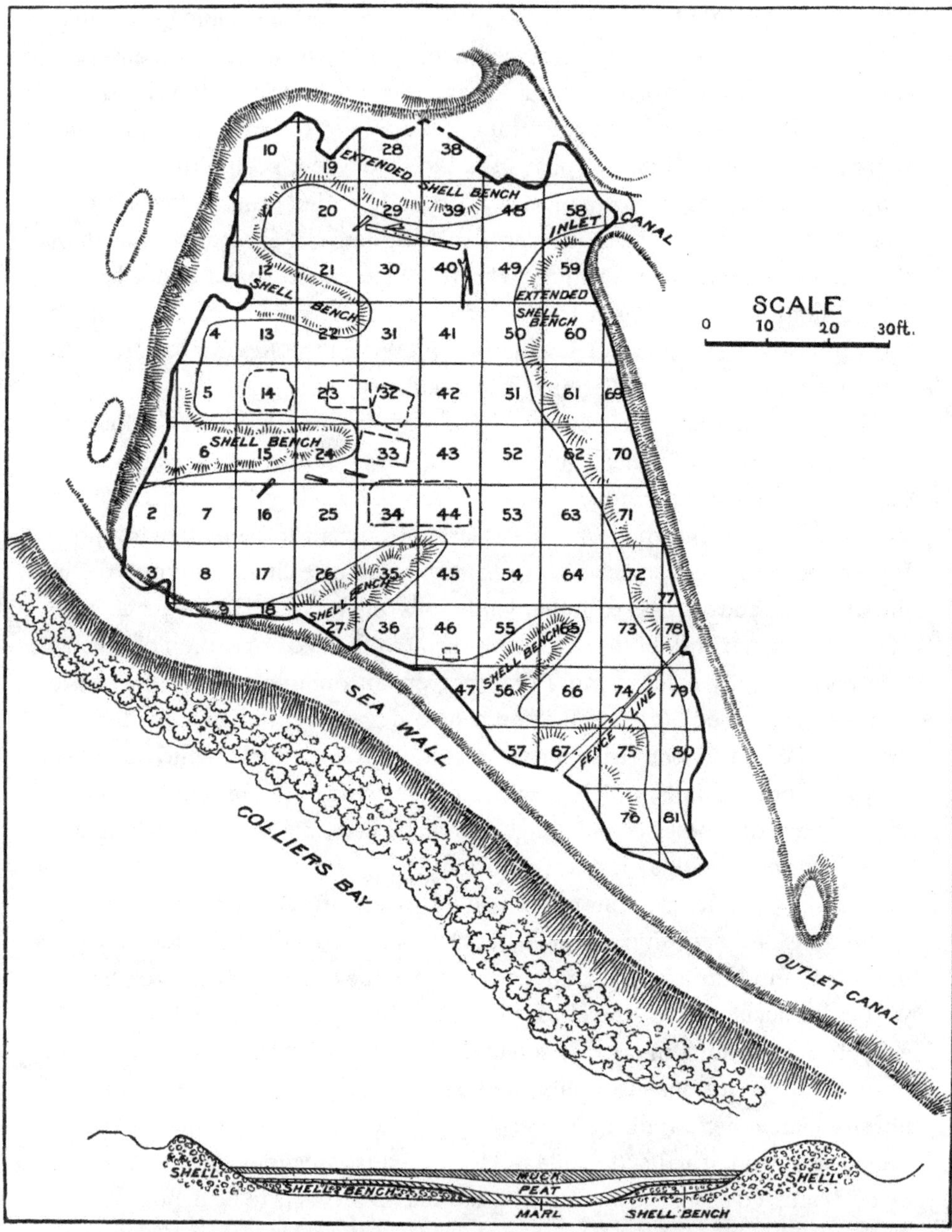

Map 4. Cushing's grid system at the *Court of the Pile Dwellers*. Map by Wells Sawyer, 1896. By permission of the American Philosophical Society.

organic soils because once the matrix dries and allows for the reintroduction of oxygen, oxidization (and thus, decomposition) of the remaining organic compounds begins.[50] There was also probably a lack of major "tidal action" or regular strong water movement across the site's surface during the artifacts' depositional period.[51] This may indicate a lower sea level—or a more elevated overall site—at the time of deposition, preventing a loss of artifacts. On June 4, 1895, seeing the muck pit for the very first time, Cushing describes it as, "covered with water surface and brackish backed up by the tide."[52]

The nature of finds at waterlogged sites also depends heavily on the chemical compositions of the deposits themselves, which often have varying hydrogen-ion concentrations—or pH levels. In more acidic wet sites, bone artifacts generally dissolve due to the abundance of calcium carbonate in their makeups. Wooden artifacts, by contrast, are better preserved in acidic peat soils. Yet at Key Marco, both materials are found in abundance. This indicates that conditions were likely "just right": an alkaline environment capable of preserving both floral and faunal materials, as well as those materials more typically found in Southwest Florida archaeological sites.[53]

No variable played a bigger factor in the alkalinity at Key Marco than the site's sheer abundance of shell, which "supercharged" its surrounding Florida peat with calcium carbonate.[54] In the absence of limestone, shell may have also helped create the marl, or calcitic mud, that Cushing identifies. Nearly all the forty-four-acre site was constructed with shells, portions of which laid below sea level. Cushing describes compacted shell "benches" that once formed long ridges, acting in some instances as "piers" or perimeter walls, but likely used more commonly as waterfront foundations beneath dwellings or other structures. A long shell "seawall" framed the southwestern boundary of the site, notably encircling and protecting the low elevation *Court of the Pile Dwellers*. Shell sloped downward from these benches and walls into and under the *Court*, forming a protective shell basin or "bowl" and allowing calcium carbonate to leach into the soil that filled it. Sawyer drew an example of these benches in profile to give an idea of their composition (map 4).[55]

Cushing believed the spaces between benches to be access points to the water, "open and deep, as if for the free passage of canoes."[56] One might assume then, that with the presence of the seawall on the southwestern border, the area of the site that became the *Court* might once have been a harbor of sorts, a protected water basin for safe and easy access to a fleet of docked canoes. The lack of canoe remains found at the site, however, does little to confirm this notion. Instead, the *Court* might have functioned as an area for fish capture and storage. The narrow inlets between each of Cushing's so-called shell benches could have been closed off with netting, thereby trapping fish and shellfish. Keeping live fish would have enabled the residents of Key Marco to maintain a surplus, as has been documented at the Calusa capital at Mound Key.[57]

Other contributing factors to the site's remarkable preservation include low light, stable temperature, and protection from predation, all provided by the thick surface level of muck that essentially sealed in the "relic-bearing" peaty marl strata underneath.[58] Combined with alkaline anaerobic conditions in a permanently waterlogged location with little tidal activity at deposition, Key Marco presented a "perfect storm" of ideal conditions that created the ultimate waterlogged site. Since *most* of the Key Marco artifacts were made of perishable materials, they offer the most "complete" known representation of material culture in pre-Columbian Florida. Had they not been protected by an unusual combination of muck, peat, marl, and shell, they would have fully decomposed in a matter of weeks or months.

Back to the Future

Time travel has long been a popular trope in works of science fiction, from H. G. Wells's *The Time Machine* (1895) to Marvel's *Avengers: Endgame* (2019). One could argue that artifacts like the Key Marco Cat are the closest things to real-life time travelers known to science *fact*. When it left its own time, European colonists had yet to reach Florida's shores. When it reached its destination, Florida was part of the United States of America, a nation of immigrants so long established that it had declared independence more than a century earlier. The object became a literal bridge between two of the most dramatically different periods in human history: pre- and postcolonial America.

During what otherwise might seem a dull and quiet fifth life, the Key Marco Cat embarked on an epic journey, a one-way voyage into the future. The fate of the object was decided through a series of large-scale conflicts and resolutions that also shaped the modern world, all while a fortunate blend of chemistry and hydrogeology safeguarded it. As the surface over the Cat's ears buzzed with activity, its cell walls filled with water, its chemical composition changed, and it somehow avoided decay for *centuries* through an incredible fusion of natural forces and luck. To me, that sounds an awful lot like science fiction.

Born Anew

The circumstances that led to the Key Marco discoveries are the stuff of legend. The sheer number of personal coincidences and serendipitous turns of events make the story read like a work of fiction. It is a story that has been well documented and well told, but some of it bears repeating, with special deference paid to the Key Marco Cat and an enhanced focus on the immediate aftermath of its recovery.[1] For as the archaeologist's exciting road to glory is often told, in truth, the less-heralded return journey *from* Florida was far more treacherous to the object itself.

This chapter highlights the sensational results of the now-famed Pepper-Hearst Expedition and details the extraordinary measures to which the Cat's finders went to preserve it and the hundreds of other priceless Key Marco artifacts. Of the Cat's nine lives, this one probably presented its greatest existential threat. Removed from the safe confines of its oxygen-free environment, the acclimatizing object became entirely reliant on people who were wholly unprepared to care for it. Not only was Cushing hard pressed to figure out a way to prevent artifacts from deteriorating on the spot, he then had to figure out how to ship them safely more than 900 miles back to the museums in Philadelphia and Washington. The seventy days between the Cat's discovery and its arrival at the Smithsonian Institution were, aside from the day it was cast into the muck, some of the most perilous of its very long life.

Frank Hamilton Cushing

Frank Hamilton Cushing (1857–1900) is a prominent figure in the field of anthropology. Hired as a curator in the National Museum's Department of Ethnology at just nineteen years old, Cushing was described as a "genius" by his peers. He is probably best known for his ethnographic fieldwork with the Zuni

Figure 20. Thomas Hovenden, *Portrait of Frank Hamilton Cushing*, oil on canvas, 16 × 22 in., Smithsonian American Art Museum, Gift of Mrs. F. H. Cushing.

people of the American Southwest. Though sometimes controversial in his approach, Cushing became one of anthropology's first practitioners of "participant observation"—the method of learning about another culture by living and taking part in it. Long lambasted for perceived inadequacies in the field, Cushing's brilliance and merit as an anthropologist, particularly regarding his discoveries and interpretations in Florida, have seen a reappraisal in recent years.[2]

In 1896, Cushing directed one of the most important excavations in the history of North American archaeology to remote and sparsely populated Marco

Island, Florida. At the time, the village at the north end of Marco Island was known simply as "Marco," and Cushing dubbed the forty-four-acre archaeological site there "Key Marco." The primary focus of Cushing's excavation was a triangular area of "muck" in the southwestern portion of the site, which he called the *Court of the Pile Dwellers*. The crew's discoveries were, as Cushing described, "literally startling"—and despite many archaeologists' best efforts, have not since been duplicated in Florida.[3]

Cushing's team uncovered "more than a thousand . . . precious examples," including painted wooden masks and figureheads, netting, rope, atlatls, wooden bowls, mortar and pestle kits, toy canoes, trays, tablets, gourds, stools, shell tool handles, shark-tooth slashing weapons, and more—all centuries old and improbably well preserved. The list is as staggering as the artifacts are stunning and the result is a spectacularly comprehensive assemblage of Native American artifacts that, to this day, offers unparalleled insight into Southwest Florida's indigenous people. As Cushing put it, "apparently, everything the people had used, had for one cause or another found its way into the deposits underlying their places of abode."[4]

"The objects found by us in these deposits were in various conditions of preservation, from such as looked fresh and almost new, to such as could scarcely be traced through or distinguished from the briny peat mire in which they were embedded. They consisted of wood, cordage and like perishable materials associated with implements and ornaments of more enduring substances, such as shell, bone and horn—for only a few shaped of stone were encountered during the entire search. Articles of wood far outnumbered all others." As Cushing would soon realize, finding the artifacts was the easy part. The real trick would be getting them back to the museum intact.

The Initial Discoveries

In February 1895, "Captain Bill" Collier (or one of his workers) ventured out to the southwestern edge of his Marco property to gather muck, presumably for fertilizing his abundant fruit trees and vegetable crops. Out of a roughly sixty-square-foot hole in the earth, unusual traces of wood, cordage, and shell began to appear—items that could have only been crafted by human hands. Collier, given his keen eye for detail and recent experiences at the World's Fair, probably soon recognized them as archaeological artifacts of some antiquity and importance.[5]

In April 1895, shortly after Collier's discovery, Charles Day Durnford was vacationing in Southwest Florida when he organized an amateur exploration of archaeological sites in the Naples area. Charles Wilkins, of Rochester, New York, participated in that expedition and, several days later, went tarpon fishing near Marco Island. Wilkins soon caught wind of Collier's finds and given his recent interest in archaeology, made a brief investigation of his own, about six feet east of Collier's digging spot. Sure enough, he found wooden cups, shell tools, and even a carved animal figurehead.[6]

Durnford quickly organized his own trip to Marco, where with the help of two of Collier's employees, he excavated more than a dozen artifacts from the muck, including rope, netting, float pegs, shell tools, and a complete wooden vessel (Durnford called it a "trencher"). Excited by his finds, Durnford still wanted a professional opinion. On his return trip to England, he stopped at the Penn Museum in Philadelphia to show his finds to curator Henry C. Mercer, a prior acquaintance. Mercer, however, was absent. Instead, Durnford ran into the museum's director, Stewart Culin (1858–1929), and his friend, the visiting Frank Hamilton Cushing.[7]

The perpetually ill Cushing was in Philadelphia visiting his personal physician, William Pepper (1843–1898), who also happened to be provost of the university and founder of the Penn Museum. He was invited to the Durnfords' hotel room with Pepper, where he immediately recognized the artifacts as "indubitably Indian and Pre-Columbian." Still, other archaeologists already had a stake in Florida, most notably Clarence Bloomfield Moore (1852–1936), to whom Pepper apparently offered the opportunity. One day after Moore declined to lead the reconnaissance, Pepper wrote to John Wesley Powell (1834–1902), director of the Smithsonian's Bureau of American Ethnology (BAE) and Cushing's boss, recommending that something be done about his ailing health: perhaps a trip to Florida was in order.[8]

Cushing was granted leave from the BAE to investigate Key Marco, with the added hopes that warm weather might improve his physical condition. His expedition, however, was funded by the Penn Museum, a fact not forgotten by Cushing when it came time to divvy artifacts between institutions years later. The arduous two-week journey to Marco, via steamship, riverboat, locomotive, horseback, and schooner, reads like a dime novel and has been retold in rollicking glory elsewhere. Cushing arrived in Punta Gorda on horseback on May 26, 1895, his rear end probably sore from the hours-long ride of thirty miles. There were no roads to Marco at that time, so he had to find his own passage by boat for the remaining seventy miles to Collier's.[9]

From Punta Gorda, Cushing sailed southward along the Southwest Florida coast, documenting other archaeological sites along the way and turning a one-day trip into eight.[10] At roughly four o'clock on June 3, 1895, his sloop rounded the corner at Big Marco Pass, the inlet from the Gulf of Mexico to the northern end of Marco Island.[11] There, an hour later along the Marco River, he found Collier at his Marco homestead.[12] Collier was "most civil and interested beyond question," agreeing to show Cushing around the following morning. The following day's weather was not so civil, however, forcing Cushing and Collier only to tour the site and discuss logistics before dining together. Cushing retired for the evening after reporting "more mosquitos than [he] ever saw before."[13]

The next morning, June 5, Cushing set about excavating the muck pit where Collier, Wilkins, and Durnford had made their discoveries. With the paid help of two of Collier's men, Cushing excavated in what would become Units 33, 34, 44, and 46 of his 1896 grid system, due south of Durnford's April excavation.[14] Unbeknownst to him, Cushing's excavation in Unit 33 was less than twenty feet away from the Key Marco Cat. But he did not have to wait long before making his first discovery. "We struck relics almost immediately and found [them] from time to time all day."[15] "After only six or seven hours of search I left this prolific place with a collection of fifteen or twenty almost absolutely unique specimens of Pre-Columbian art; for this collection consisted in the main of such objects as in nearly all other equally ancient deposits have wholly disappeared."[16]

Despite the oppressive heat, maddening bugs, and soggy working conditions, Cushing's brief reconnaissance was so fruitful that after only two days, he vowed to return for a full-scale excavation. "Thus I was more than satisfied with the results of these two days of investigation, alone, more than justified the reconnaissance I had undertaken for I even thus early realized that here was a field in which wholly new discoveries in American Archaeology or Pre-Historic Ethnology awaited the careful explorer."[17] He also apparently took pictures of the "canals and lagunes [*sic*] and . . . one to excavate," but it is unclear whether these images are amongst those now held in the National Anthropological Archives, which are generally attributed to Wells Sawyer, possibly erroneously.[18] Cushing made sure to obtain Collier's permission to return and fully excavate the site before departing on June 6, stopping again numerous times on the way back to Punta Gorda before ultimately making it to Philadelphia on July 2, 1895.[19]

Clearly, in terms of 1890s archaeology, a lot went *very* right to bring Cushing to Florida. Major credit is owed to Durnford for bringing the artifacts to the attention of professionals, as well as for his unusually expedient donation to the British Museum on July 17, 1895.[20] Had Durnford kept the artifacts for himself, failing to bring them to Cushing's attention, Collier may have let amateurs continue to disturb the site. Wilkins, too, apparently intended to donate his finds to the "Rochester Museum (of which Ward is Curator!)," referring to Ward's Natural Science Establishment in Rochester, New York, and its founder, Henry Augustus Ward.[21] Ward's enterprise, however, was known for mounting and selling specimens to other universities and museums, and the present whereabouts of Wilkins's finds, if they ever *were* donated to Ward, are unknown. Not to be overlooked, Collier's allowance of numerous strangers to pillage his property is what ultimately brought Durnford, Culin, and Cushing together, and the rest is history.[22]

The Pepper-Hearst Expedition

Cushing returned to Philadelphia on July 2, 1895, where Pepper greeted his finds with enthusiasm. Realizing the potential for further exploration, Pepper again wrote to Powell, asking for approval to send Cushing to Florida a second time. Powell granted Cushing formal permission on October 19, 1895, and funding was again to be provided by the University of Pennsylvania's Archaeology Department. Joseph Disston also volunteered the use of his schooner, the *Silver Spray*, a sponge-fishing vessel based out of Tarpon Springs. Since the expedition was a joint venture between the University of Pennsylvania and the Smithsonian Institution, the two parties agreed to an "equal division" of any recovered artifacts.[23]

Cushing left for Florida on December 6, 1895, but when he arrived in Tarpon Springs, the *Silver Spray* was away on a sponging excursion. The trip to Marco was delayed three months—until late February—but Cushing made the most of his time. With the help of his crew, he excavated important archaeological sites at Safford Mound and Hope Mound in the Tarpon Springs area, founding now-spectacular museum collections. Unfortunately, Cushing only had enough funding for three months of work, all of which were supposed to be at Key Marco. His expedition was in jeopardy until philanthropist Phoebe A. Hearst, mother of publisher William Randolph Hearst, agreed to fund the remainder of the expedition. Thus, the Pepper-Hearst Expedition, as it is now known, finally set sail for Marco.[24]

Cushing and his thirteen-person crew, including his wife Emily Tennison Magill Cushing (1860–1920), departed Tarpon Springs on February 23, 1896, bound for Marco. The trip took three days due to rough seas and a stop in St. James City, but they finally arrived at Marco at about two o'clock on February 26, 1896. They anchored the *Silver Spray* offshore in the southerly inlet to Collier Bay, between Collier's waterfront store on the east and his scenic coconut palm grove on the west. Upon arrival, Cushing made note of Collier's "fine new hotel," a building that still stands on Marco Island and would serve as "home base" for the Pepper-Hearst crew. In fact, its steps can be seen in the background of many photographs by expedition artist Wells Sawyer, in which he laid out objects on a sheet, using the angled steps to create a uniform background behind the objects.[25]

Cushing wasted little time in putting the crew to work, up early the following morning to begin the excavation. He had clearly learned something from the difficult working conditions of his reconnaissance trip and came armed with a plan to combat the site's perpetually saturated state.

Figure 21. The Key Marco site during its excavation. Photo by Wells Sawyer, 1896. National Anthropological Archives, Smithsonian Institution (NPC096911.00).

> To begin, I had a few of the trees cleared away from the outer and south-westerly corner, and . . . had a trench cut through the sea-wall to as great a depth as possible without letting water in from the bay outside. I then had a long trough of ship planks constructed and placed on stakes driven deep into the muck bed, so that one end rested over the excavation and the other, lower end, in the mouth of the sluice-way through the sea-wall. Then laying heavy planks over the boggy surface to furnish foothold for the men, I set them at work baling out the old excavation with buckets. It was at first like trying to bale out the sea itself, for water flowed in as fast as taken out; but after two or three hours of steady work, it began to lower, not only in the excavation, but over the entire court.[26]

The crew "struck relics almost immediately," which were reported daily by Cushing in his journals, each day seemingly more exciting than the last.

> Three or four of us worked side by side in each section, digging inch by inch, and foot by foot, horizontally through the muck and rich lower strata, standing or crouching the while in puddles of mud and water; and as time went on we were pestered morning and evening by swarms and clouds of mosquitoes and sand-flies, and during the midhours of the day, tormented by the fierce tropic sun heat, pouring down, even thus early in the season into this little shut-up hollow among the breathless mangroves.

The working conditions were miserable, but the incredible nature of what they were finding kept them motivated.[27]

Cushing's remarkable discoveries are well known and have been reported in exhaustive detail.[28] The vast assemblage of waterlogged artifacts, most of them made from organic materials, remains the most complete and comprehensive ever discovered in a pre-Columbian Florida deposit. Between February 26 and March 3, 1896, the crew found such objects as shell "picks" with wooden handles still attached, bone pins, wooden bowls, mortar and pestle sets, palm fiber netting, palmetto thatch, gourd floats, wooden line reels, part of a wooden canoe paddle, a wooden carving of a human figure, and *many* more wholly unique treasures. Motivated though they were, and putrid working conditions aside, there was one intensely stressful drawback to their otherwise rewarding work: artifacts were disintegrating before their very eyes.[29]

Cushing estimated that roughly 25 percent of all perishable artifacts were destroyed during the excavation. When the crew "broke the seal" of Marco's muck, objects began degenerating almost immediately upon contact with the air and light. On top of that, many articles were practically indistinguishable from the surrounding muck, turning to mush as soon as excavators uncovered them with their fingers and small garden tools. Even when artifacts were successfully extracted from the earth, "not more than one-half retained their form for more than a few days." The team's primary concern quickly shifted from "will we find anything?" to "will we save anything?" The objects, in their abundant glory, were clearly special, but the earth was not going to give them up so easily.[30]

As if the excavation weren't already exciting enough, by March 4, 1896, Cushing would begin uncovering some of the artifacts that would change his expedition from *a* monumentally important one into perhaps *the* monumentally important one, at least in the annals of Florida archaeology. That Wednesday was the day he first found a *painted* wooden facemask, followed soon after by another, and then *another*. Cushing's great foresight in acquiring Wells Sawyer's artistic services for the expedition would finally pay off. Not only did Sawyer photograph most of the artifacts soon after they were unearthed, he painted vivid watercolors of the most noteworthy in their original colorized states. Many of the same objects are now damaged beyond recognition, Sawyer's images the only surviving records of their original magnificence. Cushing ended March 4, 1896, in his journal by writing, "Greatest day of my life in exploration." Little did he know that Thursday would be even better.[31]

"A Happy Day"

The date of the Cat's discovery *appears* to be March 5, 1896. Of course, like most everything associated with the expedition, there is some uncertainty. Cushing's Key Marco field journals end on March 4, 1896—the day before the Cat was found.[32] He no doubt began a new journal on March 5, as his entries resume in another field journal on April 24, 1896, but the present whereabouts of the intermediate journal are unknown.[33] It is possible that it was relocated in response to accusations of forgery surrounding a painted human figure in a clam shell, which was discovered on March 6, 1896. Who withdrew it from the series, and for what purpose, remains a mystery.[34] Fortunately, George Gause, an "unusually careful excavator" and key member of the expedition, kept his own account of the work at Key Marco.[35] His account largely jibes with Cushing's prior to March 5, so there is no reason to doubt his journal entry on March 5: "Thursday doings went work early got some very interesting speciments 1 lyons

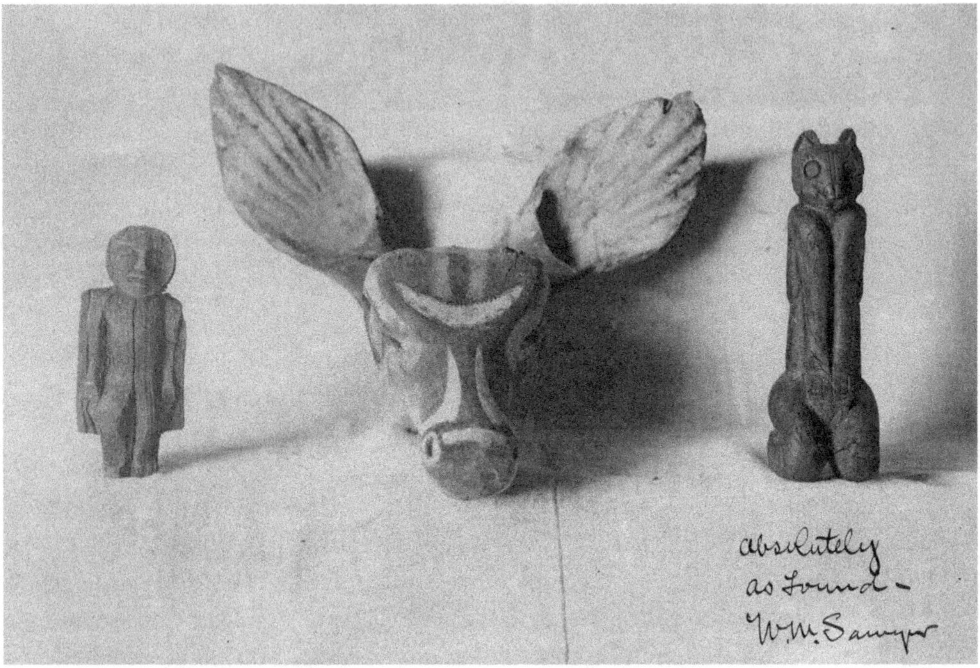

Figure 22. Three noteworthy wooden artifacts "absolutely as found," including the Key Marco Cat. Photo by Wells Sawyer, 1896. National Anthropological Archives, Smithsonian Institution (NPC096574.00).

image 1 womans image 1 turtle head all of good hard wood 6 bowls 2 pessells some carved boards 1 ball wax 2 little cannos 1 plumett rapped with thread and waxed found by Robt Day went off nice bowls found by Alfred bowls and pessell by George Turtle George Lyon and woman found by Mr. Cushing. Mrs. Cushing seams well dilighted."[36]

Given Gause's consistent misspellings of other common words, it is safe to assume that "lyon" is intended to mean "lion," which is likely a reference to the Key Marco Cat. Cushing refers to it four times as a "mountain-lion" or "lion" in his *Preliminary Report*, making him the likely source of Gause's species attribution.[37] In fact, much of Cushing's language at the site is reflected in the separate accounts of his crew. For example, when Cushing called March 4, 1896, "the greatest day of my life in exploration," the less experienced Gause similarly called it, "The happies day ever gleaned on Marco."[38] It also appears, from Gause's account, that Cushing himself is the actual discoverer of the Cat, the first person to unearth it from the muck and lay eyes on it after hundreds of years.

Cushing would go on to single out March 5 as a "happy day" in his formal presentation to the American Philosophical Society for no other reason than it was the day that he found the Cat.[39] Given the stress that Cushing was under due to intense working conditions, uncertain finances, and the rapid deterioration of the artifacts, the Cat seems to have revealed itself to Cushing and his crew at the perfect time. Indeed, Wells Sawyer's feelings about the whole adventure seem to change before and after this little window in time. In letters home, Sawyer writes from aboard the *Silver Spray* at Marco in early March 1896, "I very much fear that the dreams I had as to my getting something . . . out of this is not going to materialize."[40]

Sawyer also doubts his own work at the time, stating in a letter postmarked March 4, 1896, "My painting is simply awful," and in another letter postmarked March 8, "I haven't painted a thing worth doing. Some way I don't seem to be in it at all."[41] Given how slowly mail was delivered to and from Marco at the time (as Sawyer reports "only a couple of times a week" and by boat), these letters were likely written before the truly incredible finds began in earnest on March 4, 1896. By March 17, in a letter to his fiancée Kathleen Bailey, he raves about the Key Marco dig, saying "the wonders which this old key has given up are unique in N. American archaeology."[42] Recognizing the importance of the finds and likely inspired by Cushing's enthusiasm over them, by April 12, 1896, he declares, "I am doing the best work of my life so far. It's the only work of any distinction which I have ever done and it is going to do us both good."[43] Finding an artifact like the Cat in an otherwise hot, damp, and smelly muck pit can have that effect.

Lion in Wait

The Key Marco Cat is one of less than two dozen artifacts of "more than a thousand" that Cushing provides any individual provenience for in the grid system published with his *Preliminary Report*: "I found this gem of our art collections—on a happy day—at a depth of not more than twenty inches, just between the overlying muck and the middle stratum of peat-marl, near the edge of the shell-bench—in section 15."[44] Sawyer later confirms what little stratigraphy is known, probably echoing or even directly citing Cushing's own assertions: "It was found by Mr. Cushing at a depth of some twenty inches between the overlying muck and the peat marl."[45]

Section 15 in the detailed topographical map by Wells Sawyer is (map 4) largely defined by a subterranean feature that Cushing calls a "shell bench."

Cushing presumed the shell benches to be "piers or the foundations for long, pile-supported quays or scaffolds; upon which . . . had been constructed, side by side all around the court, comparatively long, narrow, and low, thatched and latticed houses."[46] The 10' x 10' unit, in the west-central portion of the muck pit, is intersected by the bench from west to east, underlying at least three-quarters of the unit's surface area. A long "sea wall" that Cushing describes elsewhere lies about twenty feet to the south of the unit.[47] Shell benches are spaced relatively evenly around the rest of the court, with one about seventeen feet to the north of section 15 and another about seventeen feet to the southeast.

Cushing is somewhat fortunate to have recovered the Key Marco Cat *at all* given that section 14, the neighboring 10-by-10-foot area sharing the same shell bench, was excavated prior to Cushing's arrival. As he communicates in his *Preliminary Report*, "The locations of preliminary excavations by Collier, Wilkins, Durnford and myself, [were] in sections 14, 23, 32, 33, 34 and 44."[48] The four other opened units are all within fifteen feet of section 15. In fact, according to an early draft of the map at the Brooklyn Museum (figure 15), both Collier and Wilkins excavated from section 14 in February 1895, in all likelihood walking directly on top of the ground encapsulating the Key Marco Cat at some point during their work.[49] Cushing describes finding the Cat "near the edge of the shell bench," presumably the southern edge, placing it only about ten feet from where section 14 was dug up in 1895.[50]

Maybe the lighting or breeze was just right in (what would become) section 14 that day, or maybe there was a lack of vegetation that made it ideal for digging, or maybe it was just the first place Collier and crew stumbled upon. Maybe it was a combination of factors. Cushing writes about the site, "It was covered with a dense grove of mangroves, the long skinny roots of which were interlocked to such an extent that on investigation save in the two or three very small open spaces where Capt. Collier and Col. Durnford and his friends had dug small holes, it was almost impossible to penetrate it."[51] Whatever their reasons for choosing those spots, the Cat would lie in the protective embrace of the mangroves for another thirteen months, unbeknownst to the diggers making so much commotion just a few feet to its north. Had Collier or Wilkins decided to face a different direction, or struck an impenetrable root, or moved to get the sun out of their eyes, the Cat might well have been destroyed, if not collected by someone entirely different. As with Wilkins, who discovered an undisclosed animal figurehead that was never seen again, it could have walked off and vanished.

A Game Changer

Heading into the first week of March 1896, Cushing was distressed. The *Silver Spray* delays had drained expedition resources and postponed the trip to Marco by twelve weeks. Two days before arriving, to paint a picture of his mood, Cushing writes in his journal, "There is no longer anything but evil fortune for me on this [expedition]."[52] To compound the issue, some of his crew were starting to get restless. Sawyer, in letters to his fiancée, expressed displeasure with his own work and a recurring desire to return home as soon as possible.[53] Meanwhile, Cushing had written to Pepper in an effort to secure additional funding for the expedition, without which it couldn't continue. A few days later, Cushing received what he called a "frightfully domineering telegram" from Pepper.[54] Cushing reacted by going so far as to threaten to claim the finds personally "as the discoverer" should the museum not take further interest, writing, "The discoveries I am now daily making are not only unique but unparalleled in the annals of American Archaeology!"[55]

Due to Marco's remoteness, Cushing had received little in the way of communication from Pepper, their letters sometimes crossing each other in the mail. He passionately believed in the work he was doing but needed support and validation from his superiors to ensure the expedition's success. Meanwhile, illness, storms, anxiety, and depression were taking their toll, particularly after the receipt of Pepper's March 1 telegram, which Cushing was "awfully cut up about." His journal entry on March 2 begins, "Up at six after fearful night and with severe headache from worry. World all darkened again." In short, Cushing needed a win.[56]

The tide turned on March 4, 1896. Not only did Cushing receive a "much more agreeable" letter from Pepper, he also began to uncover the first of the site's painted wooden masks, as well as "the most finely finished nest of 5 bowls and vase all wood" and dozens of other spectacular artifacts. Although Cushing's initial reactions to finding the Cat are presumably known only in his missing field journal, March 5 is the only day that he qualitatively singles out in his *Preliminary Report*, calling it a "happy" one, and specifically in reference to the Cat. If March 3 was rock bottom on the Pepper-Hearst Expedition, March 4 was the beginning of a rapid ascent to the peak between March 5 and 7, 1896.[57]

Wells Sawyer's immediate reaction to the Cat is recorded in his field journal, his opinion likely informed by Cushing's remarks at the site. Feeling compelled to document the goings-on, presumably on March 5, 1896, Sawyer writes, "There was found today a most remarkable wood carving ~~of which I~~

Figure 23. Artist's rendering of the Key Marco Cat shortly after its discovery during the 1896 Pepper-Hearst Expedition. Artwork by Russell Beans.

~~know~~. It represents a masked figure, a man in ceremonial priest garb of the wild cat or tiger. The work is exquisite—never more skillful carving and as for convention it has all the dignity of any archaic work in the museums of the world. Egypt even has nothing of which I know which touches this real masterpiece. Were the collections, which we have made, mine; I would give all the rest for this one specimen. It throws light also on other works which we have found."[58]

Cushing afterward wrote an enthusiastic letter to Pepper, dated March 7, detailing the Cat's finding as well as many of the other now-iconic artifacts. He speaks of his "literally startling" discoveries and emphasizes their extreme importance—laying it on thicker than was probably necessary—in assuring Pepper that he would not regret his recent show of support. Cushing was likely thinking ahead to future funding requests, which he undoubtedly could already envision requiring. He also justifies an expected reduction in future correspondence, as his attention was required "constantly in the muck-beds," not even trusting some of his crew with the priceless finds. "The Collier place at least must be finished now if at all."[59]

Cushing would eventually get around to providing his "official" opinion on the Cat, doing so twice in his *Preliminary Report*. His admiration for the piece is nothing short of fawning: "Nothing thus far found in America so vividly calls to mind the best art of the ancient Egyptians or Assyrians, as does this little statuette of the Lion-God, in which it was evidently intended to represent a manlike being in the guise of a panther. Although it is barely six inches in height, its dignity of pose may fairly be termed 'heroic,' and its conventional lines are to the last degree masterly."[60]

"This extraordinary object of art is generally described . . . elsewhere in the text; but I would again call attention to the fact that while the head and body are not only delicately fashioned and finished, even to the extent of polishing, the legs and the ends of the paws, although smoothed outside, are simply shaped, and,—as though purposely—left unfinished; and the spaces below the tail—which is conventionally laid along the back after the manner of Zuni carvings of the same sort of animal-god—and the spaces between the legs, still show the characteristic marks of the fine-edged shark-tooth-blade with which the figure was carved."[61]

Wells Sawyer, who attempted to synthesize some of Cushing's work after his premature death, would also later write that, "the seated figure of a 'panther, or mountain-lion god' is regarded as the gem of the art collection."[62] "The workmanship is so exquisite that the best Swiss carver of today could scarcely give it a better finish and the design was so dignified and the convention so subservient that the best Egyptian work was suggested. The little figure is scarcely eight inches high yet has the dignity of a colossus."[63] "The splendid dignity of the convention is in no wise marred by the diminutive size of the figure. The forepaws stretch down to the base with a sweep which reminds one of the best Egyptian art and the pose of the head with its delicate modeling would do credit to that famed land upon which the archaeologists have feasted since the time of Herodotus. The little image is a gem and will stand in the University Museum [Penn Museum] as the finest example of American carving ever yet found."[64]

In a sense, the Key Marco Cat, along with some of the other more "startling" discoveries, saved the Pepper-Hearst Expedition. By revealing themselves in the nick of time, they enabled Cushing to justify additional funding and time, while kicking him into a higher gear—full-on "rogue curator" mode. Those objects inspired Cushing so fully that he was absolutely determined to save them, regardless of who paid for it or how long it took. With all of the superlatives applied to the Cat by Cushing and Sawyer, one has to wonder if in retrospect they stem in part, even if only subconsciously, from the relief it provided in securing the continuation of a sputtering expedition.

Sent Packing

One of the pivotal periods of the Key Marco Cat's life, and one that generally goes without much consideration, was its successful transportation over 900 miles from Marco, Florida, to Washington, D.C., during the spring of 1896. The Wright brothers would not fly at Kitty Hawk for another seven years, the first Ford Model T would not roll off the assembly line for another twelve, and refrigerated vehicles were fifty years away. Preservation standards for waterlogged materials did not exist at the time, making the care and effort necessary to relocate "more than a thousand" extremely fragile such artifacts quite stressful for Cushing.[65]

In a March 14, 1896, letter to Pepper from the field, Cushing writes, "Up to the last . . . the finds have continued increasingly rich, and have contained something new, for although many duplicates occur, there seems to be no end to the variety of types—especially of objects illustrating the arts and ceremonology of the ancient pile dwellers and shell builders of this region." Cushing also expressed to Pepper the urgency of excavating the entire site in one trip, concerned about potential looters as word of the finds continued to spread: "I fear that what we now leave unexcavated will not be reserved for another season, because, my draining of the place has made the excavating easier for these people." In the same letter, Cushing estimated that an additional three and a half weeks were necessary to finish excavation of the water court, with an additional two weeks required to ready the specimens for shipment.[66]

Cushing gave leave to his crew on March 15 and 16, but by March 22, it is clear that he is starting to think about heading home, as he informs Pepper that he has already made preliminary attempts to preserve some artifacts. For Cushing, the logistical realities of shipping the artifacts were setting in: "The whole difficulty is in the preparation of the specimens for shipment. This is a

Figure 24. Artist's rendering of the sorting and packing of artifacts by members of the Pepper-Hearst Expedition. Artwork by Merald Clark.

serious task. Merely to dry them sufficiently for packing requires days for they have lain in the brine-soaked peat and marl for centuries, and if dried in the open air of even a room, rapidly warp and check. I therefore have to pack them in dry sand for a time, size them, place them under clothes on shelves and thus proceed very slowly and cautiously."[67] Emily Cushing played an instrumental role in packing and preserving the artifacts.[68]

Cushing utilized the parlor at the Colliers' hotel to dry and photograph artifacts.[69] He also apparently attempted some measure of conservation in the field, writing to Dr. Pepper "fluid glass [sodium silicate] does not work, glue but indifferently; and I have to send away for other preservatives."[70] Those "other preservatives" included shellac.[71] He declines to say *which* artifacts he was attempting to preserve, or whether those experimented upon were amongst the collection packed for shipment.

On March 30, Wells Sawyer reports that "Mr. Cushing expects to finish the digging next week and I hope he may do so. The packing boxes are being made and today the sharpie has gone up the coast to get saw dust to use in packing the collection which is a splendid one."[72] A surprise visit from Major John Wesley Powell a week later sped the process up considerably. Intrigued by Cushing's hyperbolic language, and partially in response to his inquiries on how best to preserve the collection, Powell wanted to see the

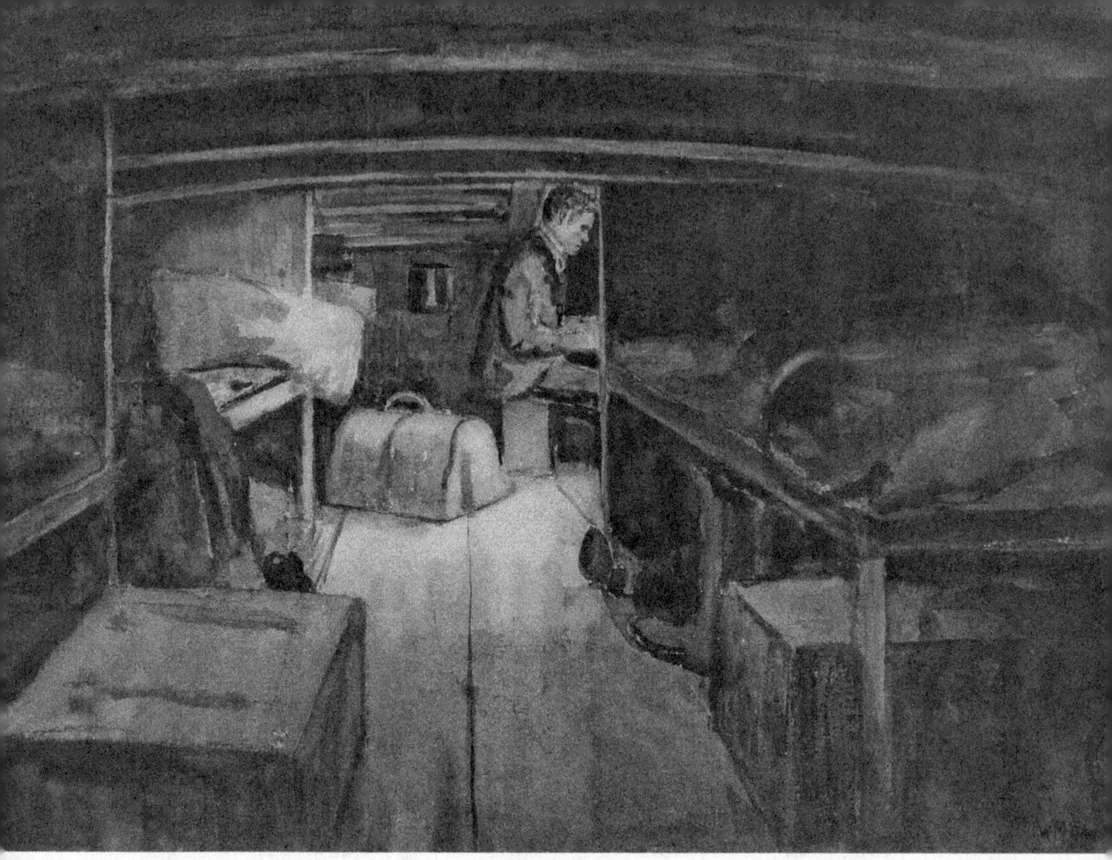

Figure 25. Cushing at work in the hull of the *Silver Spray*. Artwork by Wells Sawyer, 1896. Collections of the Anthropology Division of the Florida Museum of Natural History, FLMNH catalog number 2004-191-19B.

site firsthand. Cushing corroborates Powell's visit in a letter to Pepper, writing, "Unexpectedly Major Powell visited us Tuesday and Wednesday, and he pronounces the finds unique, and the discovery, that of a 'new culture.'"[73]

On April 8, the day after he arrived, Powell bade Cushing to stop his work, restricting it to the area of the muck court before bidding everyone goodbye and heading back out with the mail boat.[74] That same day in her diary, Maggie Collier writes, "They have finished their digging and are packing the specimens."[75] On April 10, Cushing reports to Pepper that he has completed excavations and that his crew is preparing the specimens for shipment.[76] Crew member Carl F. W. Bergmann was among those explicitly involved in packing collections, as he aided in "assorting, cleaning, and preparing specimens in one of Mr. Collier's houses."[77] Cushing apparently worked on specimens aboard the *Silver Spray* before moving them into the Colliers' parlor.[78]

On Sunday, April 19, 1896, the crew began to disperse from Marco, as Maggie Collier notes in her diary. "Three of Mr. Cushing's men left today Mr. Sayford among them."[79] George Gause's diary substantiates this departure, adding that afterward, "we get ready to sail we go shore and bade Capt Collier and family farewell. . . . We sail to Cacsimbus [Caxambas] Pass for a short stay one night we got a ground and left on the next tide."[80] Apparently, Cushing, the crew, and the artifacts made a stopover to the *south* of Marco, at Caxambas (a farming and fishing village on the southern end of Marco Island), before completely leaving the area. On April 20, Cushing writes to Pepper, "I am writing to let you know that work at Collier's is completed, the specimens packed safely on board, and we are now underway for the north."[81]

The artifacts would sit, presumably in the hull of the *Silver Spray*, for days as the crew worked its way up the Southwest Florida coastline, stopping for additional excavations and reconnaissance, as well as paying debts and tying up loose ends. Once back in Tarpon Springs, the artifacts required freight deposits. Despite a surprise increase in shipping rates from a previous agreement, Cushing was able to negotiate back down to the original rates—but not without further delay to his departure. Meanwhile, a storm on April 27 swept the *Silver Spray* off its anchor, prompting a dramatic rescue of the schooner and, presumably, its priceless contents.[82]

On May 10, Cushing wrote from Tarpon Springs that he had finally shipped via railroad eleven barrels and fifty-nine boxes of Key Marco specimens to the museum in Philadelphia.[83] As a matter of fact, he seems to have loaded the parcels onto the train car himself, sometime after dismissing his two most trusted assistants, Sawyer and Bergmann:

> I at once sent Sawyer and Bergmann home by rail (Sayford left me some weeks ago) and have been relabelling [*sic*] and loading the collections on [the] car by myself. This work has been much more arduous than I expected it to be, engrossing every moment, but it was finished yesterday, the car sealed and the bill of lading signed.

Cushing goes on to write, in a letter to Pepper,

> Each case and barrel of the collection I am consigning to you is directed as you requested according to the enclosed labels of the two boxes for greater safety retained to bring with me as extra baggage or by express.[84]

The box labels he mentions were addressed to Dr. William Pepper at the Pepper Medical Laboratory in Philadelphia. The two leftover labels, which

Cushing sent to Pepper with his letter, are from boxes 61 and 68, which Cushing decided to personally courier separately.[85] According to the original field packing lists, a majority of the most spectacular finds were included in these two boxes, including the Cat, painted masks, animal figureheads, and other works of art.[86]

Cushing was worried about the collections up until the last possible minute in Florida, due largely to the ongoing rate dispute. On May 11, he writes, "I have retained until the last hours of our stay here, the enclosed bill of lading on the possibility of having further word from the R.R. authorities. But as no message has come there will probably be no further difficulty. On the still bare possibility of such, however, I have asked both Mr. Safford our good friend here and the Agent (who is on my side also) to communicate at once with us in case the car is not speedily dispatched."[87] One can imagine the knot in his stomach as he left most of the artifacts behind, largely in the hands of strangers, hoping to be reunited with them in Philadelphia. The Cat, however, rode "shotgun" with Cushing. The "cougar or mountain lion god statuette," as it is listed on the manifest, was shipped in box 68, along with various other notable artifacts, including a single-hole atlatl with rabbit carving, wooden "woman figure doll," and a noseless wooden facemask.[88]

Cushing would return first to his home in Washington, D.C., arriving there on May 13 via train.[89] The majority of artifacts would not arrive at Philadelphia for another eleven days, Pepper acknowledging their receipt in a letter to Cushing on May 24, 1896.[90] They apparently were held until the issue of shipping rates could be resolved to everyone's satisfaction via postal mail and telegram.[91] Once they reached the University of Pennsylvania, the artifacts were housed in the Pepper Clinical Laboratory.[92] The reason that they were sent to Philadelphia immediately, rather than Washington, was the issue of storage space at the Smithsonian—or lack thereof—still one of the most common issues for museums today.[93]

On May 13, Cushing writes, "Every specimen gathered has been consigned to the address you furnished me except such precious examples as I had expressed, and they are here under my charge—or at my command, in the Express-office" in Washington, D.C.[94] Plans to see Pepper that Saturday night apparently did not materialize, as Cushing wrote an elaborate tale of having just missed him on Sunday, May 17, 1896. In his letter, he also thanks Pepper for his "kind invitation that I make your house my home whilst working up the collections in Philadelphia."[95] For the time being, the Cat would remain in Cushing's hands, at his disposal in Washington, D.C.

Wanderlust

It is unclear exactly how or when the Cat and its fellow contents of boxes 61 and 68 were delivered to Philadelphia, although eventually they must have been, because Cushing requested some of them back—including the Cat—for study in December 1897.[96] Perhaps Cushing took them to Philadelphia at Pepper's invitation, or perhaps at a later date of his own volition. He definitely visited the Penn Museum sometime before August 1896, mentioning it in a letter from Maine on August 2, but does not indicate whether or not he brought the artifacts with him.[97] In fact, while in Maine, Cushing performed experimental preservation work on what were likely the Key Marco artifacts still in his possession. These experiments are outlined in greater detail in chapter 7.

Regardless of how and when exactly the Cat arrived in Philadelphia, it would stay there for between nine and sixteen months before being returned to Cushing in Washington on loan in February 1898. Whether it spent a couple of months in Maine prior to that is still speculative, but not unlikely given the circumstantial evidence. Despite a likely *five* relocations in less than two years—from Marco to Tarpon Springs to Washington, D.C., to Haven, Maine, to Philadelphia to Washington, D.C., and all prior to becoming an accessioned museum object—the Cat endured more than 2,000 miles of travel, by boat and rail for sure, and locally, probably by horse-drawn carriage and foot. Remarkably, it seems to have logged those miles relatively unscathed, which is a credit to its courier, Cushing. One might be tempted to think that because the Cat is still with the NMNH in Washington, things calmed down for it once it landed there in 1898. On the contrary, the drama was only beginning.

7

Finding a Forever Home

People have been caring for the Key Marco Cat for hundreds of years. From its source community, where it may have been "frequently anointed with the fat of slain animals or victims," to its plush archival storage box at the Smithsonian's Department of Anthropology, people have gone to great lengths to keep the Cat "happy and healthy." Popular demand, however, dictates that the Cat be handled more frequently than other museum objects, therefore posing a regular risk to its safety. Any seasoned museum professional will agree that it is a matter of "when" not "if" a mishap occurs in collections, no matter how careful or well trained the handler. That the Cat has survived this long, in relatively unchanged condition, is a testament to all those steady hands which have held it since it was first carved from wood.[1]

In the 1890s, the most frequent handlers of museum objects were the curators who acquired them—in the Cat's case, Cushing. To his credit though, Cushing also enlisted the consistent aid of Carl F. W. Bergmann, a trusted "museum expert" with whom he had worked previously, in caring for the Key Marco artifacts. By today's definitions, Bergmann would be known as a registrar and preparator. Registrars are generally those in charge of the everyday and long-term care of the objects in a museum's collections. Preparators are generally responsible for installing and deinstalling exhibitions, which in Bergmann's time also meant such duties as restoring artifacts and fabricating dioramas.[2]

The lives of most museum objects are usually low key and uneventful. They are often in storage longer than they are on display, occasionally inspected, and less occasionally treated for conservation. There are some objects, however, that lead an abnormally busy collections life, and the Cat is one of them. Since its discovery, the Cat has been admired, fought over, inspected, mounted, studied, transported, and treated by a century's worth of museum professionals. Nowadays, handling the Cat only occurs with a registrar or collections manager's permission, usually for research purposes, using nitrile gloves over a raised, padded, and archivally safe surface.[3] Its earliest custodians, however, had the greatest influence in its trajectory, determining its "forever home" and bearing at least some responsibility for its remarkable present-day condition. The period between 1896 and 1908—outlined in this chapter—was particularly crucial to the Cat's life story, a time of uncertainty as it made the gradual transition from field site to accession log.

Object in Limbo

Cushing, the Cat, and the contents of boxes 61 and 68 made it safely back to Washington, D.C., in May 1896. The drama surrounding them, however, was only just beginning. From practically the moment Cushing returned from Florida, he was distracted by illness, financial troubles, and accusations of fraud. Not only that, but it was clear from his correspondence that Cushing was having severe withdrawals from fieldwork in the forms of anxiety, depression, and delayed progress on expected publications. Combined with a toxic blend of politics, scandal, and death, the final disposition of the Key Marco artifacts would take more than a decade to resolve.[4]

Upon first returning home, Cushing seems to have focused more on interpreting the finds than properly organizing them. He authored newspaper articles, presented to the American Philosophical Society (APS) and National Geographic Society, and published his APS presentation before the artifacts were even catalogued. Generally, this poor practice can lead to errors and inconsistencies down the road as memory fades. The Key Marco objects thus sat in a relative state of flux, not yet catalogued or formally accessioned, with Cushing intending to do the work himself when he had time. Further complicating matters, most of the collections were in Philadelphia, but Cushing lived in Washington, D.C. When the University of Pennsylvania stopped paying him, it was impossible for him to stay in Philadelphia for any significant length of time.[5]

Cushing wanted to install exhibitions at both museums, but neither could go up without first cataloging, dividing, accessioning, and preparing the specimens. He was also under pressure to publish a more comprehensive report on his findings, leading him in May 1897 to express interest in a return trip to Florida to bolster his writings. Further prodding from Pepper, who must have been growing increasingly frustrated after a year of waiting, lit a fire under Cushing, who wrote, "I will have that collection classified and catalogued within two weeks if I cough my throat raw and you will not see me until I am very sick or there is necessity."[6] Yet the scope of work, even for a healthy Cushing, realistically would have extended far beyond two weeks. So, the project dragged on.

To make things easier on himself, on December 1, 1897, Cushing wrote to Pepper requesting that the Key Marco artifacts be "referred to for temporary removal to my office and rooms in Washington" to "continue the restoration and classification of these collections" and have them illustrated for publication. He cited a lack of funds for living expenses in Philadelphia, noting that his salary was being withheld, and the need to preserve, prepare, and cast the specimens as reasons to move them.[7] He also enlisted Bergmann's aid in appropriately splitting the collection between institutions.

Pepper approved the temporary loan "for the purpose of study" in a letter to Culin.[8] Cushing acknowledged delivery of the loan on February 14, 1898, handwriting a "receipt for above collection, on arrival, and to be retained for illustration study and further restoration at Bureau of American Ethnology Washington D.C.," his signature beneath a list of objects likely prepared by Bergmann (figure 26).[9] The "above" he mentions includes, on the same page, the Key Marco Cat—or, as it is described, the "statuette of the mountain lion or panther man god, kneeling or squatting." The Cat is assigned two numbers: 790 and 40915. The field number, 790, also appears in numerical order in the second volume of the "First Catalogue of Collections from Muck-beds in the Court of the Pile Dwellers Key Marco S.W. Florida," which also appears to be written in Bergmann's hand.[10] It was the first number assigned to the Cat.

Cushing devised a numbering system that allowed him to divide the collection as equally as possible between the two institutions. There were basically two series of numbers, one for the artifacts designated to the Penn Museum (1–1,047) and another for those designated to the Smithsonian (1a–1,047a).[11] Bergmann confirms this in a letter to Culin, writing, "I was detailed to aid Mr. Cushing in cataloging it, at the time Mr. Cushing made the division . . . the lettered specimens were designated by him for the National Museum."[12] Most conspicuous is the lack of an *a* suffix in the Cat's listings, indicating that Cushing originally intended for it to live in perpetuity at the Penn Museum. He was serious about it too, surely having given it a great deal of thought before writing to Culin, "For in *no* case shall I consent to the breaking of the original series by as much as a single removal."[13]

Cushing insisted on finishing the collections himself, and he refused to re-

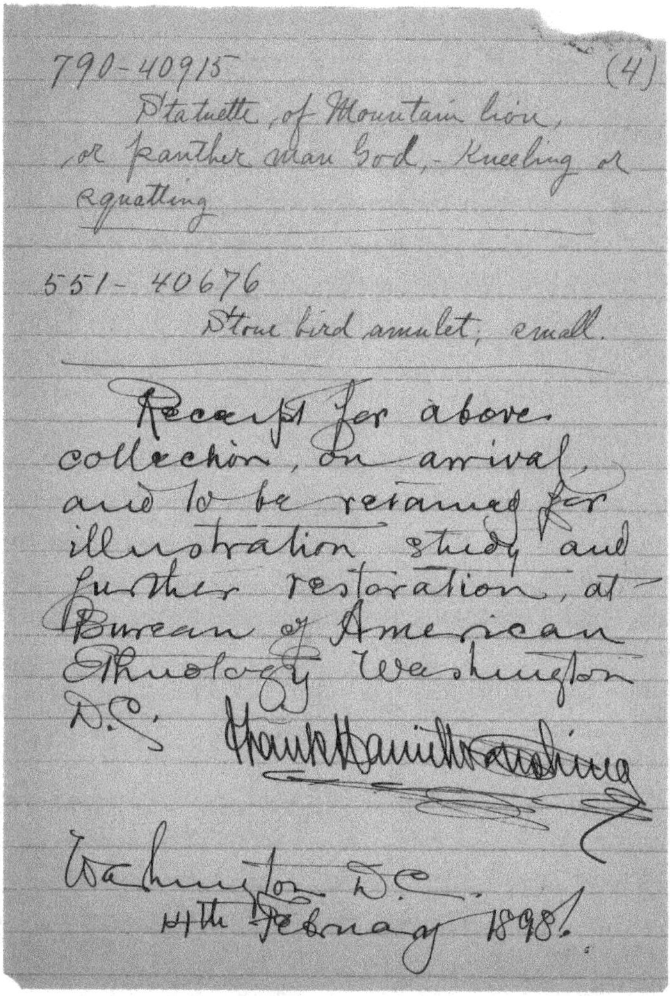

790-40915 (4)
Statuette, of Mountain Lion, or panther man God, - Kneeling or squatting

551-40676
Stone bird amulet, small.

Receipt for above collection, on arrival, and to be retained for illustration study and further restoration, at Bureau of American Ethnology Washington D.C.
Frank Hamilton Cushing

Washington D.C.
14th February 1898.

Figure 26. Courtesy of the Penn Museum, North America: Florida Explorations, 1894–1903: Box 2: Folder 2/8.

turn the items until he was completely finished, noting that by October 1898 the artifacts were "systematically arranged, labeled, and stored in glass-sealed trays awaiting further work." The Cat was likely stored in one of these "glass-sealed trays," which depending on ambient conditions, may have done more harm than good to it, particularly if in range of natural sunlight. Nevertheless, Cushing cited the objects' fragility as another reason not to transfer them back to Pennsylvania until "all of the more fragile of the specimens are mounted."[14]

As 1899 approached, both institutions were anxious to see Cushing finish his work and have the issue of dividing artifacts resolved. Powell reminded Cushing of the "conditions of his Florida work for the University Museum" in a December 12, 1898, letter and pointed out that the items remained public property until the final division was made. When Sara Yorke Stevenson, secretary of the Department of Archaeology and Paleontology at the Penn Museum, increased the pressure on Cushing in February 1899, demanding the artifacts' return with the full support of the University of Pennsylvania Museum Board of Managers behind her, Cushing cited what he believed was his agreed upon right as discoverer to continue researching and working with the collection. The July 1898 death of William Pepper, Cushing's longtime supporter and progenitor of the expedition, left Cushing high and dry regarding his oft-cited agreements, some of which were apparently verbal.[15]

Cushing continued to stall, essentially holding the artifacts "hostage" to finish his work, as well as get paid what he thought was overdue salary from the Penn Museum. Of course, Cushing had the ultimate intent of honoring his agreement with Pepper and ensuring proper care and division of the collection. But in the meantime, he took on other fieldwork, most notably in Maine in late 1899. Unfortunately, that field expedition would be his last—one final distraction from Key Marco—before dying on April 10, 1900, at age forty-two. One account, written sixty-five years after his death, claims that he choked on a fishbone while dining with his wife.[16] More contemporaneous sources indicate that after experiencing a series of hemorrhages, he passed away at his home "after but a few days."[17] This is more in keeping with the near-constant health troubles that he experienced during the final years of his life.[18]

Carl F. W. Bergmann

The only person to handle the Cat as much as Cushing after its discovery was Carl F. W. Bergmann (1856–1926). The son of German immigrants, Bergmann started out as an upholsterer in the Washington, D.C., area, where he was born and raised.[19] By 1900, Bergmann was living in Philadelphia. His occupation is listed in the census as "proprietor museum," likely a misspelling or misinterpretation of "preparator," presumably for the Penn Museum, if not as an independent contractor.[20] Five years earlier, Bergmann had joined the Pepper-Hearst Expedition practically on a whim, coincidentally available when approached by Cushing.[21]

> You will have observed that I mention a new member [to the expedition], Bergmann. I had the good luck to find him on leave. As his skill and familiarity with collections (trained by several years service—much of it under me—in the National Museum) is exceptional, and as he was willing merely at laborer's rates to join our expedition, I at once decided to engage him if passes could but be secured for him. I felt that his capacity to do what I want done would exceed that of any man or men I could secure in the field, and that therefore we could ill afford to miss having him with us.[22]

Bergmann was something of a jack-of-all-trades for the Smithsonian and the Penn Museum. His experience in preparatory work came in handy while assisting Cushing in creating the Smithsonian's exhibitions for the 1893 World's Fair in Chicago.[23] During and after the Pepper-Hearst Expedition, Bergmann acted primarily as a registrar. Like most registrars though, he probably wore many "hats."[24] The Smithsonian's Annual Report from 1897 describes his role at Marco as an "expert assistant in collecting."[25] He helped pack the artifacts in the field at Key Marco, packed them again for their trip from Philadelphia to Washington in early 1898, and a third time when artifacts were returned from Washington to Philadelphia on August 9, 1901.[26]

Bergmann also created the most comprehensive early inventories of the Key Marco artifacts, methodical and meticulous in his work. His thorough and straightforward approach balanced Cushing's flamboyant and scattershot documentation, providing some of the most important surviving records of the collection's ultimate organization and disposition. It is obvious from his correspondence with Culin that Cushing respected and relied heavily on Bergmann, trusting him like few others in the performance of his duties.[27]

Artificial Preservatives

Cushing was renowned—and in at least one case, infamous—for his ability to replicate and restore Native American material culture. His skill contributed to weighty accusations raised against him in the wake of the Pepper-Hearst Expedition.[28] (The Key Marco Cat specifically has never been accused of being a forgery.) Cushing makes no secret of his conservation attempts on the Key Marco artifacts, citing them in his 1897 *Preliminary Report* as well as his correspondence with Pepper and others. It is generally unclear, however, *which* artifacts Cushing conserved, what methods he used, and to what degrees he used them.

Cushing recounts that he and his crew "sought by every means at our disposal" to preserve the perishable items at Key Marco, apparently even experimenting and inventing techniques in the field, "for ordinary glue, shellac, and silicate of soda, proved to be comparatively inefficient."[29] His correspondence with Pepper confirms this, writing from the field on March 14, 1896, that "fluid glass [sodium silicate] does not work, glue but indifferently; and I have to send away for other preservatives."[30] Notably, Cushing's wife, Emily, who accompanied him on the expedition, "by the most painstaking care aided in preserving nearly all of such wooden articles as are preserved in the Free Museum of Science and Arts at Philadelphia [Penn Museum]."[31]

The experimentation continued well after the artifacts were extracted from Florida, with Cushing ordering more supplies from afar with Culin's help. In a July 29, 1896, letter to Culin, Cushing writes from his retreat in Haven, Maine: "I have not yet experimented enough to find out what is the best adopted to the preservation of the specimens. When the tool-chest comes and I get regularly at it I will know better I suppose. Meanwhile I wish you would get me some borax—say two pounds, some shellac (white) say an equal amount, and a gallon of glycerene [*sic*] if you can get it cheaply. The latter does better than anything I have struck yet. Some liquid cellulose would be good to experiment with too, perhaps. If we can find a way of preserving things in the condition of the Marco objects, we will have made a discovery of tremendous importance."[32]

Four days later, Cushing again writes to Culin from Maine, saying: "I am experimenting on the specimens."[33] Given that most of the artifacts were sent immediately to Philadelphia after the excavation, and that Cushing went back to Washington, D.C., it is possible that Cushing was experimenting on the contents of boxes 61 and 68, which he personally couriered from Florida and had the most immediate access to. This would explain how he was able to work on artifacts in Maine, asking Culin only for supplies and not mentioning anything about a loan, which he would request the following year. However, it does appear that Cushing may have visited Pepper in Philadelphia in late June or early July 1896—*before* heading to Maine.[34] Could Cushing be talking about experimenting on *other* Key Marco specimens? Or non-Key Marco specimens? Did he drop the Cat off in Philadelphia? If not, then the Cat likely visited Haven, Maine, where it may have received an undocumented conservation treatment.

By early December 1896, back in Washington, Cushing is *definitely* experimenting on the Key Marco collections, writing to Culin, "You will be glad to learn by the use of dilute glycerene [*sic*] with a little alcohol, I have succeeded in completely restoring several of the warped and even crumbling objects; for example the war club, the little atlatl, the twisted canoe toy. There was but one difficulty remaining the tendency of the fluid to mildew. I found that about an ounce of carbolic acid to the gallon of glycerene [*sic*] and water corrected this, and have now learned (by telling about it) that this is just the formula used in the treatment of cadavers."[35]

In his correspondence with Culin and Pepper, Cushing does not describe which artifacts are in his possession at the NMNH, nor—save for three—which ones were restored or experimented upon with glycerin. It is certainly possible that the Cat was one of them, given his mention of working with some of the "most important" specimens in a letter to Pepper, although it seems he was first and foremost concerned with those visibly deteriorating.[36] In a December 18, 1896, letter to Culin, Cushing writes from his home in Washington, D.C.: "I took from the pickle today several of my choicest specimens that had suffered so much from drying and warping, almost completely restored. I am coming over there to get the choicer of the specimens into this kind of soak at as early a date as is manageable." The "pickle" that Cushing describes was likely some sort of preservative bath, perhaps from a recipe concocted in Maine using materials provided by Culin. Cushing's enthusiasm indicates that he had settled on a solution in which to immerse many of the wooden Key Marco artifacts for stabilization.[37]

On August 7, 1897, Cushing writes Culin from Gretna, Pennsylvania, having just left the museum in Philadelphia, "I asked Mr. Bergmann to have the vat moved up from Murrays Studio to the laboratory, with your permission, and also, with your permission, to put certain classes of the wooden objects to soak in it—gelling them nearly enough in shape to enable me to fit together such as are broken and study minute parts etc. I do not think, as I told him that will take more than two days' time in each week."[38] Later that year, Cushing would request a loan of artifacts to Washington, D.C., to, in part, "continue the restoration" of the collections.[39] In his February 1898 acknowledgment of receipt from Washington, D.C., he indicates his intent to "[retain] for illustration, study, and further restoration" a select group of objects that includes the Key Marco Cat.[40]

This correspondence between Cushing and his colleagues regarding preservation attempts on the Key Marco artifacts between 1896 and 1899 corroborates an observation of a "previously undocumented treatment" on the Cat's conditions reports now on file at the Department of Anthropology, NMNH.[41] According to one conservator, "It was consolidated many years ago with an unknown material (it has an appearance of wax)."[42] It seems that, despite its relatively good condition coming out of the ground, Cushing at some point immersed the Cat in some sort of preservative glycerin bath, likely one perfected in his experimentations in Maine, Philadelphia, and Washington. Given his documented enthusiasm for the object and its relatively stable condition, it is doubtful that he would immerse it in an experimental solution, but rather would only subject it to one that had been refined after a year or two of trial and error.

Whether he treated it in Washington, Maine, or Philadelphia is unclear, and based on his purported prior behavior with a restored Zuni artifact, it is unlikely that he would have actively promoted the fact that he treated it at all.[43] Cushing was a conscientious and kind person, remarkably wary of—and sensitive to—his perception by others.[44] But he also bridged the worlds of archaeology and ethnography in an unprecedented manner, sometimes to his credit, but also sometimes to his detriment.[45] It is difficult to think he didn't learn a valuable lesson from a jeweled toad that he was accused of forging: the difference between "like new" and "like found" conditions, and the ethical gray areas between these in representation. Cushing opted for the "like new" restoration approach at Zuni with an archaeological artifact—without saying so—and paid the price for the rest of his career. He adopted more of a "like found" approach to the restoration of the Key Marco materials, but still took more liberties than would be acceptable today, where transparency trumps any illusion of authenticity.[46] For example, he outright tells Culin that he took the wooden "deer head mask" to his *hotel room* "to complete the color scheme and show an artist friend."[47] Aside from wondering what that even means, one also wonders where he might have taken the Cat in his free time!

• • •

Certainly, there are motivating factors of personal gain in pushing false narratives (or in this case, not documenting preservative work), but Cushing's concern for the long-term well-being of the artifacts was obvious. Cushing went so far as to carefully pack and ship even the most mundane items from the Key Marco site, some of which would be discarded by later curators, while constantly and vociferously demonstrating concern over their preservation beyond his own lifetime. It is quite possible that without Cushing's restorative efforts, mysterious may they have been, the Key Marco Cat would not be in the relatively excellent condition it is in today when compared to other artifacts from the same site. An object in poor condition naturally has less opportunities to travel, exhibit, educate, and inspire. So, while the Cat's original integrity may be compromised in one sense, its longevity and legend are owed largely to Cushing's long-term vision, multitude of abilities (not all museum curators can whip up a preservative solution from scratch), and willingness to take risks.

Curious Case of the Cat Castings

While Cushing and his colleagues clearly tried to preserve the Key Marco artifacts in their original "like found" conditions, they also recognized the need for a backup plan. Artist Wells Sawyer's photographs and watercolors are the best examples of this, some now more important than the objects themselves due to the objects' almost immediate deterioration. Sawyer's contributions, and Cushing's terrific foresight to bring him along, are well documented.[48] Less well known, however, are the molds and casts made of some of the most notable artifacts, including the Key Marco Cat.

The story of the casts and molds is in some ways as mysterious as that of the actual artifacts. They have been variously used, scattered, and squirreled away, only to be "rediscovered" in recent years with surprise and a renewed enthusiasm. Cushing first mentions casts in his *Preliminary Report* to the APS, saying, "The specimens themselves are now sadly warped and shriveled. But happily some of them can be fairly restored by treatment with preservatives; and happily also, our photographs, drawings and paintings, and casts, made in the field, are almost equal for study to what the originals were when found."[49]

More than a year after returning from Florida, in a September 23, 1897, letter to Culin, Bergmann provides a progress report on work he is undertaking for the museum. He mentions the Key Marco collection, saying, "Of the Florida collection 2 large, and, one small tablet have been taken away for study since last Saturday. There are also casts of piles and masks still down at the Chestnut St. studio—though I believe these are left there to have piece-molds made."[50] It seems that Cushing tasked Bergmann with having these made, at one point enlisting the services of a third party to help with their production. An August 7, 1897, letter from Cushing to Culin also refers to the studio, calling it "Murrays Studio."[51] There is no description of the process by which molds and castings were produced, but it appears that Bergmann pulled original artifacts for that express purpose. It is difficult to imagine such fragile artifacts being used to create molds, which requires the application of at least *some* surface pressure, but that apparently happened to a number of artifacts.

Nearly two years later, in an August 22, 1899, letter to Culin, Cushing writes,

"I am coloring to nature the casts of the masks and such of the figureheads as I am able to produce. You will probably therefore not want paintings of those. Sawyer made them to guide in such work."[52] This letter indicates that not only did Cushing create casts of Key Marco artifacts, he intended to paint them so that they resembled the original artifacts in their pristine conditions. The present whereabouts of these "colored" castings is unknown—if they were completed at all—during the eight months between Cushing's letter and his death.

Many Key Marco casts and molds still exist in museum collections but have been largely ignored by researchers during the past century. Gilliland mentions them only briefly in passing in 1975, and then again in 1988, writing, "Fortunately, photographs, water colors, and casts of many of the artifacts were made in the field, and later in Washington."[53] Barbara A. Purdy, curator at the FLMNH, later writes, "In 1976, I secured from the United States National Museum [NMNH] and the University Museum [Penn Museum] a number of the Key Marco casts. Molds were made of the casts at the Florida Museum of Natural History and some of the casts reproduced from these molds are on display or in storage in Gainesville."[54] It is unclear, but perhaps implicit, that these casts were originals made by Bergmann and Cushing either in the field or shortly thereafter.

The MIHS is a relative newcomer to this decades-long story by way of the generous donation of a bronze casting of the Key Marco Cat, purchased by the donors from an antique dealer near Philadelphia, Pennsylvania, in December 2014.[55] According to the dealer, Cushing made bronze replicas as gifts for crewmembers of the Pepper-Hearst Expedition. This casting was purportedly Cushing's own personal copy, perhaps made from one of Bergmann's molds, and passed on to his daughter after his untimely death in 1900. The dealer claimed to have purchased it directly from Cushing's daughter in the 1960s or 1970s in Washington, D.C. The Cushings, however, did not have a daughter, contradicting the dealer's claim and calling the item's true history into question.[56]

The casting itself is a near perfect replica of the real Cat. It features intricate and precise details, including asymmetrical features and cracks in the wood that are still visible on the original. Analysis conducted at the Smithsonian Institution in July 2018 found the bronze Cat's measurements to fall within approximately one millimeter of the original's in all directions.[57] The apparent age of the patina on the object further perplexes. Patina is a green or brown film that forms on the surface of bronze objects over long periods of time. The patina on this casting indicates that it is relatively old. Whoever made this

Figure 27. *Left:* Bronze Key Marco Cat casting, catalog number 2015-62-1, Marco Island Historical Society. *Right:* Key Marco Cat, catalog number A240915, Department of Anthropology, Smithsonian Institution. Photo by the author, July 23, 2018. By permission of the Department of Anthropology, Smithsonian Institution.

casting must have had direct access to either the real Cat or extremely detailed photographs and precise measurements.

Curiously, the Smithsonian has in its collections a mysterious plaster piece mold of the Key Marco Cat of unknown age and origin.[58] However, a July 2018 examination concluded that it was likely not the mold that produced the MIHS's bronze Cat.[59] The casting did not fit comfortably within the fully assembled mold. However, the study also concluded that the plaster mold was unlikely to have been created directly from the original Cat, since the bronze casting is so similar in size and shape to the real thing. If the casting does not fit comfortably within the mold, the real artifact likely does not either. It is also possible that the real Cat's dimensions have changed since a mold was last created from it, but the aged bronze casting's remarkably similar dimensions seem to indicate otherwise. Perhaps the Smithsonian's mold is one of those

Figure 28. Key Marco Cat mold, object number CG2017-7-1825. Photo by Austin Bell, February 26, 2019. By permission of the Penn Museum.

made from the original castings in the late 1970s at the FLMNH, which would explain its slightly inaccurate shape—it is a copy of a copy of a copy.

The Penn Museum and the FLMNH *also* have molds and castings of various Key Marco artifacts, including the Key Marco Cat. On a visit to the Penn Museum in February 2019, I mentioned the MIHS's unusual bronze casting to curator Megan Kassabaum, who in turn brought it to the attention of William Wierzbowski, keeper of the museum's American Collections. A lightbulb clearly went off in Bill's head, leading us down into the museum's basement where, along with *Expedition* editor Jane Hickman, we fanned out in search of anything remotely resembling the Key Marco artifacts. Sure enough, as we came to the last aisle of the most likely candidates, we found some familiar faces—casts of the Key Marco masks—staring back at us. These are likely the original castings made either by Bergmann in the field or someone at Murray's studio in Philadelphia prior to 1900. Amongst the molds is a six-piece Key Marco Cat mold (figure 28), which may well accommodate the MIHS bronze casting. However, the pieces have not been fit together as of this writing. If the MIHS Cat casting fits into the mold, it is very likely an authentic bronze created by someone affiliated with the Penn Museum prior to 1900.

"Murrays Studio" is likely the same "Chestnut St. studio" that Bergmann mentions in his September 1897 letter to Culin regarding molds and castings. The Chestnut Street studio in downtown Philadelphia belonged to artists Samuel Murray (1869–1941) and Thomas Eakins (1844–1916), who shared it from 1892 to 1900.[60] Eakins is largely regarded as one of the most important artists in American history.[61] Culin introduced Cushing to Eakins and Murray in 1892.[62] In 1895, Eakins painted a now-famous oil portrait of Cushing.[63] He also painted a portrait of Emily Cushing, now at the Philadelphia Museum of Art, and by all accounts, had a close personal relationship with the couple.[64] Murray, Eakins's apprentice, specialized in sculpture. Some of his best-known works of art are large-scale bronzes, including a bust of Isaac Jones Wistar at the Wistar Institute on the University of Pennsylvania campus and a statue of Commodore John Barry at Independence Hall in Philadelphia. He also worked directly for Cushing prior to his trip to Florida, probably at the behest of Culin, on mending Zuni pottery.

Given Murray's propensity for bronze work, frequent access to the Key Marco artifacts, and intimate relationship with Culin and the Cushings, Murray is very likely the bronze Cat casting's founder. While it is believable that Bergmann or Cushing could have created the original molds and castings, especially given their proficiency with artifact and exhibit preparation, metal-

Figure 29. Samuel Murray, likely creator of a bronze casting of the Key Marco Cat. Carl Van Vechten, *Samuel Murray*, March 4, 1938, gelatin silver print, 7 3/8 × 9 15/16 in, Philadelphia Museum of Art.

lurgy is an entirely different process, one that even they would likely not be familiar with. Furthermore, correspondence seems to indicate that Bergmann was the intermediary between a third party in the production of castings and molds. What remains to be seen, however, is whether the bronze replica was an authorized one. Perhaps it was produced experimentally, with consent of the museum. Perhaps Cushing ordered several made as keepsakes, as the antique dealer originally reported. Or, perhaps Murray, enamored like so many others by the Cat, created it for himself or others, or experimented with a duplicate mold to his own personal satisfaction. Whatever the case, the casting—a beautiful artistic achievement in its own right—somehow found its way back to Marco Island, the place where its creative likeness was first inspired.

Long Division

With Cushing's death in 1900, the division of the Key Marco collections hit a major setback, even if Cushing was slow to deliver on promises made during the four years since his return from Key Marco. Left in the hands of others at their respective institutions, most of whom were not involved in the original procurement of artifacts, it would be another year before a formal division would be made. The major problem, and one that likely saddled Cushing with anxiety, was the unique nature of so many of the finds. Cushing originally agreed in writing to divide everything "equally" between the two museums, a wholly subjective and inherently impossible task given the nature of the artifacts. Yet, it appears that he also promised Pepper and the Penn Museum the unique and most "full and complete" specimens.[65] Perhaps Cushing felt a debt of gratitude to those who funded the dig at the cost of "some $8,000," equivalent to nearly a quarter of a million dollars today.[66]

The Smithsonian's Bureau of American Ethnology (BAE) was apparently unaware of the oral agreement between Cushing and Pepper, expecting equal division.[67] Thus, the two museums argued back and forth over the agreement and the artifacts for months after Cushing died, all while those loaned to Cushing remained in Washington. The two foremost arbiters for their respective institutions were Stewart Culin, immediate past director and then curator of the American Section at the Penn Museum, and William Henry Holmes, head curator of anthropology at the U.S. National Museum and soon-to-be chief of the BAE.[68] Cushing's old supervisor, John Wesley Powell, then director of the BAE, became involved once more, probably much to his chagrin.[69] Important new figures at the Smithsonian were Samuel P. Langley, secretary, and W. J. McGee, ethnologist at the BAE.[70] At the Penn Museum, aside from Culin, Robert C. H. Brock, chairman of the museum's board of managers, and Sara Yorke Stevenson, secretary, were the key players.[71]

Culin and Holmes met to view the collection in Washington together, where Holmes pointed out what he believed were discrepancies in the "equal division" of artifacts: "Of the 1,047 numbers of the catalogue, 591 are by this means assigned to the Philadelphia Museum and 524 to the National Museum. As indicated by these numbers the division seems appropriately just, but it is to be noted that specimens of the first order of excellence are in all or nearly all cases given to the former institution, and those of the second, third or fourth order to the latter institution. The relative scientific and museum values of the lots as they stand are perhaps two, three or four to one in favor of Philadelphia."[72]

Holmes's obvious displeasure with Cushing's division notwithstanding, the Key Marco Cat was apparently one of the marquee "first order" objects designated to the Penn Museum. Regardless, Holmes saw fit to remove himself from the situation, requesting that the artifacts be sent back to Philadelphia, where they could be divvied up more fairly alongside the artifacts that never left. Culin agreed, also asking that Holmes be replaced.[73]

The back and forth continued, with Culin suggesting that the division be left as Cushing intended and Bergmann confirming that he helped Cushing divide and label the artifacts.[74] Culin wrote to a congressman for support and was referred to a senator, while Powell railed against Culin in letters to Secretary Langley, who in turn also wrote to a congressman. With accusations and consternation flying up and down the chains of command at both institutions, Brock got involved at the behest of a congressman who had contacted the University of Pennsylvania provost. Brock traveled to Washington to meet with Holmes and Powell on April 1, 1901—a meeting that, by all accounts, went well enough that it ended with lunch and a trip to the zoo.[75] The group agreed that it was best to honor the promises made, even if they were made without proper authority, to the expedition's financial backers. But it *was* April Fool's day, and Holmes and Powell took one last look at the collection "to select a minimum typical collection to be retained by the Institution, sending to the University of Pennsylvania in final settlement the greater portion of the objects, both in number and in value."[76]

"A Personal Favor"

On April 5 and 6, Powell made a list of the specimens he intended to keep for the Smithsonian, notifying Langley via letter on April 8, 1901 (figure 30).[77] On the otherwise typewritten list, handwritten in ink, seemingly as an afterthought, is "790—Panther-headed figure"—the Key Marco Cat. This indicates that it was either Holmes, Powell, or Langley who allocated the Cat to the Smithsonian. Langley then notified Brock of the proposed retained specimens "in addition to the articles already set aside by Cushing."[78] Brock, however, happened to notice that the Key Marco Cat was now among the artifacts designated to the Smithsonian, replying to Langley in an April 13 letter: "I want to ask you, as a personal favor, and in order that the settlement of this matter may be such a one as I can heartily and unequivocally recommend to my Board of Managers, that you will strike out from the list of objects to be retained by the Smithsonian Institute and add to the objects to be sent to the University of Pennsylvania, the panther-headed figure. I very much hope you will see your way clear to do this."[79]

Amongst the hundreds of items being divided up, Brock took the time to

ACCESSION 48531

S.P.L. APR 9 1901

Objects added to the National Museum ~~Mexico~~ Series from the Marco Collection.
(April 5,6,1901)

402 Small shapely toy canoe.

553 Paddle or spatula.

507 Prong of a fishing spear.

765
40890 Circular gorget of shell; star figure left by perforated quadrants.

855
40980 Rope and textiles.

REGISTRAR'S FILE
Return to Registrar.

419
40544 Netting. 790 – Panther-headed figure

58
40183 Medium sized deep wooden tray.

168 Large shallow cooking bowl.

1052
41177 Polished shell object.

783 Necklace ornament.

294 Crozier-shaped adze object.

71959
41030 Jaw (?) of fish.

68 Wooden bowl.

64
40189 Wooden bowl, exterior ornamented by incision.

~~331?~~ 495(2)
07908 Fine carved bone awl.
439 Shell with attached string.
333 Bodkin of deer bone.

424 Several sticks with rope attachment at ends.

853
40978 Rope, string and fibres.

299 Bone whistle. "Crozier-shaped adze handle & bone socket"
452 Pendant of stone.
~~0~~ 82 A small wooden cup without catalogue number

~~00~~ 84 A small wooden pestle without catalogue number.

(Owing to exigences in collecting some articles have double numbers)

Figure 30. "Objects added to the National Museum series from the Marco Collection. (April 5, 6, 1901)." Courtesy of the Smithsonian Institution Archives. Record Unit 305, Accession 48531.

single out only one: the Key Marco Cat. This rather remarkable request must have infuriated those at the Smithsonian, who had already ceded what Langley estimated as "more than four-fifths of the whole in number and value" of the entire collection.[80] To make such a request took a lot of nerve, but at the same time, so did the Smithsonian's last-minute addition of the Cat to its list of objects to retain. The worst the Smithsonian could do was refuse. Given the absolute unique nature of the Cat, and considering its history since, one cannot blame Brock for trying.

Naturally, Langley politely refused, writing to Brock on April 15, 1901: "Some years ago when I looked at the collection of objects from San Marco Springs [*sic*], there were three which particularly impressed me as being distinctly valuable as art objects, and which I should have wished to retain for the Institution, namely, the head of a deer, the head of a duck, and the little panther figure. I have consented to the transfer of both the deer and the duck to the University of Pennsylvania, but I am going to ask you to sympathize with my wish and purpose to retain the other. I sincerely trust that you will feel, as I do, that in sending the vastly superior portion of the San Marco [*sic*] finds to Philadelphia, the decision to retain this as one of the very few objects of value in the series reserved for the Institution, does not conflict with the very liberal disposition which the Institution has already shown in this matter."[81] Langley's tactful yet stubborn reply clearly paid off for the Smithsonian, deterring Brock, who replied with a handwritten note expressing "personal disappointment" but also "gratitude for the fairness with which" the Penn Museum was treated.[82]

So decided the long-term fate of the Key Marco Cat as a museum object. It seems that it was not Cushing, nor Holmes, nor Powell that led to its permanent residence in Washington after all, but rather Secretary Langley, who in a pure power move, decided to add the Cat to Powell's list simply because he fancied it. Its exhibition, preservation, and study would thus be dictated by the Smithsonian Institution, becoming an object of the people of the United States of America in perpetuity. The hospitality exhibited by Holmes and Powell in the April Fool's Day meeting of 1901, whether strategic or not, paid dividends in retrospect. Had the meeting gone differently, say more contentiously, perhaps Brock would not have been so willing to "sympathize" with Langley's "wish" and reach such a quick compromise. In fact, it might not be a stretch to say that a trip to the zoo may have been a key to keeping the Key Marco Cat in Washington. One wonders if they saw the big cat exhibits that day.

Stranger in a Strange Land

Despite the successful resolution reached in 1901, another seven years would pass before the Smithsonian's Key Marco artifacts would be formally accessioned. Holmes, who must have needed a break from the drama swirling around the collection, eventually circled back to them. In a March 30, 1908, letter to then Smithsonian secretary Charles D. Walcott, Holmes acknowledges the need for closure: "It was arranged that Mr. Cushing should divide these collections between the contracting institutions, and in 1900 [*sic*] the portion assigned to the Bureau was transferred to the National Museum. I understand that no formal transfer of this material has been made, and, with your approval, I now have the honor to make the formal transfer. The collections are at present in charge of the Division of Prehistoric Archaeology of the Museum."[83]

Per the terms of a "Memorandum to Registrar" signed by curator O. T. Mason, the Key Marco artifacts were transferred from the BAE (via Holmes, chief) to the Department of Anthropology, Division of Prehistoric Archaeology, at the United States National Museum on April 1, 1908.[84] So began a new chapter in the Cat's life, one that would see it pass through increasingly unfamiliar—but increasingly well-trained—hands. Prior to its formal transfer, no two individuals handled the object more than Cushing and Bergmann. The duo largely did what they wanted with the Cat, including probable experimental conservation, when and where they wanted. After Cushing's death and Bergmann's consequent disassociation from the object, the Cat was left for the first time in the care of people who were not personally associated with the Pepper-Hearst Expedition. The Cat's trips back and forth for Cushing's convenience were now over, a permanent roof over its head.

Still, even as a collections object, the Key Marco Cat is often treated differently. After the artifacts were successfully divided between the Smithsonian and the Penn Museum, Langley, who orchestrated its acquisition, *literally* kept the Cat under lock and key—separate from the rest of the collection. A 1913 memo reminds Holmes of the Cat's storage in the Smithsonian's safe for "a number of years," presumably kept there since sometime between 1901 and 1908, suggesting it might be a good time to move it to the new National Museum.[85] Even today, when the Cat is "resting" at home, it is stored separately from the other Key Marco collections in a plush archival box that any housecat would find intensely alluring.[86]

Meanwhile, over the course of a century, the collections around the Key Marco Cat have continued to disperse and dwindle in number. Naturally, due to their fragile natures, an untold number of the organic artifacts have simply disintegrated in storage. Many others have shrunken or warped to such a degree that they are now unrecognizable. Others have since been intentionally destroyed or disposed of, either because they became too badly degraded or had no apparent value to the museums that housed them.[87]

A substantial portion of the Key Marco artifacts at the Penn Museum were forwarded on to other institutions in later years, furthering the dispersal of the collection. Items transferred to the Heye Foundation in New York later became part of the founding collection of the NMAI in 1989.[88] Items loaned to the Florida State Museum in 1964 for study ended up staying there permanently, formally transferred in 1971.[89] The Florida State Museum is now known as the Florida Museum of Natural History (FLMNH), where numerous original Key Marco artifacts have been on permanent display—alongside a replica of the Key Marco Cat—in the *Hall of South Florida People and Environments* exhibition since October 2002.[90]

All the while, through all the degradations, removals, and relocations of its artifactual cohort, the Cat has persisted, largely maintaining its physical integrity across more than twelve decades. Surviving the perils of late nineteenth-century railroad trips, steam room storage, experimental conservation, territorial curators, and mountains of paperwork, the Cat remains in remarkably good condition despite—and sometimes because of—its unenviable role as an immensely important waterlogged wooden artifact in a world figuring out how best to preserve it.

8

Window to the World

Museums, loosely defined, have been collecting and displaying objects for centuries. More traditionally defined, American museums have been systematically collecting objects since their rise in the late 1800s, a result of their increasing intellectual justification and public popularity. The history of the field of anthropology is closely tied to the emergence of the modern museum. At the time of the Pepper-Hearst Expedition, archaeology was in its relative infancy and museum collections were commonly exhibited in "cabinets of curiosity." This approach to material culture was rooted largely in the colonialist and voyeuristic displays of the preceding World's Fairs, which were enormously popular global events that drew millions of visitors.[1]

American anthropology collections of Native American material culture were built upon a notion of preserving the last vestiges of a "vanishing race." The BAE, created by an act of Congress in 1879 to operate under the auspices of the Smithsonian Institution, was one of the leading executors of this philosophy. At the time, however, anthropological collections were often acquired unethically—or even illegally—with little regard for the indigenous communities from which they were separated. As members of a self-critical academic discipline, anthropologists have spent the latter part of the past century acknowledging colonialist histories and "course correcting" anthropological theory and practice. As the field has evolved, so too have the roles of the museum objects collected during its formation. Now, museum collections are sometimes treated as "anthropological data banks," field sites for modern anthropologists, eager to reevaluate long-held material culture with fresh perspectives.[2] Anthropologists are also involved in the repatriation of material culture to its Native source communities.

The Key Marco Cat is unique in that, as an object at one of the formative institutions in the history of American anthropology, it has witnessed many of these changes firsthand. John Wesley Powell and Frank Hamilton Cushing, both directly involved in the Pepper-Hearst Expedition, were also pioneers in the field. Powell was the founding director of the BAE, for which Cushing was a curator, and Cushing was the one the field's first earliest practitioners of "participant observation."[3] Prominent early figures who corresponded in reference to the Key Marco collections include Daniel Brinton, Stewart Culin, Jesse Walter Fewkes, Frederick Hodge, William Henry Holmes, Otis T. Mason, William McGee, Henry Mercer, James Mooney, Frederick Ward Putnam, Mathilda Coxe Stevenson, Sara Yorke Stevenson, and even Franz Boas, known also as the "Father of American Anthropology." The Key Marco collection attracted a veritable "who's who" of early American anthropology.[4]

Aside from the academics, however, the Key Marco Cat's gaze has also met those of millions of museum visitors as a high-profile object for more than a century. Generations have come and gone, but the Cat, in its purely physical form, has remained a constant. What has changed is the world around it, and with that, the world's interpretation of it. Museums today focus largely on delivering a high-quality "visitor experience," reinterpreting or reimagining their missions in order to strike a careful balance between education and entertainment.[5] The Cat has been right in the geographical and philosophical heart of it all along, witnessing the evolution of a discipline through to the full-circle reemergence of anthropological material culture studies and the rise of museology (or "museum studies") programs in universities.[6]

As an anthropological artifact, the Key Marco Cat is one of the best-known "constants" through which to examine changing museum practices over the past century. This is due to a surprisingly lengthy exhibition history, one that soundly refutes those who decry its imagined status as being "locked away in a drawer." That assumption, though incorrect, is reinforced by the fact that *most* museums exhibit only a small percentage of their collections at any given time.[7] In fact, in all likelihood, *most* objects in museum collections are seldom, if *ever*, exhibited or researched, even during a span of more than 100 years. Even fewer artifacts are ever displayed for the length of time that the Cat has been, which as this chapter illustrates, very likely exceeds *60 percent* of its *century-plus* as a collections object.

From behind the glass in a diverse array of exhibitions, the Cat has witnessed a monumental evolution in curatorial practices. Curators over the past century-plus have admired it, studied it, and planned for its inclusion in their exhibitions, each time adding something new to the object's legacy and, in some cases, advancing their respective fields. This chapter outlines the object's exhibition history, and in so doing, examines the life of the Key Marco Cat as a participant in the ever-changing self-critical disciplines of anthropology and museology.

An American Mainstay

The Key Marco Cat's exhibition history began almost immediately after its discovery. Cushing first reported the results of his Florida expedition in a presentation to the American Philosophical Society (APS) in Philadelphia on November 6, 1896—a presentation that would be printed shortly thereafter.[8] Its publication was announced in the May 1897 *Bulletin of the Free Museum of Science and Art*: "The remarkable archaeological collections made by Mr. Frank Hamilton Cushing at Marco, on the southwest coast [of Florida], on his expeditions in the spring of 1895 and the winter and spring of 1896, are temporarily arranged in the Pepper Clinical Laboratory. A detailed report by Mr. Cushing on his explorations, with illustrative plates and maps, will shortly appear in . . . the *Proceedings of the American Philosophical Society*."[9] The report marked the first mass dissemination of the Cat's likeness.[10]

However, according to his undated correspondence at the Penn Museum, it seems that Cushing brought artifacts to his APS presentation as props for "show and tell," an early "pop-up museum" of sorts: "Thanks to Mr. Bergman's assistance I succeeded in packing up the specimens at the Philosophical Society rooms in time, and reached Washington without mishap either to ourselves or the specimens."[11]

Re-examining Cushing's published report in light of this letter, it seems that the "exhibition" of objects mentioned throughout was not only done through the use of lantern slides, but also through the *literal* display of the objects themselves.[12] Toward the end of his report, in summarizing the discussion that occurred after his lecture, Cushing describes the exhibition of three ceramic vessels, as well as a "[great] number" of wooden objects.[13] While Cushing does not mention *which* wooden specimens he packed in Philadelphia and brought back to Washington, one might infer that they were some of the same objects he had couriered himself (and had the most direct access to prior to his presentation), including those of the more spectacular variety. This, as well as the Key Marco Cat's relatively stable status in comparison to other artifacts, makes it a likely candidate for exhibition.

Cushing followed up his Philadelphia lecture with "the first public announcement in [Washington, D.C.]" at a National Geographic Society meeting at the First Congregational Church on February 26, 1897.[14] One wonders if he exhibited artifacts at that lecture as well, but a summary in the *Washington Post* the following day suggests he only used pictures: "Mr. Cushing illustrated his discourse with stereopticon views of the different scenes of the recent explorations and pictures of the ethnological specimens secured."[15]

Regardless of what he brought to his presentations, Cushing had bigger plans for museum exhibitions in both Philadelphia and Washington, D.C., stating at the APS: "Thus, after the original series is arranged and exhibited here in the Museum of the University of Pennsylvania, and after a duplicate but representative series is displayed in the National Museum at Washington, further comparative study of them will be possible, and through this study [of] the ancient key dwellers as a people, the story even of their modes of daily life, will become known to us so fully as to make it almost like unto one which might be told of a living people."[16]

Of course, planning and executing major museum installations like the ones Cushing envisioned, particularly at institutions with such prestigious reputations to uphold, requires years of planning. Cushing's colleagues and superiors were having a difficult time getting *anything* out of him beyond his initial report, although indications are that he was working on preparing specimens for display whilst drafting a more comprehensive manuscript for publication. In a February 25, 1898, letter to Culin, Cushing writes from Washington about his plans for a late-1898 exhibition at the Penn Museum: "Enclosed you will find receipt you wish for. I have signed, and send it to you on condition that the specimens be not called for or demanded until I shall have completed my study and work upon them for purposes of the Report I am now making and the better installation of the series as a whole next autumn or winter in the New Museum, Doctor Pepper having asked me to have everything ready for that by October of November next."[17]

That deadline came and went without an installation, prompting some at the Penn Museum, such as Sara Yorke Stevenson, secretary, to become restless. Her repeated letters of concern to the Smithsonian prompted Powell, Cushing's boss, to respond in writing on February 3, 1899: "Months or even years of display of the material in the cabinets of the Museum is not a matter of so much importance that all other interests should be sacrificed thereto."[18] Other museum curators might appreciate the support levied by Powell toward his own. Exhibit installations, particularly at academic institutions, are generally just a small part of what curators do. Cushing not only faced an overwhelming amount of work with regard to the Key Marco collection, he was constantly ill. Those complaining of his delays were likely not aware that he was gravely ill. Within fourteen months of Powell's letter, Cushing died without having ever produced a formal exhibition.

International Flair

The very first *true* Key Marco exhibitions were of the international variety. In fact, one of them was actually *before* the Pepper-Hearst Expedition. In 1892, Stewart Culin, on behalf of the Department of Anthropology and Paleontology at the University of Pennsylvania, displayed at least twenty-eight artifacts from "Marco Pass" (likely the Key Marco site) in "Southwest Florida" at the Columbian Historical Exposition in Madrid, Spain. The event, which ran from October 31, 1892, to January 31, 1893, commemorated the 400th anniversary of Christopher Columbus's 1492 voyage to the Americas.[19]

Many of the Marco Pass objects presented in Madrid also made it to Chicago for the 1893 World's Columbian Exposition (Chicago World's Fair). The fair, open to the public from May 1 to October 30, 1893, was an impactful social and cultural event that brought together many of the preeminent anthropologists at the time. Ironically, Frank Hamilton Cushing designed and fabricated many of the Smithsonian's anthropology exhibitions at the fair, which were later installed at the museum in Washington "to great fanfare." It was in Chicago that Culin and Cushing solidified what would become an important working relationship, dining together frequently and often with other anthropologists and influential people.[20]

After the fair, Culin would introduce Cushing to William Pepper, who in 1895 would present Cushing with the opportunity to excavate at Key Marco. In another fortuitous twist of fate, Wells Sawyer was also at the fair in Chicago (as a member of the U.S. Geological Survey), where Cushing first hired him to do sketch work. This led directly to Sawyer's later involvement as the artist for the Pepper-Hearst Expedition. Cushing also worked with Carl Bergmann in 1893, mentioning in his diary prior to leaving for Chicago that he was stopping by Bergmann's "shop" to see about some "figure work."[21] Bergmann mounted and costumed eighty mannequins for the exhibitions in Chicago, working closely with Cushing and gaining the trust that Cushing so earnestly expresses when later justifying his addition to the Key Marco crew.[22] Clearly, if not for the 1893 World's Fair, the crew of the Pepper-Hearst Expedition would have included an entirely different cast of characters.

Amazingly, Chicago would not be the last World's Fair in which Key Marco artifacts would be on display. The University of Pennsylvania accepted an invitation from the United States Commission to the Paris Exposition of 1900 to work with other American universities on an exhibition there, focusing their efforts specifically on American archaeology.[23] Cushing's sensational Key Marco artifacts, found four years earlier, were to be included in their first professionally curated exhibition:

> The American Section will be represented by illustrations of the excavations at Marco, Florida, made by Mr. Frank Hamilton Cushing in 1896. This work undertaken jointly by the University and the Bureau of American Ethnology, in Washington, resulted in the discovery of the remains of a pre-historic Key-Dweller culture, and extremely rich finds of painted wooden masks, ceremonial tablets and wood carvings of high artistic value. The photographs to be exhibited were enlarged from those taken when the objects were found. Through the courtesy of the Bureau of American Ethnology, the reproductions of a series of water-color pictures, illustrating the wooden masks from Marco as found were incorporated as part of the exhibit, and placed in a long frame above the five sections.[24]

Although only in likeness, the Key Marco artifacts—in their first exhibition—were part of a global event that drew nearly fifty million visitors in seven months. Sadly, Cushing did not live to admire or learn the results of this work, passing away on April 10, 1900, just four days before the fair opened. However, just as the histories of American anthropology and museums are rooted in world's fairs, so too is the history of the Key Marco Cat and its fellow artifacts.

A Smithsonian Staple

The Cat, now installed in the minds of some of anthropology's most influential figures, was also part of an institution undergoing its own transformation. Formally accessioned into the Smithsonian's collections in 1908, the Key Marco Cat bore witness to the establishment and evolution of the NMNH we know today.[25] When it arrived in Washington, D.C., with Cushing in 1896, the Smithsonian's U.S. National Museum (USNM) was located at what is now the Arts and Industries Building. A new $3.5 million National Museum (now the NMNH) on the Mall opened on June 20, 1911, "the greater part of the natural-history collections, including ethnology, [having] been removed to the new structure." The exhibitions, however, "[were] being opened to the public one after another as the reinstallation . . . [progressed]." By 1912, although "about one-third of the area

[was] devoted to the subject of ethnology and archaeology, illustrative mainly of the North American Indians," the exhibitions were still not open.[26]

With completion of the exhibitions pressing, H. W. Dorsey, chief clerk at the Smithsonian Institution, writes to Holmes in a memorandum on March 17, 1913: "You remember a number of years ago Mr. Langley had placed in the Smithsonian safe the little carved panther figure which I think was obtained by Mr. Cushing in his Florida explorations, which were carried on jointly with the University of Pennsylvania. Do you not wish to have this returned to you for exhibition or placing with the collections?"[27]

A notation of "received and catalogued" was made on March 19 by Neil Judd, curator-in-charge of the Division of Archeology at the USNM. This indicates that the object was desired for exhibition and likely included for the final opening of the "permanent installations" in April 1913. There, the Cat was likely reunited with some of the Smithsonian's other Key Marco artifacts for display on the National Mall in the *North American Archaeology* exhibition.

"The archeological collections are displayed in the second story, the Old World series, both historic and prehistoric, occupying the eastern side and northern end of the wing to the extent of about 7,927 square feet, and the New World series the eastern side of the wing and the entire east range, with a floor area of 22,540 square feet. The exhibition of North American archeology is especially full and important."[28]

Between the opening of the new National Museum's exhibitions in 1913 and about 1961, museum record keeping regarding specific exhibitions is practically nonexistent. The first documented visual "sighting" of the Key Marco Cat on exhibition comes from a collection of photographs in the NMNH archives. The photos, dated March 1956, show what is clearly a display of Key Marco material in the National Museum's *North American Archeology* hall, known also as Hall 22.[29] Hall 22 was situated on the second floor of the National Museum along its eastern north perimeter, its northern windows looking out onto Constitution Avenue and its southern windows into the East Court. This location is similar to that described in the 1913 annual report, indicating that the display had not moved during the intervening forty-three years. A 1911 photograph confirms that the cases themselves remained virtually unchanged after their installation, although the contents appear to have varied.[30]

One March 1956 photograph (figure 31) shows a view "looking west from [the northeastern] corner" of Hall 22. More than a dozen old-fashioned curio cases are visible in the foreground, each brimming with hundreds of ceramic and stone objects, collected with the intent to represent Native American cul-

Figure 31. Installation view looking west, *North American Archeology* exhibition at the United States National Museum, Washington, D.C., March 1956. Supplied by the author by permission of the Department of Anthropology, Smithsonian Institution.

tures from across North America. In the background on the right-hand side of the image, in the fifth vertically oriented case perpendicular to the north wall, are several of the unmistakable Key Marco watercolors by Wells Sawyer. The images appear on a horizontal banner across the top of the case, like that described at the 1900 Paris Exposition. The wolf figurehead is most clearly visible, while others are partially obscured by the cases in front of them.

A second photograph (figure 32) shows a "view from the North Stairway by [the] entrance of Hall 23, looking East into the [North American] hall." It shows the same case with the Key Marco materials, but from the opposite side and at a closer proximity. Again, Wells Sawyer's watercolors are unmistakable on a horizontal banner across the top of the case, this one showing nine different wooden facemasks. Only the top two artifact shelves are fully visible at magnification (figure 33), but one can clearly make out several wooden cups or bowls (top shelf), wooden float pegs (second shelf), and shell tools

Figure 32 (*above*). Installation view looking east, *North American Archeology* exhibition at the United States National Museum, Washington, D.C., March 1956. Supplied by the author by permission of the Department of Anthropology, Smithsonian Institution.

Figure 33 (*below*). Detail of installation view looking east, *North American Archeology* exhibition at the United States National Museum, Washington, D.C., March 1956. Supplied by the author by permission of the Department of Anthropology, Smithsonian Institution. Graphic by the author.

(end of third shelf). A familiar profile is also visible at the southern end of the case—that of what is almost certainly the Key Marco Cat. Tilted slightly forward, its position at the end of the case is logical as one of the more eye-catching artifacts available to a passerby. It is also in a fortuitous position in that it is as far away from the UV rays pouring in from the adjacent windows as possible, although the amount of natural light in the room is shocking by today's standards.

The Cat was feasibly on display in this manner from April 1913 until at least March 1956, a period of forty-three years. It is possible, however, that the Key Marco artifacts were periodically rotated in and out of display during that time. The Cat is also described as being actively "displayed at the National Museum" in a 1957 publication, and may have remained there longer.[31] "Temporary revisions" were made to the hall in 1957, although it is unclear what those were. The Smithsonian received a construction bid to renovate Hall 22 in May 1959 and work was completed in June 1960, making it unlikely that the Cat was on display during that time. The 1956 documentary-style photographs were likely motivated by impending renovations, which had become an annual focus of the museum beginning in 1953. It would take nine years to complete Hall 22's renovation, finally reopening on November 10, 1962.[32]

The Key Marco Cat was featured in the new "Wood Carvers of Southern Florida" case, also known as Case 25, alongside other artifacts from Key Marco, Belle Glade, and the Caloosahatchee River in Florida, all of which are attributed to the Calusa (figure 34). Titled "Cat Figure of Wood," the object is seated on a shelf underneath a general label that the Cat seems to best exemplify: "Wood carving reached a high level during the 15th Century. Metal tools were unknown, and the carving was done with shells and shark-tooth knives. Yet, the craftsmen fashioned masks and figures in the round with a sensitive realism unsurpassed in any other wood sculpture north of Mexico."[33]

In fact, it seems that the Key Marco Cat was central to the production of Case 25. Early exhibit script describes the "purpose of [the] exhibit" as to "present a rather unusual series of carved wooden objects and other materials collected in 1895 [*sic*] by F. H. Cushing from the muck of Key Marco, including a feline figure that is unquestionably one of the masterpieces of aboriginal art from the eastern U.S." Again, in an instructional inventory of the twenty-eight catalogued artifacts (and three watercolors) to be displayed in the case, the Key Marco Cat is singled out: "This is a superb specimen and should be the central feature of the display. Because of its very exceptional character, some way of showing all sides should be considered: mirrors, turn table, casting, or ? ?"[34]

Figure 34. Installation view of Case 25, Hall 22, *North American Archaeology* exhibition at the United States National Museum, Washington, D.C. [1962]. Image number MNH-995, Department of Anthropology, Smithsonian Institution.

It seems that a compromise was reached by painting a small contrasting rectangle behind it to make it stand out.

Remarkably, the Cat sat on display in this exhibit case for another twenty-one years, until at least March 1984. At that time, the NMNH was constructing its Museum Support Center (MSC) in Suitland, Maryland, to address a growing storage crisis. Many of the collections, especially those not on exhibition, were held at the museum on the National Mall and were slated for relocation. Additionally, the Detroit Institute of Arts (DIA) had reached out to the Smithsonian in February 1983 about a special loan exhibition of pre-Columbian Native American art.[35] By 1984, they had added the Key Marco Cat to their list of requested objects.[36] However, unlike most of the other objects requested, the Cat was still on display. A handwritten note in the NMNH loan file, presumably by curator Bruce Smith in March 1984, says, "These guys will be here on Thursday (3–29) to photograph these items—can they be pulled . . . by next Thursday? The Cat will be a hassle, since it is on exhibit."[37]

The exact number of people that saw the Cat on exhibit at the NMNH is unknown, but tens of millions of people visited between 1909 and 1984. More than 300 million people visited the Smithsonian Institution between 1970 and 1984 alone.[38] Few museums in the world can claim numbers like that, so the Cat's sixty-four-plus year display on the National Mall makes it something of a national treasure.

The Traveling Show

Since the Cat came off display at the Smithsonian in 1984, it has been incorporated into seven exhibits—four of them major—outside of the NMNH. The DIA made the first official loan request on March 20, 1984, an ideal time for the NMNH. The NMNH was in the midst of an arduous and lengthy collections move to its new storage facility in Maryland and was already considering closing its dated *North American Archaeology* exhibit, which had been on display for more than two decades. The DIA's loan proposal would see the Cat travel first to the National Gallery of Art (NGA) in Washington, D.C., before moving on to Detroit and then Houston, for an exhibition at the Houston Museum of Fine Arts.[39] While considering the loan, NMNH director Richard S. Fiske wrote an internal memorandum on March 26, 1984, to Bruce Smith outlining his rationale for approving the loan request:

> I walked over and took a look at the Key Marco cat today, and I can clearly see why the Detroit Institute wants to borrow it for their show. To my eye, it is far and away the most beautiful and captivating piece within several of those tired old exhibit cases. But, back to the question at hand! I hereby grant permission to loan this specimen as requested. I base this decision on two points. First, and less important, the piece will be included on the show when it debuts at the National Gallery here on the Mall. Second, and obviously of much greater importance, I honestly think that we will end up with no other recourse but to close Hall 22 because of MSC move and Library perturbations. Mind you, these words do not constitute the final decision on this important matter, because I want to have further discussions on the overall move strategy. Anyhow, I think it appropriate to move forward with this loan even though the larger decisions here in the Museums have yet to be made in final form.[40]

Thus began a new chapter in the life of the Key Marco Cat, one that saw it "hit the road" on a national tour of sorts, straying from its Washington, D.C., home for the first time since 1901. The exhibition, *Ancient Art of the American Woodland Indians*, began its run just down Constitution Avenue from the NMNH at the NGA. It was organized by David W. Penny at the DIA, showcasing "132 works made of mica, wood, ceramic, copper, shell, and stone . . . to explore the artistic achievements in the Late Archaic, Woodland, and Mississippian periods (3000 BCE–1500 CE) of North American Woodland Indians." The exhibit was in keeping with changing museum exhibition practices at the time, wherein Native American material culture was presented from an art historical perspective.[41]

The Key Marco Cat was exhibited in a wall-mounted case with three other Native Floridian artifacts: directly above it, a marine-shell effigy bowl (Pensacola Incised; 1350–1500 CE) from Choctawhatchee Bay in Walton County, Florida; to its proper left, a pair of effigy bowls, one featuring a pair of bird-head adornos (Fort Walton Incised; 1350–1500 CE) and the other a frog or fish effigy (1350–1500 CE), both also from Choctawhatchee Bay. All four "casemates" are striking examples of the complex artistry demonstrated by early Native Americans in Florida. But geographically, the Cat originated more than 400 miles south of the Florida panhandle. A wooden eagle effigy from a charnel house at the Fort Center site in Glades County, Florida, displayed dramatically at the entrance to the exhibit, is the only other artifact from southern Florida. Notably, it is dated much earlier (500–1000 CE) than the Cat, which is presented as an object of the late Mississippian Period (1400–1500 CE). Given the eagle's large size (157 cm) and the Cat's supposed later date, it makes sense from a chronological and practical sense to include it instead with the Mississippian Walton County artifacts in a "Florida case." But stylistically and culturally, the Cat is unique to South Florida, as the curators made clear in their uncertainty over how to interpret it.[42]

The artifact itself is given little mention in an otherwise thorough unpacking of Mississippian serpent and fertility cults—*piasas* in particular. The authors, to their credit, admit not knowing quite how the Cat fits in the larger scheme of things: "Simple depictions of panthers without the *piasa* associations are represented by a pipe from the lower Mississippi valley and by a unique, small fetish figurine from the Calusa area of south Florida."[43] *Ancient Art* was displayed at the National Gallery from March 17 to August 4, 1985 on the ground floor of the East Building. More than 107,000 people saw the exhibition in less than five months.

Figure 35. Installation view of *Ancient Art of the American Woodland Indians* [1985/86]. Museum of Fine Arts, Houston Archives.

After a successful debut in Washington, the exhibit moved on to Detroit, Michigan, on display at the DIA from September 2 to November 11, 1985.[44] Per the instructions of Smith, the Cat was hand carried by a courier the roughly 400 miles to the DIA, while all but one other artifact was shipped.[45] After a two-month stint in Detroit, the Cat was again gathered by hand and carried over 1,000 miles to the Houston Museum of Fine Arts in Houston, Texas. The concluding exhibition ran from December 16, 1985, to March 2, 1986.[46] The artifact returned home on March 14 in "fine condition," as acknowledged in an April 16, 1986, letter to the DIA from Adrienne L. Kaeppler, chair of the Smithsonian's Department of Anthropology.[47]

In 1986, with another renovation of Hall 22 under way and the recent establishment of the MSC, the Key Marco cat returned to a less familiar Smithsonian Institution.[48] Its shipping address was still NMNH on the National Mall, where it had spent most of the past eighty-five years, but at some point thereafter it was likely transferred to the MSC, where it is still housed when not on exhibit.[49]

Big Budget Blockbuster

There is no rest for the weary in the life of a famous museum object, and just four years later the Cat would find itself a part of a landmark art exhibition being developed by the Smithsonian Institution. Titled *Circa 1492: Art in the Age of Exploration*, the exhibition was a commemoration of the 500th anniversary of Christopher Columbus's arrival in the Americas, one of many being planned for 1992, some of which were protested by Native Americans and others.[50] The ambitious installation would feature "more than 600 paintings, sculptures, prints, drawings, maps, scientific instruments, and decorative arts objects . . . from five continents . . . a survey of the world's visual culture around 1492."[51] Broader in scope even than *Ancient Art*, the Key Marco Cat was requested not just as an object representative of the southeastern United States, but of all of the fifteenth- and sixteenth-century Americas. The Cat would be displayed alongside artistic creations of the Aztec, Taíno, and other cultural groups and in juxtaposition with items from Europe, the Mediterranean, and Asia. The intent was to focus on American art prior to European contact, emphasizing its aesthetic beauty and artistic merit.

In a November 1, 1990, letter, longtime director of the NGA John Carter Brown expresses excitement about the exhibition's potential to "break new ground, intellectually and culturally, in the presentation of the period. Art history too often tends to examine the contribution of each culture of this period in isolation. The exhibition presents us with the rare opportunity to broaden that approach and to examine one of the crucial ages of our civilization in a global context, to compare the culture of the Mediterranean with the venerable civilization of the Americas and of Asia which the Europeans suddenly and unexpectedly encountered. We hope that this approach will encourage our visitors to see all the works we exhibit in a new light, unencumbered by traditional classifications."[52]

Amazingly, despite the ambitious and broad scope of the planned exhibit, the *only* artifact requested from the NMNH in Brown's letter is "the wooden Cat from the Key Marco excavation." Brown continues, "We want visitors to understand that at the time of the arrival of the Europeans the Americas were populated by highly developed cultures, whose finest works can be compared directly with those of contemporary Europe. We hope to begin the section with a small presentation entitled 'First Contacts: The Antilles, Florida and Brazil,' which will survey the cultures in the lands which first came into contact with the Europeans. North American objects from this period are particularly difficult to locate and date, and the Key Marco material is therefore especially relevant. Our hope is to reunite the *Cat* with several of the pieces from Key Marco that are now in the University Museum in Philadelphia."[53]

Citing a "refreshing change from the usual plan of presenting one culture in isolation," Melinda Zeder, acting chairm of the Smithsonian's Department of Anthropology, formally approved the loan on November 28, 1990.[54] The massive exhibition consisted of loans from 210 collections and individuals in thirty-four countries, including Queen Elizabeth II of England, who lent materials from the Royal Library at Windsor Castle. Taiwan even went so far as to overturn a twenty-five-year-old law against lending to contribute objects to the exhibition. Along with the Cat, the exhibition included "work not only by European masters such as Leonardo da Vinci and Albrecht Durer, but by Asian masters such as Sesshu Toyo of Japan and Shen Chou of China. Aztec, Islamic and African artisans [were] featured, as well." King Juan Carlos I of Spain opened *Circa 1492* at the National Gallery of Art in October 1991.[55]

Photographs of the exhibition show the Key Marco Cat on display in a wall-mounted case within the "Cultures of the Southeast" section (figure 36). Curiously, there is no mention of the Calusa or Key Marco on the nearby interpretive map. Its display case, however, is home to a reunion of sorts, with three other remarkable Key Marco artifacts on loan from the Penn Museum. The deer figurehead, pelican figurehead, and wolf figurehead are reunited with an object from the Smithsonian for the first time since they were divvied up between institutions in 1901—90 years earlier.

Here, the Key Marco objects are interpreted as early Mississippian (1000 CE) and attributed to the Glades culture of South Florida. The authors compare the animal figureheads with similar mortuary carvings found at Fort Center, noting a much earlier date (200 CE) but similar form and style. The representations of a "broad range of animals having local prominence" in the Key Marco figures, rather than the more traditionally "Mississippian" animals of "pan-regional mythic significance" seem to indicate an earlier date. This is in direct contrast with the interpretation in the prior *American Woodlands* exhibit.

The Key Marco Cat is described as "perhaps a piece of shrine furniture" and posited as one of many pieces found in the ruins of what may have been a community shrine and "probably part of the building." The authors note a stylistic similarity to upright crouching feline figures found at Fort Center, which were "carved terminals of posts that were found by archaeologists in similarly submerged sites." There is no physical evidence, however, that the Key Marco Cat was ever adjoined with or part of a larger piece of wood, as it was seemingly designed to rest on its lower legs, as carved by its creator.[56]

Figure 36. Installation view of *Circa 1492: Art in the Age of Exploration* [1991/92]. National Gallery of Art, Washington, D.C., Gallery Archives.

The loan marked the Cat's second trip to the NGA in less than seven years. The blockbuster exhibition welcomed more than 568,000 visitors in just three months, between October 12, 1991 (Columbus Day), and January 12, 1992.[57] It received largely favorable reviews, *New York* magazine claiming that it "will change your thinking forever" and asking, "Has there ever been an exhibition with such grand dreams?"[58] The *Washington Post* called it "gargantuan, complicated, astounding."[59] Yet, others have pointed out its inherently Eurocentric organization and colonialist worldview.[60] The show certainly had faults, as any invariably does, but as far as museum exhibitions go, *Circa 1492* was about as big and bold as they've ever come.

Finding Your Roots

Three years after appearing in one of the most ambitious and complex art exhibitions ever produced, the Cat took a more central role in a far simpler and more locally focused historical exhibition at the Collier County Museum (CCM) in Naples, Florida. The exhibition, guest-curated by Marion S. Gilliland and co-sponsored by the CCM and the Marco Island Historical Society (MIHS), commemorated the centenary of Cushing's 1896 expedition. Its first-ever return to Florida also marked the first of two visits to the object's native Collier County over a period of less than five years, in keeping with, but not necessarily motivated by, an emerging trend of long-tenured museums addressing their colonialist collecting practices by returning objects to their places of origin.[61]

The Key Marco Expedition (1896–1996) featured the Cat as its undeniable star, but was complemented by artist Wells Sawyer's original watercolor paintings and field documents, as well as locally held shell and stone artifacts, artifact replicas, and artifact loans from the FLMNH.[62] From December 7, 1995, to May 31, 1996, 36,912 visitors from forty states and seven countries saw the arti-

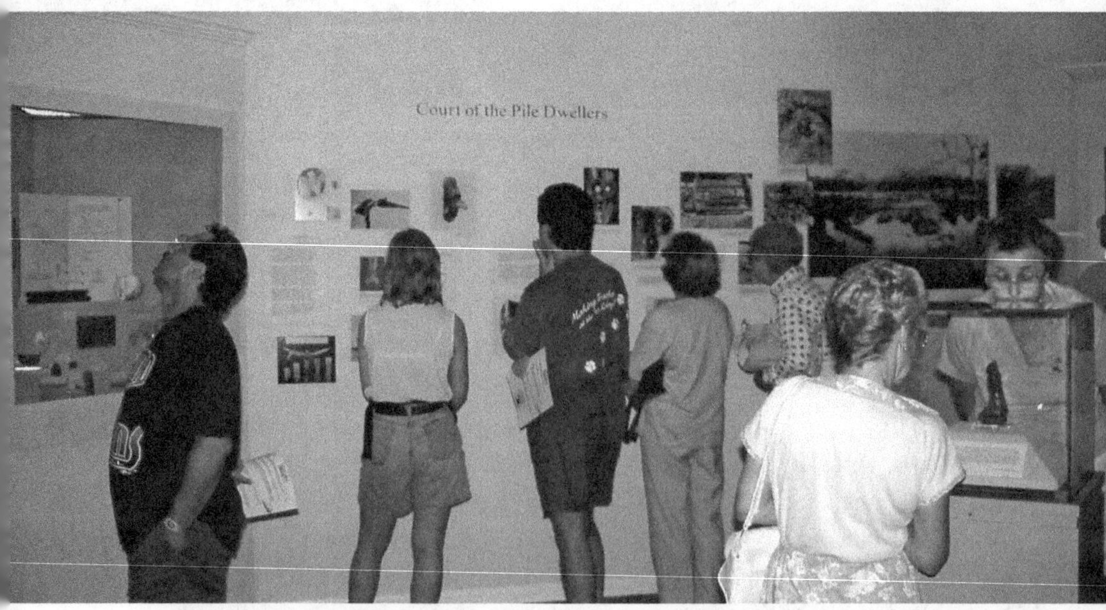

Figure 37. Installation view of *The Key Marco Expedition (1896–1996)* [1995/96]. By permission of the Collier County Museums.

fact in what was a landmark achievement for the eighteen-year-old museum.[63] While the exhibition may not have held the same cachet as those at the Cat's previous venues, and was not curated with the same academic innovations in mind, its homecoming was nonetheless a significant local cultural event. The Cat traveled an estimated 900 miles each way for the loan, on display just 11 miles north of the site in which it was found.

The MIHS brought the Cat even closer to its point of origin in 1999, when it orchestrated a second loan from November 4, 1999, to March 30, 2000. A limited "millennium" exhibition, this time on Marco Island, drew an estimated 18,000 visitors to a display at Citizens Community Bank, which was located just over one mile from the Cat's archaeological context. The five-year-old MIHS recycled the case from the CCM exhibit and agreed to bolt it—with the Cat inside—to the bank's floor, with limited viewing hours. The Cat flew relatively solo this time, displayed alongside reproductions of Wells Sawyer's artwork and a detailed village diorama, but was bolstered by a long list of volunteers eager to share its story with visitors and bank customers.[64]

With a new millennium approaching, the MIHS and its community partners believed "the Key Marco Cat represents a cultural achievement of the highest level for the original inhabitants of the area [and] . . . will serve as a beacon to point the way to Marco Islanders to improve the quality of life in the newly formed city while preserving the natural beauty and environment of the island. It is fitting to display this symbol of achievement by the original inhabitants of this Island to celebrate the beginning of a new millennium on Marco."[65] Ultimately more successful as a marketing tactic than an educational or aesthetic exhibit, the second successful return of the Cat raised awareness about Marco Island's history and gave momentum to a burgeoning movement to build a local history museum.[66] Plus, should anything have gone haywire during Y2K, as some believed it might, at least the Cat would have ended its days back where it started.

New Voices, New Perspectives

In 2004, the Cat joined another major traveling art exhibition: *Hero, Hawk, and Open Hand: American Indian Art of the Ancient Midwest and South*. The exhibition was organized by the Art Institute of Chicago (AIC) and displayed in its Regenstein Hall from November 30, 2004, through January 30, 2005. The Cat was one of twenty-five objects loaned from the NMNH, and the only one from Florida. It was insured for $800,000, more than twice the amount of the second highest artifact, and $300,000 more than it was insured for in most previous loans. The AIC first reached out to the NMNH with its exhibition proposal in February 2000, taking more than four years to bring it to fruition—a standard timeframe in the development of a major museum exhibition.[67]

Thematically, the exhibition was largely in keeping with 1985's *Ancient Art*, which was directly acknowledged as "highly significant" in the accompanying catalogue. Indeed, many of the objects were the same displayed in the 1985 exhibition. Yet, once again, in keeping current with evolving museum exhibition practices, curators employed a subtly different approach to *Hero, Hawk, and Open Hand*: "The notion of working closely with Native American cultural authorities and tribal officials, scholars from several disciplines, museum curators, and private collectors to bring diverse voices and interests together in a project of national significance."[68]

The exhibition also addressed, as AIC director and president James Cuno put it, "the myth of the wilderness," refuting the uniquely American notion of an idealized virgin landscape, conquered first by Europeans and later Americans during a period of westward expansion. This dangerous mode of thinking legitimizes nation building at the expense of the people who were there first. The exhibit's curator, Richard F. Townsend, asserts that "there never really was an untamed wilderness here—at least not since the time of the mastodon and saber-toothed cat: for North America had been in the process of being explored, populated, and exploited for thousands of years before the European migrations began."[69]

One of several themes proposed in the exhibition, in which the Cat is a pivotal figure, is the notion of "Domains of the Hunt and the Animal Powers." To Native cultures, animals are often more than a source of food and technology, they are a living connection to the spiritual realm. "Intersecting the sacred and the everyday, animals acted as intermediaries for humans." Animals are also a connection to a shared past, when "many people could understand animal languages, and could talk to reptiles, furred creatures, birds, or butterflies; animals could also change themselves into people, and people into animals."[70]

"No figure illustrates more poetically the spiritual world of animal-human correspondence than a small wooden effigy from the Key Marco site in southern Florida." In describing the Cat, the lower half is interpreted as "human" while the face is distinctly emblematic of a lifelike feline, not intended as a human wearing a feline mask. "Surely this magical effigy signals the transformation of a shaman into an animal, with the corresponding ability to travel closer, in the continuum of social and sacred space, to the great sources of power residing in the natural environment." The object is ascribed a date of 1400–1500 CE, placing it solidly in the late Mississippian Period.[71]

This exhibition is the first to interpret the Cat as an item imbued with magical powers from a Native perspective, illustrating the growth of the museum field since the Cat's previous exhibitions. As Townsend writes to Smith on March 25, 2002, "The project is encouraging a creative dialogue between specialized scholars and Native American cultural leaders at a time when it is vital to achieve an inclusive approach to this ancient form of civilization as part of our collective, national history." After showing at the AIC, the exhibition traveled 260 miles to the Saint Louis Art Museum in St. Louis, Missouri, where it was exhibited from March 4 to May 5, 2005. The exhibition then returned to Washington, D.C., for display at the NMNH, a place with which the Cat was exceedingly familiar. The exhibition on the National Mall ran from July 2 to September 17, 2005.[72]

In September 2010, the Peabody Essex Museum (PEM) in Salem, Massachusetts, "America's oldest continuously operating museum," contacted the NMNH regarding an exhibit they were developing, to be curated by PEM curator Karen Kramer Russell. Titled *Shapeshifting: Transformations in Native American Art*, the exhibit would invite visitors "to explore how Native American art is always contemporary—art of its time—constantly refreshing itself with new ideas, forms, and expressions," with the ultimate objective of "[reframing] how visitors look at and understand Native art and cultures." In the preliminary loan request letter, the "human-feline effigy" is one of three objects requested from NMNH, and by far the oldest, the other two objects dating to the nineteenth century.[73]

In the PEM's rationale for requesting the loan, special attention is paid to the Cat: "Within the thematic section, *Knowing: Expressing Worldview* [one of four sections], the powerful human-feline effigy and shield cover allow us to explore various Native ways of seeing, understanding, and experiencing the world. Artworks within *Knowing* express diverse beliefs, religions, cosmologies, and ideologies among tribal communities, and contradict the perception that all Native Americans have the same worldview. As a visual articulation of the artist's worldview, the exquisite human-feline carving underscores the dualistic relationship between humans and animals. . . . Modern in appearance, these highly stylized works will further serve to challenge visitor perceptions of what it means for art to be contemporary."[74]

This letter marks the first documented example of an exhibition giving credit to the individual artist who created the Cat. Even in the exhibition catalogue, the first piece of information presented about the object is an attribution to a "Southeastern artist." This is evidence of a still-ongoing paradigm shift within museums, giving the Native voice equal—if not greater—standing in the interpretation of Native American material culture. Several other major acknowledgements are made for the first time in this exhibition that were previously either glossed over or overlooked. The Cat is given a broader date range of 700–1500 CE, offering greater transparency over uncertainty about the object's age. It is also noted as "stylistically distinct from all other regions" in its interpretation, rather than being labeled Woodland or Mississippian, adding that little is known about the inhabitants of Key Marco in 700 CE, but by historic times, the region "was part of the greater Calusa domain, and as such, the carving was possibly made by a Calusa artist."[75]

The exhibition also, for the first time, refreshingly incorporates Native belief systems into the specific interpretation of the Cat, offering a more localized explanation for the carving's inspiration. "Panthers, indigenous to what is now Florida, would likely have inspired Native artists to create their likeness. Additionally, Native people of Southeastern North America, among others, have in their oral histories the concept of a world order kept in balance by Underwater Panthers who rule the watery Lower World and Thunderbirds who rule the Upper World. These human-animal beings are continually at war, not only to maintain the balance between the worlds but also between the elements of fire and water."[76] The concept of underwater panthers was first presented in association with the Cat in *Ancient Art*, but never applied directly to it before in an exhibition.

In March 2011, the NMNH conditionally approved the loan, requesting an alarmed and sealed case specifically for the Cat. The loan was formally approved on August 18, 2011, for display at the PEM between January 14, 2012, and April 29, 2012. The Key Marco Cat was insured for $600,000 and couriered over 400 miles each way, returning to its home in Suitland, Maryland, on May 2, 2012, in unchanged condition.

A Common Misconception

When I first moved to Marco Island in 2013, a local fascination with the Key Marco Cat was clear from the outset. To my surprise, however, conversations with residents and museum stakeholders were often laced with hints of entitlement and resentment. Entitlement to a national treasure taken from its place of origin, and resentment of the Smithsonian Institution for "keeping it in a drawer." Most Marco Islanders I spoke to felt that it belonged on Marco Island, especially now that there was a museum in which to display it. Never mind the hopeless state of our collection and exhibit spaces at the time, to which the Smithsonian Institution would never have issued a loan of even its least fragile artifacts. That Cat belonged on Marco Island, dammit, and there was no convincing people otherwise.

As the years passed and the museum completed its permanent exhibition spaces and brought its collections care up to national standards, I hoped that those feelings would subside, perhaps replaced by a new appreciation for the amount of work that goes into professionalizing a museum. In twenty-six months, with a curatorial staff of no more than two, we opened three permanent exhibitions representing an investment of more than $750,000 into the museum, hired a full-time collections manager, and received a grant from the National Endowment for the Humanities to improve the storage of our archaeological materials. Yet it seemed that with each passing event, each passing milestone, the drumbeat for the Cat only grew louder. Sure, the award-winning *Pioneer Era* exhibit was nice, but when was the Cat coming back?[77] Surely now, with all these improvements, the museum must be ready? I had been naïve about the true power of the Cat.

I must admit to at times being shocked by the local entitlement and frustrated by any negative perceptions of the Smithsonian Institution, without which the object likely would no longer exist. After all, they had been in existence for seventeen decades—the Marco Island Historical Museum (MIHM) had not even made it through one. But I also had to admire the connection that people felt to the object and their passion for local history. The Cat was not just an artifact to them, it was a source of pride and identity. In the early days of my job, I was armed with little information to refute their claims of it being locked away in a drawer. In fact, when I first saw it in person in December 2014, it was literally locked away in a drawer. Now, armed with the new information outlined here, I hope to instill a different source of pride in Marco Islanders—pride that the Cat has played such an important role in telling the stories of Florida, the Southeast, and the Americas to millions of people from around the world, as well as lending a small hand (or paw) in shaping the disciplines of anthropology and museology in their modern forms.

As it turns out, the Cat has not only *not* been in a drawer since it formally became part of the Smithsonian's collections in 1908, it has been on exhibit for shockingly long durations and displayed in at least eight different U.S. cities, part of nine different exhibitions. Millions of visitors have seen it in six states and the District of Columbia. And in December 2018, many Marco Islanders got their wish with the Cat's long-anticipated loan to the MIHM, a story best told in the context of chapter 9. In the 118 years between April 1908, when it was first accessioned, and April 2026, when its loan to the MIHM expires, it will have been on exhibit for at least seventy-four years—well more than half (63 percent) of its long life as a collections object. So long, in fact, that those who had long been clamoring for its return might now be convinced to argue that it "belongs in a drawer."

Exhibition Venues and Durations for the Key Marco Cat

North American Archaeology
National Museum, Washington, D.C., Apr. 1913–Mar. 1956[a] (42 years, 11 months)

Wood Carvers of Southern Florida
National Museum of Natural History, Washington, D.C., Nov. 1962–Mar. 1984[a] (21 years, 4 months)

Ancient Art of the American Woodland Indians
National Gallery of Art, Washington, D.C., Mar. 17, 1985–Aug. 4, 1985 (6 months)

Ancient Art of the American Woodland Indians
Detroit Institute of the Arts, Detroit, MI, Sep. 2, 1985–Nov. 11, 1985 (2 months)

Ancient Art of the American Woodland Indians
Houston Museum of Fine Arts, Houston, TX, Dec. 16, 1985–Mar. 2, 1986 (3 months)

Circa 1492: Art in the Age of Exploration
National Gallery of Art, Washington, D.C., Oct. 12, 1991–Jan. 12, 1992 (3 months)

The Key Marco Expedition (1896–1996)
Collier County Museum, Naples, FL, Dec. 7, 1995–May 31, 1996 (6 months)

Millennium Exhibition
Citizens Community Bank, Marco Island, FL, Nov. 4, 1999–Mar. 30, 2000 (5 months)

Hero, Hawk, and Open Hand: American Indian Art of the Ancient Midwest and South
Art Institute of Chicago, Chicago, IL, Nov. 30, 2004–Jan. 30, 2005 (2 months)

Hero, Hawk, and Open Hand: American Indian Art of the Ancient Midwest and South
Saint Louis Art Museum, St. Louis, MO, Mar. 4, 2005–May 5, 2005 (2 months)

Hero, Hawk, and Open Hand: American Indian Art of the Ancient Midwest and South
National Museum of Natural History, Washington, D.C., July 2, 2005–Sept. 17, 2005 (2 months)

Shapeshifting: Transformations in Native American Art
Peabody Essex Museum, Salem, MA, Jan. 14, 2012–Apr. 29, 2012 (4 months)

Paradise Found: 6,000 Years of People on Marco Island
Marco Island Historical Museum, Marco Island, FL, Dec. 2018–Apr. 2026[a] (7 years, 4 months)

Total exhibition duration: 74 years, 6 months

Note: a. Dates inferred by the author.

The Cat, through its participation in museum exhibits for more than 100 years, is a living demonstrator of changing practices in anthropology and museology, a constant in an ever-changing world. As technology has evolved, so too has the Cat's accessibility, evidenced by its traveling adventures as a loan object. Now something of a "road warrior," it has traveled nearly 12,000 miles—enough to fly from New York to Los Angeles and back *twice*—since its discovery. After being exhibited for a remarkable sixty-four years on the National Mall, the Cat has traveled 90 percent of those miles since 1985, part of seven different loans. It will be fascinating to see how the Cat is displayed and interpreted in the future as the fields of anthropology and museology continue to evolve.

9

National Treasure

I had been in talks with the Smithsonian about returning the Key Marco Cat on loan for more than three years, but the object's true power never fully hit me until I was catching a flight to Washington, D.C., on July 11, 2018. A loan of the Key Marco Cat to the MIHM had been formally approved, and I was on my way to the Smithsonian to conduct research for the accompanying exhibition. And I was not alone. I had the MIHS's mysterious bronze Cat casting in my carry-on luggage. The Smithsonian's Department of Anthropology staff had graciously agreed to humor my request to compare it in person to the real Cat.

As I approached the security checkpoint, wary that I might have some explaining to do on the other side of the x-ray machine, I wondered to myself what Cushing might make of this scenario. One hundred twenty-two years earlier, he had packed the Cat in a box and taken it from Florida by train, no questions asked, to Washington, D.C., arriving two days later. Here I was, with a *replica* of the same artifact, about to be x-rayed, scanned, swabbed, and questioned before taking it aboard two different airplanes that would get us to Washington, D.C., in less than five hours. Couriering museum collections in post-9/11 America is a very different experience than it was in Victorian America.

The TSA agent at the x-ray machine paused when my bag passed through the machine, a slight look of embarrassment creeping onto his face. I had considered the idea that its size and phallic shape might prompt this reaction, given that its solid-metal body would create an inescapably suggestive signature on x-ray. I, too, was now blushing. A second TSA agent asked me if the bag was mine, telling me that they were going to have to open it. I sheepishly consented, with a polite warning that there was a museum object in the bag, and that I would appreciate their careful handling of its contents. The agents' demeanor changed from serious to curious as they pulled nitrile gloves onto their hands, even asking if the gloves were acceptable. What happened next made a lasting impact on me.

Mercifully, it was a slow day at the security checkpoint. I was one of a few passengers weaving my way through the stanchions. As the agent pulled the bronze Cat from my suitcase, carefully unwrapping it from its acid-free tissue cocoon, they asked what I did and where I worked. Nervous, I instinctively launched into "curator mode" while they swabbed the Cat for traces of explosive residue. I explained that I was on my way to the Smithsonian, and that the object they were holding was a bronze replica of a famous wooden object found on Marco Island. Before I knew it, a small crowd of TSA agents had gathered to listen to my impromptu lecture on the Cat's history. None were familiar with it, but most expressed a polite interest in seeing the real thing when it came back to Florida. Satisfied by my excessively thorough explanation of the contents of my luggage, they handed it back to me, at which point I packed it back up, put my belt and shoes back on, and continued toward my gate.

When I sat down at the gate, a wave of relief washed over me. It was my first time couriering any museum object on a plane, and after giving what had to be a local record for "longest historical explanation of luggage contents," I had not ended up in detainment. In fact, I had ended up doing a pop-up exhibit of sorts for a few government employees who seemed genuinely engrossed in the subject matter. It was certainly an educational experience for me. I could not help but think back again to Cushing's time on Marco, when he reportedly visited with the Colliers and their guests in the parlor at the Marco Hotel, gushing with excitement over his finds of the day. He must have enjoyed that, for it is far more gratifying to personally engage with excited members of the public than it is to verbally joust with other academics.[1]

In that moment, I felt that I fully comprehended the modern power of the Cat. Pulling it out of a suitcase before a diverse group of completely unsuspecting people—with no preconceptions, prior knowledge of the subject, or even awareness that they would be seeing it at all—immediately changed their day. Its charisma so obviously universal and its story so remarkable, the object was almost impossible not to at least take a cursory interest in. I soon realized though, from the questions they began asking, that the Cat is more than just an interesting looking thing, it is a "gateway artifact." Most of the questions were not about the Cat itself, but rather the people who made it. I ended up talking more about the Calusa and their ancestors than the object itself. The Cat had acted as a conduit through which to explore these other subjects, igniting curiosities and sparking imaginations. It became an object of free-choice learning, or "learning for fun," the Cat at the center of any number of outwardly radiating educational avenues for exploration.[2]

Invigorated by my atypical act of interpretation, I thought to myself, "Maybe I should travel with this thing more often. What a great way to educate the public." The element of surprise can really work to one's advantage when trying to teach people something new, much like hiding healthy ingredients in kids' dinner recipes and telling them afterward what they ate. Maybe I could take a viral marketing approach to interpretation, popping up with the bronze Cat in airports around the country. My less-eventful return trip through Washington-Reagan International Airport—where I was not even asked to open my bag—brought me quickly back to reality.

Legend Status

Archaeologist Barbara Purdy writes that "idiosyncratic objects are not significant, no matter how interesting they are, because social scientists cannot determine what they represent to the culture." She writes this not about the Key Marco Cat specifically, but while defining culture in anthropological terms and establishing the importance of anthropological work generally.[3]

However, when it comes to public education, particularly at museums, where everyday people come face-to-face with the "real thing," idiosyncratic objects *can* be significant. Just as I experienced at the airport, when people in a vacuum are presented with the Cat—thereby making it temporarily idiosyncratic—they often respond by wanting to know more *because* of how interesting it is. It instills a sense of wonder that leads to resonance, whereas most objects must first earn resonance before instilling wonder.[4]

That charisma—the "it factor"—also likely had a lot to do with the Cat's special treatment over the years. It was personally couriered nearly 1,000 miles from field site to museum by the archaeologist who found it. It has been adored and protected by its museum caretakers of all generations, as documented in decades of correspondence. It has been stored separately, away from the rest of the Smithsonian's Key Marco collection, at various times since 1908. It has been featured in numerous exhibitions and publications, putting it in the spotlight far longer than most other artifacts or works of art. Combine all that with its near-miraculous preservation, healthy number of mysteries, unusual level of public attention, and the brilliance and controversy of the archaeologist who found it and *voilà*: the Cat has become a modern-day cultural icon.

In fact, the Key Marco Cat has become so well known that it was even fea-

Figure 38. First day of issue Key Marco Cat postage stamp, San Juan, Puerto Rico (October 12, 1989). Catalog number 2020-2-2A, Marco Island Historical Society. By permission of the United States Postal Service and the Department of Anthropology, Smithsonian Institution.

tured on a 1989 United States Postage Stamp, celebrating pre-Columbian art in the Americas. The forty-five-cent airmail stamp was designed by Lon Busch of St. Louis, Missouri, and produced by the Bureau of Engraving and Printing in Washington, D.C., with permission of the Smithsonian Institution. The Cat is assigned a date of 700–1450 CE and is described on the stamp simply as a "Southeast carved figure." The stamp also features the logo of the Postal Union of the Americas and Spain (PUAS), of which twenty-three countries printed their own similar stamps to commemorate the Columbus quincentenary. The Cat stamp was released on October 12, 1989 (Columbus Day), in San Juan, Puerto Rico, one of only two objects chosen to represent the Americas prior to Columbus's arrival.[5]

As a symbol of regional history and culture, the Key Marco iconography—and the Cat in particular—are ubiquitous throughout Florida. I have personally seen Key Marco replicas on exhibit in museums from the Florida Keys to Sanibel Island, from Tallahassee to Naples.[6] The Cat has become more than just an artifact: it is a symbol of Florida's Native American history and heritage. Its likeness is emblazoned on book covers and widely distributed ephemera produced by historical societies, museums, professional affinity groups, and

Figure 39. Florida Archaeology Month 2019 poster. Designed by Becky O'Sullivan. By permission of the Florida Public Archaeology Network.

other organizations. In 2019, the Florida Anthropological Society made the Cat the sole subject of its annual Florida Archaeology Month poster (figure 39), celebrating "the museums and institutions across the State making their collections accessible to the public." Roughly 12,000 copies of the poster were given away for free across the state.[7] Davis, in his 2018 Pulitzer Prize–winning book *The Gulf: The Making of an American Sea*, alludes to the Cat in a chapter dedicated to Cushing's explorations at Marco: "Statuettes, carved from stock of local buttonwood trees, combined human and animal characteristics."[8]

On Marco Island, the iconography is even more prolific, long seeping into local advertising, jewelry, street signs, and more.[9] A blue sign (figure 41), engraved with an image of the Cat, welcomes drivers and pedestrians to "Olde Marco Historic Village," the area of the original Key Marco site.[10] A local hardware store's walls are adorned with handmade Key Marco artifact replicas and a large Calusa mural painting. The City of Marco Island installed a brown tourist sign with an image of the Cat at the island's main intersection, with an arrow pointing to Olde Marco.[11] Presumably, the sign leads drivers to the site of a humble marker on the ground along Bald Eagle Drive that denotes (incorrectly) the location of the 1896 archaeological dig.[12] The sign points in the exact opposite direction of the MIHM, particularly ironic during the real Cat's loan to the museum. For many years, these uses of the figure's likeness on Marco Island were thought to be "technically illegal." NMNH curator William Sturtevant even started a folder with examples of the carving's unlicensed use in 1993. In recent years, however, the Smithsonian has focused on an open-access policy, especially with objects in the public domain.[13]

Clearly, the Cat is now engrained in the identity of many modern Marco Island residents, part of the 16,000-resident city's public consciousness.[14] Many take pride in it as a source of local identity, despite being created centuries earlier in an entirely different context. Its commodification not only helps build community, but also generates revenue and helps keep Marco Island's seasonally driven tourism-based economy afloat. A 2017 impact study by the Southwest Florida Regional Planning Council's Regional Economic Analysis Program estimated that the Cat's loan to the MIHM would help generate an average output in Collier County of more than $6 million per year over five years, contributing an average of $3.71 million annually to the gross county product.[15] Awareness of the Cat, and Marco Island's history in general, has escalated since the establishment of the MIHS in 1994, which uses the artifact's famous profile in its logo. The Cat's likeness has also appeared in coffee shops, street parades, ice sculptures, and hotel banquets. Simply put: the Cat sells.

Figure 40. "Rotary Club's 1982 Edition Marco Island Guide." By permission of the Marco Island Rotary Club and the Department of Anthropology, Smithsonian Institution.

Figure 41. This sign welcomes visitors to "Olde Marco Historic Village"—location of the Key Marco archaeological site—on Marco Island. Photo by the author, October 28, 2013.

Figure 42. The Key Marco Cat in chalk at a coffee shop on Marco Island. Artwork by Katherine Ebaugh. Photo by the author, January 10, 2019.

Figure 43. The Key Marco Cat in ice at the Marco Island Historical Society's annual gala. Photo by Erin Wolfe Bell, February 9, 2019.

The Marco Island Historical Museum

The proliferation of museums in the United States—small museums in particular—has skyrocketed during the past three decades. A 2014 report by the Institute of Museum and Library Services (IMLS) revealed that there are about 35,000 museums in the United States—more than the total number of Starbucks and McDonald's in the country *combined*.[16] That number had more than doubled from an estimate done in the 1990s, due largely to the establishment of small museums led by local historical societies, which made up nearly 17,000 (48 percent) of the total reported.[17] Clearly, Marco Island was no exception to the trend, establishing the MIHS as a chapter of the Collier County Historical Society in 1994.

The MIHS became an independent nonprofit organization in 1996. One of its first major initiatives was to partner with Collier County Museums (CCM) in bringing the Key Marco Cat "home" on loan for the Pepper-Hearst

Expedition's centennial anniversary. Using the Cat's successful returns as a fundraising platform, the MIHS garnered momentum over the following eight years to build a local history museum on Marco Island. By 2008, the MIHS had raised enough of its $4.5 million goal to begin groundbreaking on a new 15,500-square-foot facility, executing an agreement with Collier County to operate the Marco Island Historical Museum (MIHM) on three acres of county-owned property in central Marco Island. Completed in 2010, the museum opened full-time in 2011 and is presently staffed by both CCM and MIHS employees. The exterior of the building is designed to resemble the wood "pile dwelling" structures with thatched palm roofs that Cushing so vividly imagined.[18]

Ambitiously, the museum was also designed specifically with an eventual return of the Cat in mind. Architects included a secure central display "vault" as the building's crowning architectural feature. Per its agreement with CCM,

Figure 44. Aerial photograph of the Marco Island Historical Museum. Photo by Joey Waves, December 5, 2018.

the MIHS maintains its own museum collections on the premises and has largely dictated the content of the museum's permanent exhibitions.[19] A six-foot-tall bronze statue of the Cat, created by artist Carl Wagner, was installed in the museum campus's central courtyard in 2010 (figure 45). One of the museum's primary attractions when it first opened, it has since become a local landmark, favorite photo spot, and even a "gym" in the popular augmented reality game Pokémon Go.[20] Salt air from Hurricane Irma accelerated corrosion of the statue in 2017, necessitating a complete restoration in May 2020.[21]

By 2013, the museum had been open for nearly two full years with minimal interpretive content, as additional funds and planning would be required to develop and complete three planned permanent exhibitions. After the MIHS acquired $250,000 from the Collier County Tourist Development Council and the City of Marco Island to fund the MIHM's empty "Calusa Gallery," I was hired as an independent contractor in June 2013 to guide those projects to completion. The first finished exhibition, *Paradise Found: 6,000 Years of People on Marco Island*, opened in November 2014, receiving the prestigious Museum Excellence Award and generating the positive momentum necessary to begin funding and developing the museum's other two permanent exhibitions.[22] Its successful debut also led to my retention as the MIHS's first full-time employee. The MIHS presently has four full-time employees. All our positions are, in some sense, byproducts of the Cat's existence.

The credibility gained both publicly and professionally during this window of growth also put the MIHS and CCM in a position to pursue a long-shared dream of seeing the Cat back on Marco Island for an extended period.[23] In 2014, the MIHS again initiated discussions with the Smithsonian Institution to return the artifact on loan to Marco Island, finally reaching an agreement on June 27, 2017, per the terms of a joint request with CCM.[24] The MIHS's 2016 "CATapult Campaign" raised more than $1 million in private funds to support the loan effort.[25] The driving force behind this fundraising initiative was a straightforward but ostensibly powerful ambition: the fulfillment of a community's shared vision of seeing the Cat on display just three miles from where it was found, in a space designed specifically to accommodate it. Once again, the museum's fate would be tied largely to the Key Marco Cat, regardless of the outcome.

Homeward Bound

In 2018, with a formal commitment in place, the MIHS and CCM underwent the process of preparing the MIHM for the Cat and four other notable

Figure 45. MIHS interns and University of Florida Museum Studies graduate students Kristin Conwill and Casey Wooster pose with a six-foot-tall statue in the Key Marco Cat's likeness on the grounds of the MIHM. Photo by the author, August 1, 2017.

Key Marco artifacts from the Penn Museum. The artifacts, to be reunited on Marco Island for the first time since their excavation, would be exhibited from December 2018 until April 2021, a period of twenty-eight months. When completed, it would be the longest single loan *ever* of the Key Marco Cat to an outside institution, traversing two full hurricane seasons in South Florida. After absorbing a direct hit from Hurricane Irma, which made landfall at Marco Island on September 10, 2017, the CCM and MIHS staff felt confident that, with a few facilities upgrades, the museum could safely accommodate the artifacts. Chief amongst the upgrades were a network of security cameras, new display cases, a sophisticated new alarm system, and a backup generator that would power the museum and its HVAC system in the event of an outage. A full-time security guard was also required in the loan agreement.

The most important stipulation of the loan agreement was a guarantee of consistently safe environmental conditions, including temperature, relative humidity (RH), and light level—even in the event of extreme power loss. The Smithsonian requires the Key Marco Cat to be kept at 70°F (±8°F) with an RH of 45 percent (±8 percent) and light levels not to exceed ten foot-candles. Anyone who has ever sweated in a South Florida September, where the average relative humidity is 92 percent in the morning and 61 percent in the afternoon, can imagine just how challenging those conditions are to maintain.[26] To ensure the safety of the Cat and other artifacts, the MIHS retrofitted its artifact cases with inert materials to prevent off-gassing and created a microclimate within the tightly sealed cases using desiccant trays and preconditioned silica gel. Wireless dataloggers inside the cases continuously recorded conditions (34,950 readings per year), sending notifications via e-mail and text alerts if they fell outside of the prescribed ranges.

Collier County fronted the cost of the backup generator, provided the requisite security guard, installed security systems, and paid loan and shipping costs. Combined, the two organizations spent upward of $1 million on the project. All of this is only to say that, thanks to the Cat, not only did the museum exhibits and facilities receive permanent improvements that will pay dividends for years, standards were raised across the board at the museum. In the long run, this benefits not only the public that the museum serves, but all the thousands of archaeological and historical materials preserved there in perpetuity by the MIHS. They say that a rising tide lifts all boats; for the other artifacts at the MIHM, the Key Marco Cat was a tsunami.

Dreams Realized

The revamped *Paradise Found* exhibition formally opened to the public on January 26, 2019. Street banners around the City of Marco Island decreed "The Return," helping draw in record-breaking crowds.[27]

The successful return of the Key Marco Cat also produced unprecedented visibility and an overall increase in the awareness of and interest in Marco Island history. Media coverage included stories in Lee and Collier county print publications and numerous national publications, including *American Archaeology* (cover story), *Forbes*, *Smithsonian*, *USA Today*, and others. The museum was featured in the public television series *How to Do Florida* and *Florida Frontiers*.[28] Educational programming at the MIHM, as well as other organizations, revolved heavily around the artifact's return.[29] In 2019, the MIHS produced a self-reflective temporary exhibit, *Building a Dream: The 25 Year History of the Marco Island Historical Society*, spotlighting the community group's deter-

Figure 46. Installation view of *Paradise Found: 6,000 Years of People on Marco Island*. Photo by Seamus Payne, June 9, 2019.

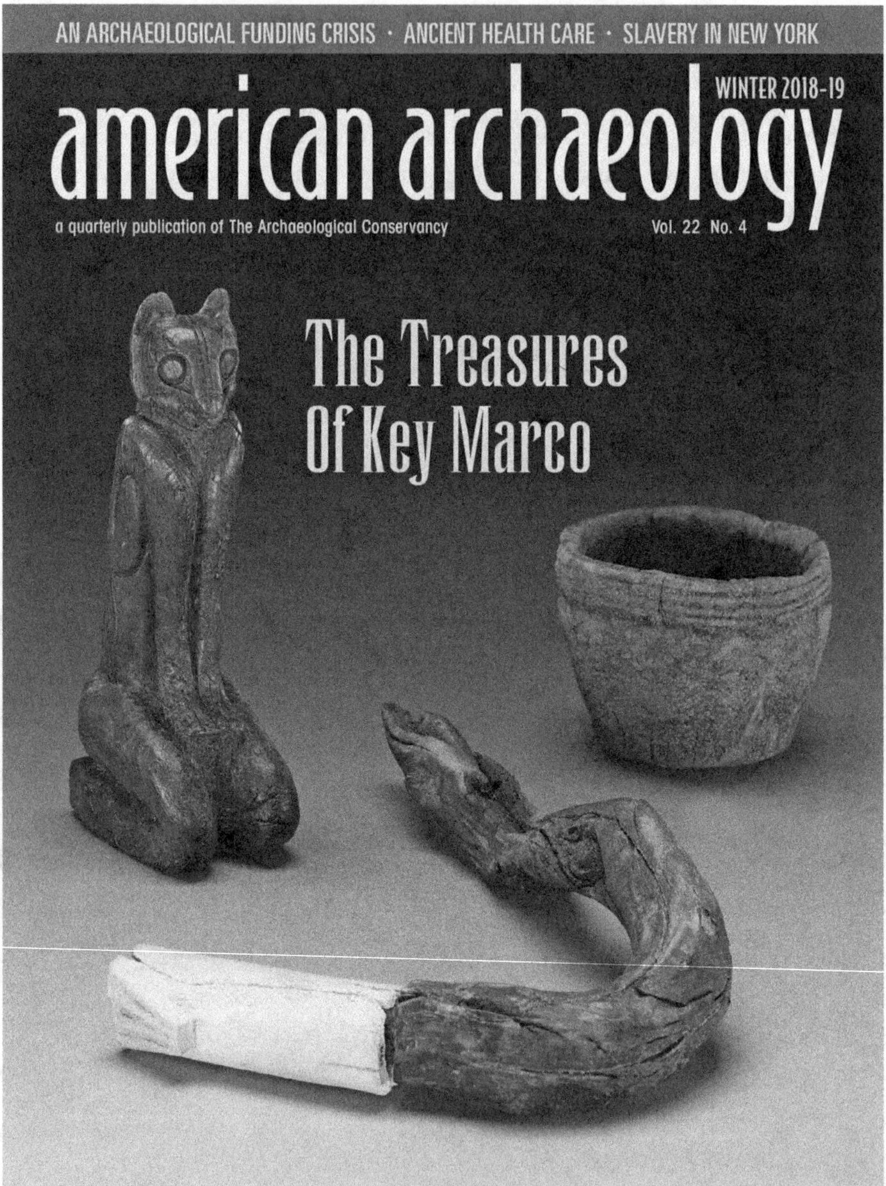

Figure 47. Cover of the Winter 2018–19 *American Archaeology* magazine. By permission of *American Archaeology* and the Department of Anthropology, Smithsonian Institution.

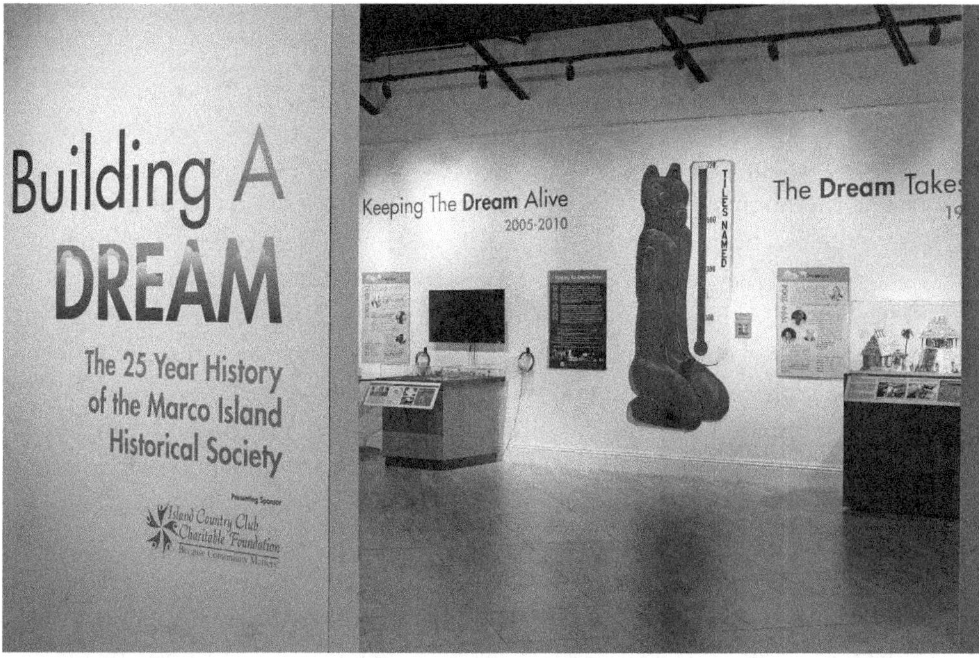

Figure 48. Installation view of *Building a Dream: The 25-Year History of the Marco Island Historical Society*. The exhibition featured a large Key Marco Cat fundraising "thermometer," used during the campaign to build the MIHM, as its visual centerpiece. Photo by Seamus Payne, June 9, 2019.

mined efforts to build the MIHM and obtain the Cat on loan three separate times. Meanwhile, the overhauled *Paradise Found* exhibition was recognized for excellence by both the Florida Association of Museums and the Southeastern Museums Conference.[30]

The Key Marco loans have unquestionably been a transformative event for the small but dedicated MIHM and its community. Recognizing its local impact, in October 2020, the Smithsonian Institution formally extended the loan for another five years, through April 2026. However, as visitation begins to trend toward historic norms, with a twenty-five-year mission "accomplished," the initial excitement of the Cat's "blockbuster" return wearing off, and the effects of a global pandemic dramatically impacting visitation, the MIHM faces new challenges in engaging its constituents.[31] This is a common reality for many museums around the world, but one thing is certain at the MIHM: whether the Cat is still physically present or not, its shadow will undoubtedly loom large over the museum's next chapter, wherever it leads.[32]

The Truth Is Out There

The Key Marco site was excavated in 1896, about seventy years before Marco Island would be dramatically transformed by one of the most ambitious and dramatic development projects in Florida history. In fact, even before the Deltona Corporation began literally reshaping the island itself, much of the Key Marco site had been developed or partially destroyed. Shell from the mounds was used by earlier pioneers to pave roads for the fifteen automobiles on the island by 1918. Anthropologist Aleš Hrdlička writes of his 1918 visit to Marco that the site "had been so affected by removal of shell and the activities of the adjoining settlement that little value could now be said of it." The Olde Marco area was extensively developed during the 1940s and 50s when it changed ownership several times. In 1957, historian Charlton Tebeau reports the shell mound sites at Marco Island "taken over by modern man." The site was also probably ravaged by looters in the wake of Cushing's sensational finds.[33]

Yet, in some publications, the Key Marco site is described as if there is nothing left of it at all. Gilliland writes that that "due to extensive development of the area . . . no further work is likely to be possible." Others describe the site as "devastated," which to an extent is true.[34] However, Widmer's 1995 dig proved that there are some underlying strata still intact, and because the entire northern half of Olde Marco is an area of known probability, state and county ordinances suggest surveying, monitoring, and in some cases, mitigation, by a registered professional archaeologist.[35] These protective safeguards were not in place to protect cultural resources during Cushing's era. Ironically, now that the site is significantly depreciated, it also has more protection—but that does not mean it is not holding on to any more secrets.[36]

In fact, the MIHS is home to more than 130 cubic feet of archaeological materials, most of which have been excavated during the past two decades. Notable sites represented in the MIHS collections include Key Marco, Caxambas Point Shell Midden, and Horr's Island Archaic Village.[37] These materials were the beneficiaries of a 2016 Preservation Assistance Grant from the National Endowment for the Humanities (NEH), which allowed for the rehabilitation of their archival housing.[38] I am optimistic that they will be analyzed and researched by archaeologists in the future, as they hold considerable potential for comparative analysis with legacy collections at other institutions.[39]

While most of the archaeological materials in its possession were donated by private landowners, the MIHS still acquires some Key Marco–related objects the old-fashioned way—with cash. For example, the MIHS purchased a (now priceless) autographed first edition of Frank Hamilton Cushing's *Preliminary Report* on eBay for $103.99 in November 2015.[40] Along with the bronze Cat casting, these objects are proof that original Key Marco–related materials are still "out there."

New School, Old School

Of course, the potential for new discoveries lies not just in archaeological digs and online garage sales. Much of the potential still lies in the objects themselves. As promising new technologies continue to emerge, there will be new opportunities to add to our understanding of the site's many mysteries. In the case of wooden animal carvings from Hontoon Island in Florida, it has been demonstrated that artifacts can be sufficiently prepared for radiocarbon dating to eliminate contaminants such as alvar, turpentine, linseed oil, and other solvents, practices not observed when the Key Marco radiocarbon dates were made.[41] Or perhaps there are altogether uncontaminated wooden samples waiting to be tested in Durnford's Key Marco collection at the British Museum.[42] Technologies such as gas chromatography, infrared spectrometry, and strontium-isotope analysis might reveal information that could lead to specific inferences about the object's age and geographic origins. Additionally, with the advent of the noninvasive and relatively affordable X-ray fluorescence (XRF) analysis, perhaps a new array of wooden artifacts can be selected for radiocarbon dating, particularly those with the lowest detectable amounts of pesticides.

The emergence of three-dimensional printing has created potential for fast and accurate replication of otherwise fragile objects. In fact, the Key Marco Cat was one of the first artifacts to receive this treatment, scanned by the University of South Florida and the Smithsonian Institution in 2018. This practice should be applied to other Key Marco artifacts to aid in their preservation, and scans of the original castings and molds could help reproduce to scale some of the artifacts that disintegrated long ago.[43]

Alternatively, new answers may lie in more traditional but as-yet-unutilized approaches. Ironically, although most of the Key Marco materials are made of wood, dendrochronology—the practice of counting tree rings to achieve the precise date of when a tree was harvested—has not been attempted on the artifacts. Researchers at the Fountain of Youth Park in St. Augustine, Florida, were able to successfully apply dendrochronology to a cross section of waterlogged pine discovered in 2002 (18 cm in diameter), dating it to between 1620 and 1668 CE, a period of Spanish occupation.[44]

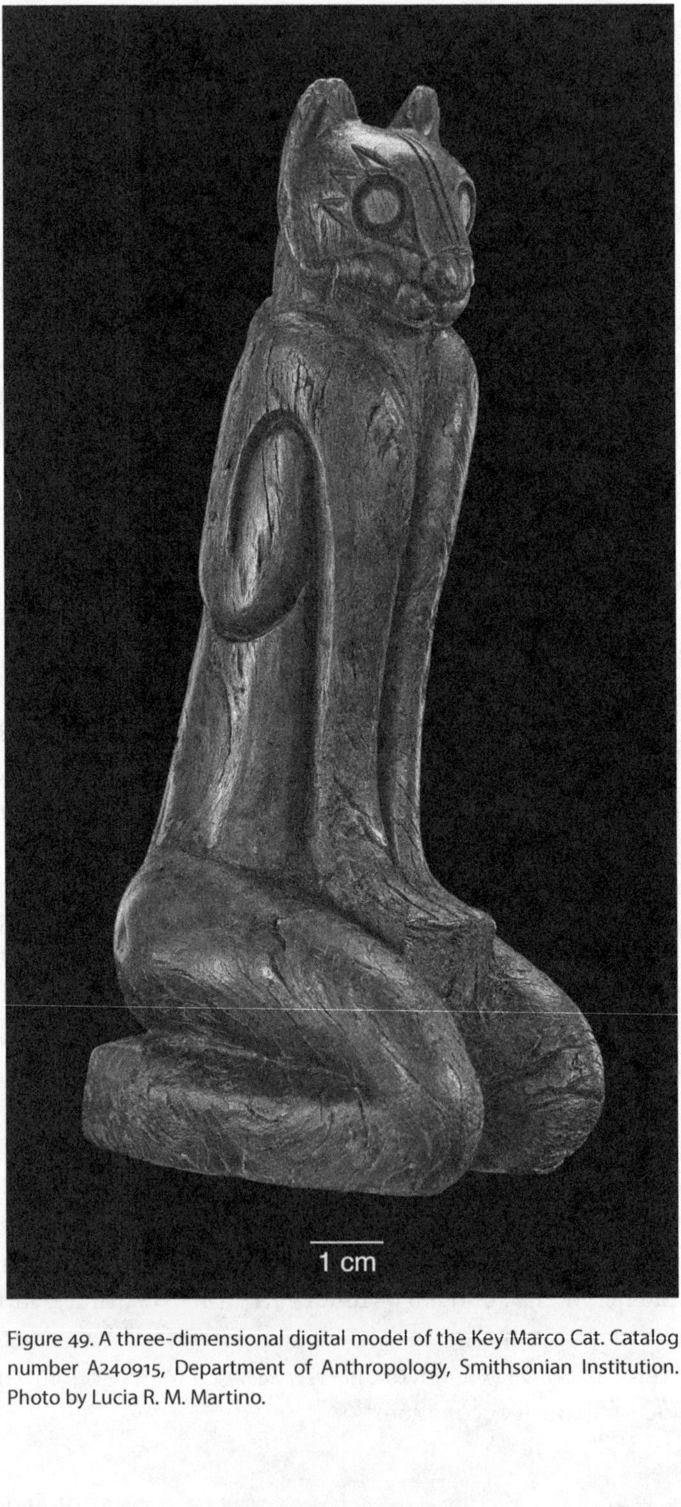

Figure 49. A three-dimensional digital model of the Key Marco Cat. Catalog number A240915, Department of Anthropology, Smithsonian Institution. Photo by Lucia R. M. Martino.

Complicating the potential for Key Marco dendrochronology are the poor states of most objects. Irreversible damage has occurred on a cellular level to the artifacts, likely impacting any attempts to cross-section or analyze the wood. The specimen successfully dated at St. Augustine was immediately preserved in polyethylene glycol after recovery, something Cushing did not have the capability of doing in 1896. Additionally, if the Key Marco artifacts are much older, as some have suggested, they will likely not match up with any existing wood chronologies, making a date impossible. However, it should be noted that Cushing did collect several large timbers, which if still intact, would make the most ideal candidates for any dendrochronological attempts.[45]

Understandably, the wood and plant artifacts from Key Marco receive most of the attention in analysis and interpretation, but a renewed focus on the non-plant-based artifacts from the site, particularly those of bone, ceramic, and stone, might yield surprising results. While considerably fewer in number, numerous examples of each were found at the site and most are still in museum storage. Could it be possible that some of these artifacts were not treated as intensely with pesticides and other contaminants due to their inherently more stable conditions?

Cushing describes the presence of charred food residue on some of the pottery from Key Marco, which is precisely how the MIHS was able to radiocarbon date three ceramic vessels from its collections eleven years after their excavation. Cushing's ceramics could be reexamined in search of usable traces of charred organic material. Archaeologist Robert Tykot has also demonstrated success in distinguishing local from nonlocal wares from Northwest Florida sites, determining their origins at Poverty Point in Louisiana through the use of nondestructive XRF analyses.[46] The application of this process to Key Marco ceramics could theoretically tell us more about their origins.

Success in obtaining elemental composition data from stone has been achieved through the use of nondestructive means such as scanning electron microscopy and XRF.[47] Although stone at Key Marco was sparse, Cushing did recover several flint specimens in addition to an abundance of limestone and coral artifacts. Further study of these pieces might illuminate previously unknown postdepositional processes or geographical origins that could inform our understanding of the site's chronology.[48]

The same strategy applies to bone from the site. The analysis of stable carbon and nitrogen isotopes in human teeth is a reliable method of learning about dietary practices and has been conducted on human remains from nearby sites in Southwest Florida, including Horr's Island. This could be applied to Key

Marco human remains and, in the absence of permission to perform destructive analysis, could instead be attempted using XRF.[49]

If some of these cutting-edge techniques (or a new as-yet-undeveloped technique) were successfully implemented and systematically applied to individual specimens, we might even get an idea as to which theory of deposition holds truest, whether the artifacts are all generally the same age, whether they are all from the same place, and a better overall understanding of the Key Marco site.

The Road Ahead

Not to be a downer, but while time presses forward, the Key Marco Cat is fighting a losing battle. Like all material culture, and all human life that produces it, it will at some point completely degrade and turn to dust. However, as we have seen, careful practice by its museum caretakers can prolong that lifetime for decades or centuries, perhaps even to a point beyond which it is still necessary (i.e., outliving humans). In the meantime, the most significant threats to its life will continue to be the conditions of its surrounding environment, over-exhibition, and human fallibility. As the world faces the global threat of human-induced climate change in the coming century, it will become increasingly difficult and expensive to protect fragile artifacts like the Cat.

As much promise as there is in technology gleaning new information from the Key Marco artifacts, there is also likely to be further controversy. The proliferation of digital media, particularly in the world of photography, has already created headaches for the Smithsonian. When Wells Sawyer photographed the Cat in 1896, he did so by making a negative image onto a glass plate. Nowadays, nearly everyone has a high-quality handheld imaging device on their person, posing what the Smithsonian might perceive as both a physical and intellectual threat. High-intensity light flashes can damage artifacts and inaccurate interpretation or representation—or even unauthorized capitalization—is just a "send" or "upload" away. Yet, the Smithsonian, for its part, is more concerned with the physical integrity of the object, as the Cat's likeness is rightfully in the public domain.[50]

There is also a remote possibility that the Key Marco Cat could someday qualify as a "sacred object" or "object of cultural patrimony" under the terms of the Native American Graves Protection and Repatriation Act (NAGPRA). The return of artifacts to their "places of origin" is a practice that the museum field has increasingly favored in recent decades, particularly regarding the material culture of indigenous communities. Colonialist collecting practices utilized by many museums in the late nineteenth and early twentieth centuries resulted in the accumulation of artifacts in localities far from the cultures and landscapes in which they originated. Many well-established institutions in the United States have addressed past collecting techniques through the repatriation or loan of anthropological collections to their communities of origin, especially after the implementation of NAGPRA in 1990.[51]

In the case of Cushing's Key Marco artifacts, no extant indigenous population has laid claim to them, so there is little controversy over their extraction from a Florida archaeological site in 1896. Cushing also collected the artifacts with the permission of the landowner, W. D. Collier, so there is no question over the legality of the Smithsonian's (and others') possession of the objects. However, human remains *were* found at the site, and should the Key Marco artifacts one day meet the criteria of NAGPRA or the Smithsonian's evolving repatriation policies, it is possible that the Cat could be the subject of such a discussion or dispute.[52]

Finally, the rise of the local history museum in America might continue to play a role in the Cat's life. Marco Island is happy to have its Cat home for now, but what happens when it must return to Washington, D.C., in 2026? How content will the public be to let it sit in storage again? How many new MIHS board and staff members will have to come and go before it becomes part of another strategic plan at the museum? Does it even matter? By that time, maybe it will have been repatriated, transferred to another institution, put on long-term exhibition, or deemed unsuitable for travel. Or, perhaps it will get a much-needed "cat nap" in collections storage, buying it a few more years for the next generations of Smithsonian patrons. Whatever the future holds for the Cat, there will be a lot of interested stakeholders, each with their own opinions on the most appropriate outcomes.

A Legacy of Transformation

All museum artifacts—and all material culture, for that matter—have a life cycle. From the moments they are produced by human hands to the moments of their inevitable destructions, just like humans, so too do objects live. Not all objects, however, hold the power that the Key Marco Cat now holds. Indeed, even fewer have seen their power transformed, reinvented, and redefined as often and as powerfully as the Cat.

That is the great thing about museums and the objects they preserve. Artifacts are constantly being contested, interpretations challenged, narratives overthrown. Undoubtedly, this will happen in some fashion with the Key Marco Cat. But museums, thanks to their tireless preservation efforts and the general public's awareness of and stake in their collections, are the sites where those dialogues, however pleasant or unpleasant, can and should happen. They ensure legacy, and not just of individuals or nation-states, but of cultures past and present, of dreams and ideals, and of objects ephemeral and singular.

The Cat's legacy is one of improbability and universality, a timeless masterpiece of staggering simplicity that has survived impossibly long odds. People have worshipped it in entirely different ways in entirely different worlds for entirely different reasons. It has changed the lives of people in ways that its creator could never have foreseen, traveling thousands of miles, moving millions of dollars, and bringing complete strangers to tears. Yet, it retains an elusive deeper meaning that its modern worshippers will never truly understand, obfuscated by centuries of complicated human history. Its artisan might appreciate—or maybe even find humorous—the profound efforts and technologies now dedicated to preserving it, having already lost it to the elements once. Modern museum visitors still yearn for a greater understanding of the artist's intent, sadly lost at the very same moment.

The Key Marco Cat is an inspiring and poignant link to the past, a testament to the artistry and complexity of Florida's indigenous peoples, a reminder of the fleeting nature of our own fragile lives, and a demonstration of the timelessness of art. Works of art like the Cat elicit single-word descriptions of the highest order, its descriptors futilely searching the depths of their internal thesauruses for adequate adjectives. No one word can truly do it justice, but combined, they give an idea: "heroic," "masterly," "extraordinary," a "gem," "captivating," "exquisite," "magnificent," and "compelling."[53] To those adjectives, and with the benefit of a more extended hindsight, I might only add the word "transformative."[54] Not only is the Cat thought to represent a human-panther deity in literal transformation, it has undergone its own transformation since its discovery, demonstrating that it in turn has the capacity to transform the world around it. From its original perch at Key Marco village to its mount behind bulletproof glass at the MIHM, the Cat has impacted the lives of human beings for hundreds of years by transforming our collective understandings of the world around us.

Acknowledgments

The majority of this book was written in Marco Island, Florida, the ancestral homeland of the Archaic, Glades, Calusa, Miccosukee, and Seminole Indians. Not only that, it was written largely *about* them by a non-Native author. I would like to acknowledge that both the Marco Island Historical Museum and my home rest on land that variously belonged to these cultures for centuries, and that my career, the museum, and this publication have benefitted from the material culture of Florida's indigenous peoples. It is my sincere hope that this publication will foster greater appreciation and awareness of Florida's diverse Native American communities past and present.

Travel expenses, image licensing, professional proofreading, and indexing for this book were funded by a generous grant of $8,000 from the Island Country Club Charitable Foundation (ICCCF) in Marco Island, Florida. The ICCCF has been a loyal supporter of the Marco Island Historical Society (MIHS) for years, and I am particularly grateful to its board of directors, especially Gary Landis, Karen Blackwell, and Ronald Rutledge.

This book would not have been possible without the generous support of the MIHS, its board of directors, and staff. The flexibility and faith they showed in allowing me to produce this publication during the regular course of my duties—at a small nonacademic institution with many other pressing needs—is uncommon, but not unappreciated. In particular, I would like to thank Patricia Rutledge, Heather Otis, and Susan Pernini. I'd also like to thank my former coworker and "museum bestie" Katie Romey, who supported this project in its nascent stages, as well as former MIHS interns and collections assistants Morgan Andrews, Meagan Boritz, Kyle Bostick, Cameron Buxton, Kristin Conwill, Rosemarie Fusco, Kathryn Ivanovich, Ivy Johnson, Lauren O'Neill, Alissa Mittl, Joseph Morelli, Angela Paola, Mara Reynolds, Bailey Rodgers, and Casey Wooster for their contributions to preserving and sharing Marco

Island's history. Former MIHS board presidents Kathy Miracco, Alan Sandlin, Tom Wagor, and Craig Woodward have supported my endeavors since they hired me as the MIHS's first full-time staff member in 2013. My family and I owe them a lifetime of gratitude for taking a chance on me.

I also owe a great deal to the Florida Museum of Natural History (FLMNH) and the University of Florida, which shaped my career between 2003 and 2013. I had the privilege of working at the FLMNH beginning in 2007, first as a volunteer, and then for more than five years as a collections assistant, where I met so many lifelong friends and colleagues, including Melissa Ayvaz, Krista Church, Andrea Cohen, Ann Cordell, Gypsy Price, Paul Morse, and Elizabeth Olson. Memories of time spent with my Museum Studies cohort of Vivian Gornik, Renee Keifer, Amanda Kimble, Natália Marques da Silva, and Hannah Soh still influence everything I do professionally. I also had the good fortune to work for some incredible mentors, who through their brilliance, enthusiasm, and professionalism, inspired me to pursue a career in museums. To Elise LeCompte, Darcie MacMahon, William Marquardt, Susan Milbrath, Dixie Neilson, Donna Ruhl, Karen Walker, and Glenn Willumson, I can only say thank you.

In 2012, I had the opportunity to attend the Smithsonian Institution's Summer Institute in Museum Anthropology (SIMA). During my time at the National Museum of Natural History (NMNH), I learned new ways of looking at and thinking about material culture. The lessons realized during those ten invigorating weeks manifest themselves tenfold in the pages of this book. I am especially grateful to Candace Greene, Nancy Parezo, and the faculty and staff that put together such an outstanding program.

My appointment as a consulting scholar to the University of Pennsylvania Museum of Archaeology and Anthropology in 2019 has been one of the great honors of my professional life. This book would not have been possible in its current form without the opportunities and resources that institution has provided. The faculty and staff at the museum and library, including Anne Brancati, Jane Hickman, Megan Kassabaum, Allison McLaughlin, Evan Peugh, Alessandro Pezzati, Eric Schnittke, and others have proven to be warm and welcoming colleagues. In particular, I would like to thank Meg and her cat Tux for their hospitality and enthusiastic collegiality.

At the Smithsonian's NMNH, special thanks are owed to Allison Butler, Michele Dennehy, James Di Loreto, Felicia Pickering, Dave Rosenthal, James Krakker, Kim Cullen Cobb, Kristen Quarles, Torben Rick, Pamela Steele, Heidi Stover, and Barbara Watanabe, who invariably assisted not only with image and research requests for this book and other publications, but also facilitated access to the Key Marco artifacts and helped orchestrate a loan of the Key Marco Cat to the Marco Island Historical Museum in 2018. The staff at the National Anthropological Archives probably tire of my image and research requests, but they always deliver courteously and professionally, especially Daisy Njoku.

Thanks to my colleagues at the Collier County Museums, who have partnered with the MIHS unfailingly on ambitious endeavors that other museums might shy away from. I owe thanks to Steve Carnell, Jennifer Guida, Ron Jamro, Lisa Marciano, Pam Miner, Jessica Patel, Jennifer Perry, and Amanda Townsend for their support in developing the MIHM's permanent exhibitions, as well as making the Key Marco loans a reality in 2018. Retired Collier County commissioner Donna Fiala has been a vocal proponent of the museum since its inception and rarely misses a museum event. Her kindness and support are felt in person just as much as they were in policy.

The incomparable Merald Clark's creativity, imagination, and thoughtfulness bring the Calusa and their ancestors to life in a way that few others can. It is an honor and joy to work with Merald, who puts so much time and research into his artwork. Thanks also to the talented artists Amanda Wagner-Pelkey and Russell Beans for their delightful contributions to this work.

The following individuals helped bring other information or images to the pages of this book: Vicki Singer (*American Archaeology* magazine), Joe DiLullo and Mary McDonald (American Philosophical Society), Elizabeth Bray (British Museum), Monica Park (Brooklyn Museum), Diane Bonar and Richard Davis (Collier Family Archives), Becky O'Sullivan (Florida Public Archaeology Network), Durrell Buzzini and Linda Sandlin (Marco Island Noontime Rotary), Stratton Meyer (Museum of Fine Arts, Houston Archives), Laura Pavona (National Gallery of Art), Claire Blechman (Peabody Essex Museum), Kathleen Foster and Rick Sieber (Philadelphia Museum of Art), Jessica Rahmer (Saint Louis Art Museum), and Tad Bennicoff (Smithsonian Institution Archives). I am probably missing a few.

Kudos to the nonprofit statewide organizations that I have had the privilege of becoming involved with over the years, which do so much to promote the history and heritage of the State of Florida. These organizations include the Florida Anthropological Society, the Florida Association of Museums, the Florida Public Archaeology Network, the Florida Trust for Historic Preservation, and the Trail of Florida's Indian Heritage.

Special thanks to my peer reviewers, Barbara Purdy and Torben Rick, as well as to William Marquardt, for their valuable criticisms, edits, and feedback. This book is far better for their contributions, and in fact, is built upon the decades of work they've each contributed to their respective fields. This story, wherever it succeeds, does so because of their expertise, knowledge, and scholarship, some of which was written before I was born. Thanks also to my fearless editor, Sian Hunter, who handled my years of excuses like a true professional. Her encouragement and positivity kept this project alive in the moments I feared I had lost it. I'd be remiss if I didn't also thank the rest of the University Press of Florida staff, particularly project editor Michele Fiyak-Burkley and editorial assistant Mary Puckett, as well as freelancers Kerry Smith, Sue Baldwin, and Suzanne Coffman for their copyediting, proofreading, and indexing.

Finally, I would like to thank my loving Bell, Lubitz, Thimmer, Verner, and Wolfe families, whose unfailing support over a lifetime of curiosity has empowered me to chase after that which I find enthralling. In particular, I send thanks and love to my parents, Dave and Linda Bell, for believing in their eldest child (the "guinea pig") even after he switched from engineering to anthropology in college. To my sisters, Allison and Angela Bell, both superior writing talents, please do not point out your brother's grammatical errors, problematic prose, or typos until well after he retires.

And most thanks of all, of course, go to my wondrous wife, Erin Wolfe Bell. While I was writing this book, we bought our first house, had our first child, and then, like everyone else, found ourselves in the midst of a global pandemic. While we were working from home, struggling to stay afloat and make sense of it all, it was difficult not to think that there were more pressing matters than bringing a 2017 "shower idea" to fruition. That this book was completed at all is a minor miracle considering how often I felt like quitting. It only exists because of her encouragement, love, and support. I am honored to dedicate it to our beautiful daughter, Chloe Evelyn Bell.

Any errors in this book are the author's own. Everyone listed here is off the hook.

Notes

List of Abbreviations

1. Woodbury and Woodbury, "Rise and Fall," 283–96.

2. "About the Museum," Collier County, accessed March 26, 2020, https://www.colliercountyfl.gov/your-government/divisions-f-r/museums/about-the-museum.

3. "Brief History of the Museum," Florida Museum of Natural History, accessed March 26, 2020, https://www.floridamuseum.ufl.edu/about/history/.

4. "Marco Island Historical Museum," Collier County Museums, accessed March 26, 2020, https://colliermuseums.com/locations/marco-island-historical-museum.

5. "Fast Facts," Marco Island Historical Society, accessed March 26, 2020, https://themihs.info/mihs-business/.

6. "History of the Collections," National Museum of the American Indian, accessed March 26, 2020, https://americanindian.si.edu/explore/collections/history.

7. From 1881 to 1910, the U.S. National Museum was in what is now known as the Arts and Industries Building.

8. "A Brief History of NMNH," About the Museum, National Museum of Natural History, Smithsonian Institution, accessed April 20, 2020, https://naturalhistory.si.edu/about/brief-history-nmnh.

9. Alessandro Pezzati, Jane Hickman, and Alexandra Fleischman, "A Brief History of the Penn Museum," *Expedition* 54, no. 3 (2012): 4–19, https://www.penn.museum/documents/publications/expedition/PDFs/54-3/A_Brief_History.pdf.

Introduction

1. An "object," by definition, is "a discrete visible or tangible thing." An "artifact" is a *type* of object "showing human workmanship or modification." "Material culture" is "the totality of physical objects made by a people for the satisfaction of their needs," or in anthropological terms (as noted by Thompson and Parezo), "physical objects that provide us with insights into how culture operates and that help us interpret human behavior." These three-tiered terms are used frequently throughout this publication in reference to archaeological artifacts. I follow Webster's definitions of these terms, and their definitions are important to keep in mind, as this book is a material culture study through the lens of a single artifact.

2. Ambrose and Paine, *Museum Basics*, 134; Burcaw, *Museum Work*, 24–31; Alexander and Alexander, *Museums in Motion*, 1–19.

3. Ambrose and Paine, *Museum Basics*, 6.

4. Appadurai, "Introduction," 3–63; Ingold and Hallam, *Making and Growing*, 1–3.

5. "Smithsonian Snapshot: Hope Diamond Mail Wrapper," *Snapshot* (blog), November 16, 2010, https://www.si.edu/newsdesk/snapshot/hope-diamond-mail-wrapper.

6. Iran Cultural & Press Institute, "Canoe Unearthed by Hurricane Irma Could Be Hundreds of Years Old," *Iran Daily* (Tehran, Iran), September 16, 2017.

7. Marquardt, "Padgett Figurine," 159.

8. The term *Key Marco Cat* is the unofficial nickname for the Smithsonian object number A240915-0. It is treated in this volume as a proper noun and is accordingly abbreviated as *Cat* (with a capital *C*).

9. Hrdlička, *Anthropology of Florida*, xiv.

10. The Marco Island Historical Museum closed to the public on April 3, 2020, and reopened on June 9, 2020.

11. Fewkes, "Aboriginal Wooden Objects," 1.

12. Brose, Brown, and Penney, *Ancient Art*, 127–29; Pels, "Spirit of Matter," 94–95; Ingold, "Materials against Materiality," 12.

13. Knappet, *Thinking through*, 1–10, 167–70; Woodward, "Object Interviews," 363.

14. Horse Capture, "Time-Honored Expression," 76.

1. Nature Made

1. *Webster's Third New International Dictionary* (2002), s.v. "provenance"; Alexander and Alexander, *Museums in Motion*, 200.

2. *Pre-Columbian* = prior to the arrival of Christopher Columbus in the Americas (1492); *BCE* = Before Common Era; *CE* = Common Era. Archaeological time periods are largely based on Marquardt, "Shell Mounds," 559.

3. Wilder and Roche, "Floristic Inventory," 873; "Present Day Marco Island," City of Marco Island, accessed March 25, 2020, https://www.cityofmarcoisland.com/community/page/present-day-marco-island; Davis Jr., "Geology of the Florida Coast," 162; Widmer, *Evolution of the Calusa*, 207.

4. Wilder and Roche, "Floristic Inventory," 873–77; Waitley, *Last Paradise*, 37–79; Bell, *Marco Island* (2018), 9–24; Scarry and Newsom, "Archaeobotanical Research," 376.

5. MacMahon and Marquardt, *Calusa and Their Legacy*, 102; Purdy, *Florida's Wetlands*, 1–2.

6. Cushing, "Ancient Key Dweller," 350, 358, 362, 423, 428; Gilliland, *Material Culture of Key Marco*, 47.

7. Gilliland, *Material Culture of Key Marco*, 47–168; Purdy, *Florida's Wetlands*, 31; Newsom, Brown, and Natt, "Pineland Cordage," 605, table 6.

8. Gilliland, *Material Culture of Key Marco*, 47, plate 40; Brown, *Florida's First People*, 27, 228; Milanich, *Precolumbian Florida*, 304; Milanich, *Ancient Times*, 126; Newsom, Brown, and Natt, "Pineland Cordage," 604–5, table 6; Kolianos and Weisman, *Lost Florida Manuscript*, 107.

9. Newsom, Brown, and Natt, "Pineland Cordage," 603, table 4; Brown, *Florida's First People*, 103; Wilder and Roche, "Floristic Inventory," 882–93, appendix 1.

10. Cushing, "Ancient Key Dweller," 362, 423.

11. "Black Ironwood," Natives for Your Neighborhood, accessed May 22, 2020, https://www.regionalconservation.org/beta/nfyn/plantdetail.asp?tx=Krugferr.

12. Cushing, "Ancient Key Dweller," 423, 429; Gilliland, *Buried Treasure*, 73.

13. Lee Newsom, e-mail message to author, May 20, 2018.

14. Purdy, "Experiment and Reflection," 108.

15. Lee Newsom, e-mail message to author, May 20, 2018.

16. Marquardt, "Padgett Figurine," 154; for more on density of South Florida woods, see Scarry and Newsom, "Archaeobotanical Research," 389–90.

17. "NOTES," *Popular Science Monthly (1872–1895)* 28 (1886): 430.

18. Cushing, "Ancient Key Dweller," 429; Michelle Austin Dennehy, April 12, 2018, Condition Report, Outgoing Loan File, Marco Island Historical Museum, on file with Accession No. 48531, Registrar's Office, Department of Anthropology, National Museum of Natural History, Smithsonian Institution.

19. Marquardt, "Padgett Figurine," 152–55, 170; Fewkes, "Aboriginal Wooden Objects," 1; Purdy, *Florida's Wetlands*, 241.

20. *The Concise Oxford Dictionary of Archaeology*, s.v. "experimental archaeology," accessed December 1, 2020, https://www.oxfordreference.com/view/10.1093/acref/9780199534043.001.0001/acref-9780199534043-e-1436.

21. Brown, *Florida's First People*, 102–4.

22. "Exothea paniculata," Florida Native Plant Society, accessed July 2, 2020, https://www.fnps.org/plants/plant/exothea-paniculata; "University of Florida Herbarium Collections Catalog," FLAS Accession No. 94147, Florida Museum of Natural History, Gainesville, Florida, https://www.floridamuseum.ufl.edu/herbarium/cat/search.asp?accno=94147.

23. Newsom, Brown, and Natt, "Pineland Cordage," 593; Marquardt, "Padgett Figurine," 163.

24. Thomas Becnel, "A Fierce People," *Sarasota Herald Tribune*, May 6, 2013; Michael Coleman, *Marco Island: Florida's Gulf Playground* (self-pub., Marco Island Ink, 2014), 27; Davis, *Gulf*, 39; Harriet Howard Heithaus, "The Year of the Cat: Key Marco Cat Returns, This Time to a Home Built for It," *Naples Daily News*, April 21, 2018, https://www.naplesnews.com/story/entertainment/arts/2018/04/21/year-cat-key-marco-cat-returns-time-home-built/523476002/; Chelle Koster Walton, "The Year of the Calusa," *Florida Weekly*, August 1, 2018, https://fortmyers.floridaweekly.com/articles/the-year-of-the-calusa/; Cushing, "Ancient Key Dweller," 362, 423, 428; Bell, *Marco Island* (2017), 21. I regret perpetuating the myth to an extent, identifying it as "probably buttonwood" in print and "possibly buttonwood" in a museum exhibition at the Marco Island Historical Museum from November 2014 to November 2018. In November 2018, the exhibition was corrected with more conservative language and the book, if ever reprinted, will bear the same corrections.

25. Marquardt, "Padgett Figurine," 175.

26. Widmer, *Evolution of the Calusa*, 207; Russo, "Archaic Sedentism"; Alan Yuhas, "Sinkhole Discovery Suggests Humans Were in Florida 14,500 Years Ago," *Guardian*, May 14, 2016, https://amp.theguardian.com/science/2016/may/14/archaeology-florida-sinkhole-ancient-humans-mastodon-knife-bones-bering-strait; Duggins, "Modeling Submerged Landscapes," 45. There are three well-known Paleoindian sites within about 100 miles ATCF from Marco Island, including Little Salt Spring and Warm Mineral Springs in Sarasota County, Florida, and the Cutler Fossil Site in Miami; Griffin, *Archaeology of the Everglades*, 144–45.

27. Milanich, *Precolumbian Florida*, 58–59, 61–104; Widmer, *Evolution of the Calusa*, 167–69, 206–13; Marquardt, "Tracking the Calusa," 7.

28. The Horr's Island Archaic Village is a complex of seven sites including 8CR201, 8CR205–9, and 8CR211; Russo, "Archaic Sedentism," 1, 375–76.

29. Widmer, *Evolution of the Calusa*, 67; Milanich, *Precolumbian Florida*, 86; Russo, "Archaic Sedentism," 244–49, 367, 492, 596–611, table C.2; Russo, *Archaic Shell Rings*, 94–95.

30. Cockrell, "Settlement and Subsistence," 67–69; Widmer, *Evolution of the Calusa*, 67–73; Griffin, *Archaeology of the Everglades*, 146–47; Russo, "Archaic Sedentism," 502–4.

31. Milanich, *Precolumbian Florida*, 275–79, 298–323; Griffin, *Archaeology of the Everglades*, 150–54; MacMahon and Marquardt, *Calusa and Their Legacy*, 77–78.

32. Widmer, "Recent Excavations," 19; Marquardt and Walker, "Southwest Florida During the Mississippi Period," 45–46; Griffin, *Archaeology of the Everglades*, 75–87, 152–53, 159; Cordell, "Pottery Variability at the Pineland Site Complex," 383–543, table 37, 402, 465–67; Marquardt, "Environmental and Cultural History," 885. These Glades types have also been observed by the author in ceramics from Key Marco (8CR48) in the collections at the Marco Island Historical Society, Marco Island, Florida.

33. Griffin, *Archaeology of the Everglades*, 327; MacMahon and Marquardt, *Calusa and Their Legacy*, 6; Marquardt, "Tracking the Calusa," 7, 15.

34. Goggin, "Cultural Traditions," 31.

35. MacMahon and Marquardt, *Calusa and Their Legacy*, 63–64, 79–80; Hann, *Missions*, 280.

36. Thompson et al., "Midden to Midden-Mound," 1. Distances represented in the text were made by the author using Google Maps and are straight-line approximations.

37. Goggin and Sturtevant, "Calusa," 183–86; Marquardt, "The Calusa Domain," 2; Marquardt, "Tracking the Calusa," 9; Hutchinson et al., "Calusa and Prehistoric Subsistence," 55–73.

38. Griffin, *Archaeology of the Everglades*, 72–122.

39. MacMahon and Marquardt, *Calusa and Their Legacy*, 1, 78, 82.

40. Austin, "Lithic Acquisition," 671–72.

41. The author has observed St. Johns series ceramics from Marco Island sites in accessions 2014–7 (Key Marco, 8CR48) and 2014–8 (Caxambas, 8CR107) at the Marco Island Historical Society, Marco Island, Florida. Accession 2014–8 also contains ceramics identified in the field as Englewood Incised. The entirety of these collections should be analyzed by an archaeologist or ceramic technologist for confirmation.

42. Hann, *Missions*, 219–85; Griffin, *Archaeology of the Everglades*, 327.

43. Hann, *Missions*, 312; Worth, *Discovering Florida*, 204.

44. Milanich, *Invasion from Europe*, 40–41; Worth, *Discovering Florida*, 3, table 1, 4, figure 1, 6–7.

45. Wheeler, *Treasure*, 11; MacMahon and Marquardt, *Calusa and Their Legacy*, 6; Austin J. Bell, *Paradise Found: 6,000 Years of People on Marco Island* (Marco Island, FL: Marco Island Historical Museum, 2014), permanent exhibition, text on file at the Marco Island Historical Society.

46. Worth, *Discovering Florida*, xi-xii, 204.

47. Hann, *Missions*, 177; Milanich, *Invasion from Europe*, 41.

48. Hann, *Missions*, 312.

49. MacMahon and Marquardt, *Calusa and Their Legacy*, 6.

50. Howe, "Los Cayos De Muspa," 13.

51. Williams, *Territory of Florida*, 33; Sturtevant, "Chaikaka and the Spanish Indians," 41; Worth, "Creolization in Southwest Florida," 142–60.

52. Gilliland, *Material Culture of Key Marco*, 257.

53. Griffin, *Archaeology of the Everglades*, 151–54.

54. Austin J. Bell, *Paradise Found: 6,000 Years of People on Marco Island* (Marco Island, FL: Marco Island Historical Museum, 2014), permanent exhibition, text on file at the Marco Island Historical Society.

55. Moore, "Certain Antiquities," 369–77.

56. Moore, "Certain Antiquities," 369; Schwadron, "Landscapes of Maritime Complexity," 149.

57. Widmer, "Planned Shell Mound Community," 15; Cushing, "Ancient Key Dweller," 358.

58. Cushing, "Ancient Key Dweller," 350, 362–63.

59. Hrdlička, *Anthropology of Florida*, 21.

60. Marquardt, "Tracking the Calusa," 11; Marquardt, Krus, and Thompson, "Rethinking the Estero Island Site," 7.

61. Purdy, *Florida's Wetlands*, 49; Widmer, "Woodland Archaeology," 391.

62. Widmer, "Planned Shell Mound Community," 11, 19–20.

63. Marquardt and Walker, *Archaeology of Pineland.*

64. Widmer, "Planned Shell Mound Community," 14, 18, 19.

2. Springing to Life

1. Cushing, "Ancient Key Dweller," 387, 429; Richard S. Fiske to Bruce Smith, March 26, 1984, Outgoing Loan File, Detroit Institute of Arts, Ancient Art of the American Woodland Indians, on file with Accession No. 48531, NMNH; Gilliland, *Material Culture of Key Marco*, 116; Milanich, *Precolumbian Florida*, 308; Milanich, *Ancient Times*, 126; Marquardt, "Padgett Figurine," 161.

2. Bill McAllister, "Stamping Out Competition," *Washington Post*, September 8, 1989, 58; Dominic Sama, "U.S. Joins in Celebration with New Columbus Issue," *Chicago Tribune*, October 15, 1989, M11.

3. MacMahon and Marquardt, *Calusa and Their Legacy*, 85.

4. Wallis et al., "Weeden Island," 140–41.

5. Marquardt, "Padgett Figurine," 167.

6. Measured by the author with permission at the Museum Support Center in Suitland, Maryland, on July 23, 2018, using handheld calipers; originally measured in centimeters: height = 15.2 cm, maximum width = 4.5 cm, depth at base = 7.0 cm.

7. Measured by the author with permission at the Museum Support Center in Suitland, Maryland, on July 23, 2018, using an OHAUS Scout (Model SPX421) digital scale.

8. Michelle Austin Dennehy, April 12, 2018, Condition Report, Outgoing Loan File, Marco Island Historical Museum, on file with Accession No. 48531, NMNH; Gilliland, *Material Culture of Key Marco*, plates 69–71.

9. Cushing, "Ancient Key Dweller," 387; Gilliland, *Material Culture of Key Marco*, 116, 117, plates 69–71; Brose, Brown, and Penney, *Ancient Art*, 107, plate 75; Levenson, *Circa 1492*, 583; Wheeler, "Trail of the Panther," 143; Marquardt, "Padgett Figurine," 159.

10. *Webster's Third New International Dictionary* (2002), s.v. "anthropomorphic."

11. Cushing, "Ancient Key Dweller," 387.

12. *Webster's Third New International Dictionary* (2002), s.v. "zoomorphize"; *Webster's Third New International Dictionary* (2002), s.v. "zoomorphic."

13. Carr, "Mississippian Influence," 78–79.

14. "Hero Pose," *Yoga Journal*, updated January 7, 2019, https://www.yogajournal.com/poses/hero-pose.

15. Cushing, "Ancient Key Dweller," 387.

16. Purdy, *Florida's Wetlands*, 257–59; Purdy, *Indian Art of Ancient Florida*, 32, plates 23, 36; Marquardt, "Padgett Figurine," 153, figure 8.1, 155–56, figure 8.3, 159, 165, figure 8.8.

17. Clark, "Mechanical Waterbird," 639–40, figure 17; Marquardt, "Padgett Figurine," 152–55, 158–59.

18. Purdy, *Florida's Wetlands*, 259, figure 104.

19. Cushing, "Ancient Key Dweller," 388.

20. Marquardt, "Padgett Figurine," 160; Wheeler, "Trail of the Panther," 143.

21. Cushing, "Ancient Key Dweller," 387.

22. The Florida panther has five toes on its front paw, but only four register in its track impression. The missing digits on the Key Marco Cat's front paws are probably due to artistic or practical reasons.

23. Cushing, "Ancient Key Dweller," 429; Schwehm, "Wood Effigies of Fort Center," 77; Brown, *Florida's First People*, 227; Russell et al., *Shapeshifting*, 113.

24. Griffin, *Archaeology of the Everglades*, 93–108; Marquardt, "Shell Artifacts," 191–227.

25. Purdy, *Florida's Wetlands*, 1–2; Dietler, "Craft Specialization," 145.

26. Dietler, "Craft Specialization," 70, table 2.2, 109–11, 145–59; Marquardt and Kozuch, "The Lightning Whelk," 5.

27. Dietler, "Craft Specialization," 436–43.

28. Sturtevant, "Woodsmen and Villagers," 122–23; Ostapkowicz et al., "Pre-Columbian Wood Sculpture," 605.

29. Pané, "How They Make and Keep," 25–26.

30. Marquardt, "Shell Artifacts," 193–94.

31. Marquardt, "Shell Artifacts," 193–94.

32. Brown, *Florida's First People*, 85–91.

33. Cushing, "Ancient Key Dweller," 368; Gilliland, *Material Culture of Key Marco*, 47.

34. Brown, *Florida's First People*, 102.

35. Marquardt, "Shell Artifacts," 194.

36. Marquardt, "Shell Artifacts," 204, 207, 208, 211.

37. Brown, *Florida's First People*, 99; Austin, "Lithic Acquisition," 657, 662–71.

38. Austin, "Lithic Acquisition," 666.

39. Widmer, "Recent Excavations," 23, figure 12; Russo, "Archaic Sedentism," 369. The MIHS has in its collections a chert core from a disturbed context at Horr's Island, excavated by the Archaeological and Historical Conservancy Inc., AHC Project Number 2010.14, MIHS catalog number 2012-6-55.

40. Brown, *Florida's First People*, 73, 98. Fossil shark teeth were also sometimes used as cutting blades.

41. Ostapkowicz et al., "Pre-Columbian Wood Sculpture," 605.

42. Marquardt, "Shell Artifacts," 211–12; Thompson et al., "Rise of the Calusa," 35–36.

43. Cushing, "Ancient Key Dweller," 364.

44. Brown, *Florida's First People*, 102–3.

45. Cushing, "Ancient Key Dweller," 429.

46. Brown, *Florida's First People*, 103.

47. Gilliland, *Material Culture of Key Marco*, 48; Marquardt, "Shell Artifacts," 207; Thomp-

son et al., "Rise of the Calusa," 35–36. Possible shell tools used for smoothing include bivalve scrapers, spokeshaves, or columella planes.

48. Kozuch, *Shark Products*, 2–3.

49. Brown, *Florida's First People*, 104.

50. Cushing, "Ancient Key Dweller," 371.

51. Marquardt, "Shell Artifacts," 204, 211.

52. Gilliland, *Material Culture of Key Marco*, 47, 133, 207, 221–22; Griffin, *Archaeology of the Everglades*, 101, 109.

53. Gilliland, *Material Culture of Key Marco*, 205; Griffin, *Archaeology of the Everglades*, 112.

54. Gilliland, *Material Culture of Key Marco*, 48.

55. Cushing, "Ancient Key Dweller," 429.

56. Kozuch, *Shark Products*, 1.

57. Brown, *Florida's First People*, 99, 102.

58. Gilliland, *Material Culture of Key Marco*, 205; Kozuch, *Shark Products*, 1, 3; Brown, *Florida's First People*, 102.

59. Kozuch, *Shark Products*, 1.

60. Cushing, "Ancient Key Dweller," 370.

61. Wells M. Sawyer, Pepper-Hearst Expedition: Notes on the "Shell Hammock" Keys, [ca. 1895–96], Wells M. Sawyer Collection, University of Florida, https://ufdc.ufl.edu/AA00021036/00010/11j; Gilliland, *Buried Treasure*, 71.

62. Gilliland, *Material Culture of Key Marco*. 48; Kozuch, *Shark Products*, 3.

63. Gilliland, *Material Culture of Key Marco*. 48.

64. Cushing, "Ancient Key Dweller," 370.

65. Wallis and O'Dell, "Swift Creek Paddle Designs," 202.

66. Cushing, "Ancient Key Dweller," 371.

67. Wells M. Sawyer, Pepper-Hearst Expedition: Notes on the "Shell Hammock" Keys, [ca. 1895–96], Wells M. Sawyer Collection, University of Florida, https://ufdc.ufl.edu/AA00021036/00010/11j; Gilliland, *Buried Treasure*, 71; Brown, *Florida's First People*, 99.

68. Kozuch, *Shark Products*, 1, 31; Widmer, "Off-Shore Fishing," 249–50.

69. Kozuch, *Shark Products*, 25, 32; deFrance and Walker, "Zooarchaeology of Pineland," 319–20.

70. Kozuch, *Shark Products*, 39.

71. Kozuch's study does not include the Caxambas site (8CR107) on Marco Island, likely because materials from the site were not available for study at the time. The MIHS has in its collections hundreds of shark remains from this site, including dozens of centra and several examples of perforated sharks' teeth. These shark remains, some preliminarily identified by the author, are in MIHS accessions 2014-6 and 2014-8. The entirety of these collections should be analyzed by an archaeologist or zooarchaeologist.

72. Gilliland, *Material Culture of Key Marco*, 135; 4 inches converted from 10.6 cm; 11 inches from 28.1 cm.

73. Brown, *Florida's First People*, 102–3.

74. Gilliland, *Material Culture of Key Marco*, 47.

75. Gilliland, *Material Culture of Key Marco*, 205–20.

76. Walker, "Bone Artifacts," 242; Griffin, *Archaeology of the Everglades*, 112–15; Walker, "Precolumbian Fishing," 24–45.

77. Cushing, "Ancient Key Dweller," 429.

78. Gunnerson, "Mountain Lions," 230, 240–42.

79. Mills and White, *Organic Chemistry*, 35.

80. Michelle Austin Dennehy, April 12, 2018, Condition Report, Outgoing Loan File, Marco Island Historical Museum, on file with Accession No. 48531, NMNH.

81. Michelle Austin Dennehy, April 12, 2018, Condition Report, Outgoing Loan File, Marco Island Historical Museum, on file with Accession No. 48531, NMNH.

82. Kavich, "p-XRF," 2.

83. MacMahon and Marquardt, *Calusa and Their Legacy*, 86.

84. Brown, *Florida's First People*, 107.

85. MacMahon and Marquardt, *Calusa and Their Legacy*, plate 38.

86. Karacic and Duggins, "Colorful Past," 151–60.

3. A Life with Purpose

1. *Webster's Third New International Dictionary* (2002), s.v. "agency."

2. Thompson and Parezo, "Material Culture," 33.

3. Sturtevant, "Anthropological Data Banks," 40–55.

4. *Webster's Third New International Dictionary* (2002), s.v. "material culture"; Herskovits, *Man and His Works*, 245; Schlereth, "Material Culture Studies," 2; Thompson and Parezo, "Material Culture," 34.

5. This assumes that in the distant future, *Star Wars* is no longer a well-known pop-culture phenomenon, an admittedly absurd idea.

6. Cushing, "Ancient Key Dweller," 387, 429, plate XXXV; Gilliland, *Material Culture of Key Marco*, 116, plates 69, 70; Milanich, *Precolumbian Florida*, 308; Russell et al., *Shapeshifting*, 113; Kolianos and Weisman, *Florida Journals*, 59; Harriet Howard Heithaus, "The Year of the Cat: Key Marco Cat Returns, This Time to a Home Built for It," *Naples Daily News*, April 21, 2018, https://www.naplesnews.com/story/entertainment/arts/2018/04/21/year-cat-key-marco-cat-returns-time-home-built/523476002/.

7. Clark, "Mechanical Waterbird," 639.

8. Wheeler, "Trail of the Panther," 143.

9. Davenport, "Proto-Underwater Panther," 59–60.

10. Milanich, *Ancient Times*, 126; Russell et al., *Shapeshifting*, 113.

11. Gross, "Science Failed"; Johnson et al., "Genetic Restoration," 1641–42.

12. "Florida Panther Program," Florida Fish and Wildlife Conservation Commission, accessed July 16, 2020, https://myfwc.com/wildlifehabitats/wildlife/panther/.

13. Wheeler, "Trail of the Panther," 139–62.

14. Culver et al., "Genomic Ancestry," 196; Johnson et al., "Genetic Restoration," 1641–45.

15. Clark, "Mechanical Waterbird," 633, figure 11.

16. Cushing, "Ancient Key Dweller," 388.

17. Hamell, "Long-Tail," 264, 271; Wheeler, "Trail of the Panther," 140, 141, 149, 151, 160.

18. Gilliland, "Material Culture of Key Marco," 130; Gilliland, *Material Culture of Key Marco*, plate 89.

19. Wing, "Animal Bones," 21–28; Wheeler, "Trail of the Panther," 141.

20. Katherine Moore, e-mail message to author, August 5, 2020; Nicole Cannarozi, e-mail message to author, August 6, 2020.

21. Gilliland, *Material Culture of Key Marco*, 215.

22. Gilliland, "Material Culture of Key Marco," 130; Gilliland, *Material Culture of Key Marco*, plate 89.

23. Cushing, "Ancient Key Dweller," 393, 399; Clark, "Mechanical Waterbird," 634, figure 12, 639.

24. Cushing, "Ancient Key Dweller," 388, 393.

25. Clark, "Mechanical Waterbird," 646–47, figure 18f.

26. Purdy, *Indian Art of Ancient Florida*, 33, plate 36; Wheeler, "Trail of the Panther," 143; Marquardt, "Padgett Figurine," 159.

27. Marquardt, "Padgett Figurine," 158–59; Wheeler, "Trail of the Panther," 144.

28. Sears, *Fort Center*, 186; Wheeler, "Trail of the Panther," 145.

29. Moore, "Northwest Florida Coast," 261; Wheeler, "Trail of the Panther," 145.

30. Davenport, "Proto-Underwater Panther," 59–61, 64. The author also suggests armadillo or alligator as alternatives due to the presence of what might be perceived as a carapace or osteoderms on the figure's back.

31. Lord, "Zoomorphic Bone," 263–64; Davenport, "Proto-Underwater Panther," 61.

32. Kind et al., "Smile of the Lion Man," 129–45.

33. Baldwin, "Notes and Speculation," 428–48.

34. "The Gayer-Anderson Cat," Online Collection, British Museum, accessed August 14, 2019, https://www.britishmuseum.org/research/collection_online/collection_object_details.aspx?objectId=153429&partId=1.

35. Saunders, "Introduction," 2–3; Diesel, "Felines and Female," 71–94.

36. Cushing, "Ancient Key Dweller," 387.

37. Saunders, "Introduction," 4–6.

38. Wheeler, "Trail of the Panther," 146; Brose, Brown, and Penney, *Ancient Art*, 78, plate 61.

39. Brose, Brown, and Penney, *Ancient Art*, 78, plate 61, 206; Seeman, "Hopewell Art," 63.

40. Cushing, "Ancient Key Dweller," 387; Townsend, "American Landscapes," 28–29; Milanich, *Precolumbian Florida*, 308; Dietler, "Craft Specialization," 126; Wheeler, "Trail of the Panther," 143; Russell et al., *Shapeshifting*, 113; Clark, "Mechanical Waterbird," 639; Marquardt, "Padgett Figurine," 159–60; Davenport, "Proto-Underwater Panther," 61.

41. Marquardt, "Padgett Figurine," 159.

42. Milanich, *Precolumbian Florida*, 308; Clark, "Mechanical Waterbird," 639.

43. Cushing, "Ancient Key Dweller," 387; Townsend, "American Landscapes," 28–29; Russell et al., *Shapeshifting*, 113.

44. Schwehm, "Carved Wood Effigies," 60; Gunnerson, "Mountain Lions," 230–33; Wheeler, "Trail of the Panther," 151.

45. Saunders, "Architecture of Symbolism," 16.

46. Wheeler, "Trail of the Panther," 143

47. Hann, *Missions*, 287–88.

48. Griffin, *Archaeology of the Everglades*, 327.

49. Levenson, *Circa 1492*, 583.

50. Goggin and Sturtevant, "Calusa," 197–99.

51. Gilliland, *Material Culture of Key Marco*, 247.

52. Cushing, "Scarred Skulls," 18.

53. Marquardt, "Tracking the Calusa," 14.

54. Wheeler, "Trail of the Panther," 151.

55. Gunnerson, "Mountain Lions," 234; Wheeler, "Trail of the Panther," 147, 150; Cushing, "Ancient Key Dweller," 429.

56. Vega, *Florida of the Inca*, 68; Wheeler, "Trail of the Panther," 149, 151. Engravings by Theodore de Bry in 1591, which he claimed were French colonist Jacques Le Moyne's representations of indigenous Floridians, are the most commonly reproduced ethnographic images of sixteenth century Florida, including one showing a man wearing a panther headdress and cape (Wheeler, "Trail of the Panther," 147, figure 8).

57. Milanich, "Devil in the Details," 26–31; Wheeler, "Trail of the Panther," 148.

58. Hamell, "Long-Tail," 271, 282.

59. Fairbanks, *Archeology of the Funeral Mound*, 46.

60. MacMahon and Marquardt, *Calusa and Their Legacy*, 121, 134–35.

61. Billie, *Legends*, 7–9; Wheeler, "Trail of the Panther," 148.

62. Speck, "Aboriginal Culture," 289–90; Wheeler, "Trail of the Panther," 150.

63. Spoehr, "Camp, Clan, and Kin," 16; Wheeler, "Trail of the Panther," 148.

64. Schwehm, "Carved Wood Effigies," 58–59; Wheeler, "Trail of the Panther," 150.

65. Thompson et al., "Rise of the Calusa," 38–39.

66. Townsend, "American Landscapes," 21; Gunnerson, "Mountain Lions," 230–31.

67. Gunnerson, "Mountain Lions," 231–32.

68. Brown, "Mississippian Period," 96.

69. Brown, "Mississippian Period," 104.

70. Marquardt, "Introduction," xvi.

71. Cushing, "Ancient Key Dweller," 387; Gunnerson, "Mountain Lions," 234–35; Wheeler, "Trail of the Panther," 148, 150.

72. *Webster's Third New International Dictionary* (2002), s.v. "shamanism"; Cushing, "Ancient Key Dweller," 387, 391; Saunders, "Architecture of Symbolism," 29–33; Gunnerson, "Mountain Lions," 235; Seeman, "Predatory War," 181–82; Wheeler, "Trail of the Panther," 150; Clark, "Mechanical Waterbird," 643.

73. Becker, "Olmec Were-Jaguar," 57–58; Wheeler, "Trail of the Panther," 150.

74. Clark, "Mechanical Waterbird," 644; Wheeler, "Trail of the Panther," 150–51. Public lecture titled "Key Marco in Living Color" on April 15, 2019, at the Rose History Auditorium, Marco Island Historical Museum, Marco Island, Florida.

4. Moment of Truth

1. Cushing, "Ancient Key Dweller," plate XXXI; Kolianos and Weisman, *Lost Florida Journals*, 84–87.

2. Cushing, "Ancient Key Dweller," 358–60; Gilliland, *Material Culture of Key Marco*, 37; Milanich, "Temporal Placement," 682.

3. Mason, "Primitive Wooden Masks," 5.

4. Gilliland, *Material Culture of Key Marco*, 37–38.

5. Carr and Beriault, "Utility Trenching North Marco," 17, 32. Secondary identification made by Gifford Waters, e-mail message to author, June 6, 2014. Confirmed by Waters on July 14, 2014, at the FLMNH, Gainesville, Florida.

6. Gilliland, *Material Culture of Key Marco*, 231–36.

7. Griffin, *Archaeology of the Everglades*, 138.

8. Hann, "Indians of Central and South Florida," 17; Weisman, *Pioneer in Space and Time*, 72–94.

9. Gilliland, *Material Culture of Key Marco*, 128, 231; Gilliland, *Buried Treasure*, 127–28; Milanich, *Precolumbian Florida*, 247, 301; "St. Johns Check Stamped," Florida Museum of Natural History, last updated November 19, 2019, https://www.floridamuseum.ufl.edu/ceramiclab/pottery-types-gallery/st-johns-check/.

10. John M. Goggin to Harriet Newell Wardle, May 12, 1946, box 4, folder 4/11, Florida Explorations, Penn Museum; Mason, "H. Newell Wardle," 40.

11. Van Beck and Van Beck, "Marco Midden," 5–7, 11; Griffin, *Archaeology of the Everglades*, 152.

12. Widmer, "Recent Excavations," 19–20; Carr and Beriault, "Utility Trenching North Marco," 16; Sweeney, "Archaeological Testing," 42–45.

13. The three vessels described are a round Glades Plain vessel (cat. no. 2014-12-8-1), round Key Largo Incised vessel (cat. no. 2014-12-7-9), and square Glades Plain vessel (cat. no. 2014-12-7-10). These are housed in the permanent collections of the MIHS at the Marco Island Historical Museum, Marco Island, Florida.

14. The author submitted samples to Beta Analytic for radiocarbon dating, which were received there on February 23, 2015. The results were reported back to the author on March 10, 2015. The final report, ID number 55171, is on file at the MIHS.

15. American Chemical Society National Historic Chemical Landmarks, "Discovery of Radiocarbon Dating," accessed April 10, 2020, http://www.acs.org/content/acs/en/education/whatischemistry/landmarks/radiocarbon-dating.html.

16. Crane and Griffin, "Radiocarbon Dates," 93; Gilliland, *Material Culture of Key Marco*, 257.

17. Crane and Griffin, "Radiocarbon Dates," 93.

18. Gilliland, *Material Culture of Key Marco*, 257; Griffin, *Archaeology of the Everglades*, 153; Purdy, *Florida's Wetlands*, 29.

19. Gilliland, *Material Culture of Key Marco*, 257.

20. Milanich, "Temporal Placement," 682; Griffin, *Archaeology of the Everglades*, 153.

21. Cushing, "Ancient Key Dweller," 361.

22. Purdy, *Florida's Wetlands*, 29–30.

23. Gilliland, *Buried Treasure*, 127–28.

24. Widmer, "Recent Excavations," 25.

25. Kavich, "p-XRF," 1.

26. Milanich, *Precolumbian Florida*, 269; Brown, "Cahokian Expression," 106; Kassabaum, "Early Platforms," 187.

27. Widmer, "Ceremonial Artifacts," 172.

28. Newsom and Knight, "Foreword," xxi.

29. Marquardt and Walker, "Mississippi Period," 29–61; Carr, "Mississippian Influence," 62–80; Spivey-Faulkner, "Fort Center's Iconographic Bestiary," 279.

30. Widmer, "Ceremonial Artifacts," 172, 179–80; Milanich, "Temporal Placement," 682; Carr, "Mississippian Influence," 78–79.

31. Anderson and Mainfort, "Woodland Archaeology," 1; Hutchinson, *Bioarchaeology*, 2.

32. Anderson and Mainfort, "Woodland Archaeology," 10, 18–19.

33. Hutchinson, *Bioarchaeology*, 2; Anderson and Mainfort, "Woodland Archaeology," 1, 9; Wheeler, "Trail of the Panther," 151.

34. Schwehm, "Carved Wood Effigies," 73; Widmer, "Ceremonial Artifacts," 180; Townsend,

"American Landscapes," 29–30; Dietler, "Craft Specialization," 126; Carr, "Mississippian Influence," 78–79.

35. Kassabaum, "Early Platforms," 211; Spivey-Faulkner, "Fort Center's Iconographic Bestiary," 263–71.

36. Widmer, "Woodland Archaeology," 394.

37. Widmer, "Recent Excavations," 20–21; Kassabaum, "Early Platforms," 187, 198.

38. Kassabaum, "Early Platforms," 211.

39. Welch and Butler, "Borne on a Litter," 2.

40. Anderson and Mainfort, "Woodland Archaeology," 1; Marquardt and Walker, "Mississippi Period," 29.

41. Griffin, "Buzzard Cult," 295–301; Crane and Griffin, "Radiocarbon Dates," 93; Gilliland, *Material Culture of Key Marco*, 257; Widmer, *Evolution of the Calusa*, 89.

42. Griffin, "Buzzard Cult," 298–300.

43. Milanich, "Temporal Placement," 682.

44. Wheeler, *Treasure of the Calusa*, 150; Carr, "Mississippian Influence," 79. It should be noted that the cross in precontact Native American societies is emblematic of a belief in the "four cardinal directions," not a crucifix associated with Christian religions, which would have emerged in imagery only after European interference. The Key Marco site, as has been discussed previously, is believed to predate contact due to the lack of European goods at the site.

45. Wheeler, "Trail of the Panther," 147.

46. Brose, Brown, and Penney, *Ancient Art*, 126–27; Townsend, "American Landscapes," 21; Walker, "Prehistoric Art," 222.

47. Cushing, "Ancient Key Dweller," 387; Wheeler, "Trail of the Panther," 150.

48. Waring and Holder, "Prehistoric Ceremonial Complex," 4; Widmer, "Ceremonial Artifacts," 172; Reilly, "People of Earth," 127–30; Wheeler, "Trail of the Panther," 143.

49. Goggin, "Archaeological Areas," 120; Goggin and Sturtevant, "Calusa," 198; Widmer, *Evolution of the Calusa*, 89, 92–93; Carr, "Mississippian Influence," 78–79.

50. Marquardt and Walker, "Mississippi Period," 45–47, 56.

51. Gilliland, *Material Culture of Key Marco*, 33.

52. Walker, "Environmental Contexts," 30, 37–38.

53. Walker et al., "Episodic Sea Levels," 171–73.

54. Marquardt, "Pineland Site Complex," 816–17.

55. Cushing, "Ancient Key Dweller," 358.

56. Cushing, "Ancient Key Dweller," 361.

57. Cushing, "Ancient Key Dweller," 349.

58. Cushing, "Ancient Key Dweller," 361.

59. Moore, "Certain Antiquities," 380; Cockrell, "Settlement and Subsistence," 27.

60. Wardle, "Pile Dwellers," 186.

61. Milanich, "Temporal Placement," 682.

62. McGoun, "Medals of Conquest," 13.

63. Widmer, "Woodland Archaeology," 393.

64. Gilliland, *Material Culture of Key Marco*, 33.

65. Purdy, *Florida's Wetlands*, 48–49.

66. Cushing, "Ancient Key Dweller," 361.

67. Wells M. Sawyer, "The Court of the Pile Dwellers," [ca. 1897]: 10, Wells M. Sawyer

Collection, Special and Area Studies Collection, George A. Smathers Libraries, University of Florida, https://ufdc.ufl.edu/AA00021036/00014/19x.

68. Cushing, "Ancient Key Dweller," 361; Gilliland, *Material Culture of Key Marco*, 33.

69. Gilliland, *Material Culture of Key Marco*, 33.

70. Speck, "Aboriginal Culture," 293; Gilliland, *Material Culture of Key Marco*, 34.

71. Cushing, "Ancient Key Dweller," 360–61.

72. Cushing, "Ancient Key Dweller," 357–58.

73. Swanton, "Indians," 101; Gilliland, *Material Culture of Key Marco*, 33; Ewen, "Anhaica," 111.

74. Schober, *ArtCalusa*, 52.

75. Goggin and Sturtevant, "Calusa," 197; Gilliland, *Material Culture of Key Marco*, 33, 213; Widmer, "Planned Shell Mound Community," 20.

76. Gilliland, *Material Culture of Key Marco*, 247.

77. Milanich, *Invasion from Europe*, 105–7; Milanich, *Ancient Times*, 134; MacMahon and Marquardt, *Calusa and Their Legacy*, 115.

78. William H. Marquardt, e-mail message to author, May 1, 2020.

79. MacMahon and Marquardt, *Calusa and Their Legacy*, 6.

80. Marquardt, "Tracking the Calusa," 15–16.

81. Marquardt, "Tracking the Calusa," 13.

5. Four Hundred Years of Solitude

1. Worth, *Discovering Florida*, 16.

2. Hutchinson, *Bioarchaeology*, 55–60.

3. "Henry Laurens Mitchell," Florida Department of State, accessed July 28, 2020, https://dos.myflorida.com/florida-facts/florida-history/florida-governors/henry-laurens-mitchell/.

4. Milanich, *Invasion from Europe*, 213–31; MacMahon and Marquardt, *Calusa and Their Legacy*, 115–21.

5. Tebeau, *Florida's Last Frontier*, 140.

6. "Legal History," Smithsonian Institution, accessed July 28, 2020, https://www.si.edu/ogc/legalhistory; "The Smithsonian Institution Fact Sheet," Smithsonian Institution, last updated February 13, 2020, https://www.si.edu/newsdesk/factsheets/smithsonian-institution-fact-sheet.

7. Patrick, *Florida under Five Flags*, 25–73.

8. Tebeau, *Florida's Last Frontier*, 207–8; Schafer, "U.S. Territory," 202.

9. "Seminole Wars History," Seminole Wars Foundation, accessed July 28, 2020, https://seminolewars.org/index.php/history/; Missall and Missall, *Seminole Wars*, 162–66.

10. Tebeau, *Florida's Last Frontier*, 207–19.

11. Cushing, "Ancient Key Dweller," 329.

12. Wells M. Sawyer, "The Court of the Pile Dwellers" [ca. 1897], 2, Wells M. Sawyer Collection, University of Florida, https://ufdc.ufl.edu/AA00021036/00014/3j.

13. Tebeau, *Florida's Last Frontier*, 140–43.

14. Tebeau, *Florida's Last Frontier*, 162–63, 216–17. In a remarkable coincidence, it appears that Cushing had the opportunity to meet Watson during his excavation at Marco. According to Margaret Collier's diary, a "Mr. Watson" visited Marco with local pineapple farmer Frederick Ludlow and Walter Langford on March 15, 1896, just ten days after the Cat's discovery

(Collier, *Diary*, 16). For more on Watson, see Peter Matthiessen's fictional Watson trilogy, including *Killing Mr. Watson* (1990), *Lost Man's River* (1997), and *Bone by Bone* (1999).

15. Typed facsimile of *Collier County News*, Thursday, July 21, 1927, on file in the Collier Family Archives, the Marco Island Historical Society, Marco Island, Florida.

16. Gilliland, *Buried Treasure*, 3.

17. Ironically, the 1893 Chicago World's Fair would also play a pivotal role in the formation of the Pepper-Hearst Expedition (see chap. 8).

18. Kolianos and Weisman, *Florida Journals*, 23.

19. Davis, *Gulf*, 30; W. T. Collier, "Reflections of W. T. Collier," on file in the Collier Family Archives, Marco Island Historical Society, Marco Island, Florida.

20. Cushing, "Ancient Key Dweller," 350–51; Kolianos and Weisman, *Florida Journals*, 23.

21. Kolianos and Weisman, *Florida Journals*, 48, 50, 138. The Colliers' "fine new hotel" is still standing, now the Olde Marco Inn and Suites. Sawyer drew the building into his topographical site map (Cushing, "Ancient Key Dweller," plate XXXI).

22. Kolianos and Weisman, *Florida Journals*, 50.

23. Kolianos and Weisman, *Florida Journals*, 50, 52.

24. Gilliland, *Buried Treasure*, 81–82. The Olde Marco Inn & Suites, previously known as Hotel Marco, the Marco Hotel, and the Old Marco Inn, is located at 100 Palm Street, Marco Island, Florida. Since 2017, the Marco Island Historical Museum has featured a history of the hotel in its permanent exhibition, *The Pioneer Era: A Tale of Two Villages*.

25. Collier, *Diary*, 25; Gilliland, *Buried Treasure*, 88.

26. It is no wonder that Collier had great vegetable crops on Marco. His land was likely largely pH neutral to slightly alkaline due to high amounts of archaeological shell. Many farmers must add lime in the form of crushed limestone or shell to their soils to make them more suitable for growing vegetables. Coupled with an abundance of organic material buried within the surrounding muck pits, it is easy to see why Collier was so excited about the fertilizer being collected by Cushing's team.

27. Cushing, "Ancient Key Dweller," 355–56.

28. Gilliland, *Buried Treasure*, 84. The whereabouts of this written agreement, or any copy of it, if it exists, is presently unknown.

29. Davis, *Gulf*, 24.

30. Durnford, "Anthropology," 1032–39; Cushing, "Anthropology," 1132-35; Snapp, "Durnford Collection," 267–73.

31. Griffin, *Archaeology of the Everglades*, 56–62.

32. Harrington, "Shell Implement," 218–21. The Heye Foundation transferred its collections to the Smithsonian Institution's new NMAI in 1989. The object is catalog no. 127366.000 (12/3766) at the NMAI.

33. Perdichizzi, *Island Voices*, 18; Coleman, *Marco Island*, 73.

34. Tebeau, *Florida's Last Frontier*, 143.

35. The Marco Island Cemetery is located at 489 W. Elkcam Circle, Marco Island, Florida.

36. Coleman, *Marco Island*, 73–80.

37. McIver, *Death in the Everglades*, 46–53; "Lee County Official Records Search," Lee County Clerk of Court, FL, book D, 142–43, accessed July 30, 2020, https://or.leeclerk.org/LandMarkWeb/.

38. Kolianos and Weisman, *Florida Journals*, 23.

39. Cushing, "Ancient Key Dweller," 350.

40. Collier, *Diary*, 5–6; Gilliland, *Buried Treasure*, 80; Kolianos and Weisman, *Florida Journals*, 58, 143, note 34.

41. Purdy, *Florida's Wetlands*, 1.

42. Milanich, *Precolumbian Florida*, 304–8.

43. Purdy, *Florida's Wetlands*, 9.

44. Cushing, "Ancient Key Dweller," 358.

45. Wells M. Sawyer, "Memories" [ca. 1900], 3, Pepper-Hearst Expedition: Frank Hamilton Cushing Memorial by Sawyer, Wells M. Sawyer Collection, University of Florida, https://ufdc.ufl.edu/AA00021036/00005/17j.

46. Cushing, "Ancient Key Dweller," plate XXXI.

47. Purdy, *Florida's Wetlands*, 10.

48. Purdy, *Florida's Wetlands*, 10, 15, 17.

49. Purdy, *Florida's Wetlands*, 18.

50. Purdy, *Florida's Wetlands*, 18–19.

51. Purdy, *Florida's Wetlands*, 37.

52. Kolianos and Weisman, *Florida Journals*, 23.

53. Purdy, *Florida's Wetlands*, 13, 18, 37.

54. Florida peat, often called fen peat, is materially different from peat found in other places, as its name suggests (Brown, *Florida's First People*, 175). Typically acidic, Florida peat is often charged with alkaline calcium carbonate from underlying limestone, rendering its pH neutral. Large amounts of shell can have the same effect. This was likely the case at Key Marco, where the entire forty-four-acre settlement was essentially a network of human-engineered shell mounds. In the absence of limestone, encapsulating and underlying shell introduced the calcium carbonate that neutralized the Key Marco peat.

55. Cushing, "Ancient Key Dweller," plate XXXI.

56. Cushing, "Ancient Key Dweller," 357.

57. Thompson et al., "Ancient Engineering," 8374–81.

58. Brown, *Florida's First People*, 175.

6. Born Anew

1. Gilliland, *Material Culture of Key Marco*, 3–6; Gilliland, *Buried Treasure;* 1–54; Davis, *Gulf*, 23–40.

2. Chamberlain, "In Memoriam," 129-34; Gilliland, *Buried Treasure;* 26, 103; Davis, *Gulf*, 25; Kolianos and Weisman, *Lost Florida Manuscript*, 1–13.

3. Cushing, "Ancient Key Dweller," 350; Frank Hamilton Cushing to William Pepper, March 7, 1896, box 2, folder 2/3, Florida Explorations, Penn Museum.

4. Cushing, "Ancient Key Dweller," 360; Kolianos and Weisman, *Lost Florida Manuscript*, 108.

5. Frank Hamilton Cushing, cartographer, draft of *Plan and Section of the "Court of the Pile Dwellers," at Key Marco, Showing Locations of Excavations and Finds* (Cushing, "Ancient Key Dweller," plate XXXI), Brooklyn Museum Archives, Culin Archival Collection: Cushing Collection [6.3.026]: A143; Durnford, "Anthropology," 1033; Davis, *Gulf*, 23–24; Cushing, "Ancient Key Dweller," 329; Gilliland, *Material Culture of Key Marco*, 3; Tebeau, *Florida's Last Frontier*, 29.

6. Durnford, "Anthropology," 1033; Read, "Antiquities from Marco," 406–7; Snapp, "Durnford Collection," 267.

7. Durnford, “Anthropology,” 1034–36; Cushing, “Anthropology,” 1132-35.

8. Cushing, “Ancient Key Dweller,” 330; Gilliland, *Buried Treasure*, 45. The project appears to have, on April 13, 1895, been offered to Clarence B. Moore, a well-known archaeologist already operating in Florida. Moore declined the opportunity in a letter to Pepper on April 21, 1895, box 2, folder 2/2, Florida Explorations, Penn Museum.

9. Kolianos and Weisman, *Florida Journals*, 15; Gilliland, *Buried Treasure*, 44–54; Davis, *Gulf*, 27.

10. Davis, *Gulf*, 28.

11. Cushing hired a small sloop named *Florida*, owned by Capt. John Smith, for this excursion.

12. The Marco River forms Marco Island’s north and eastern borders and once encircled the entire Key Marco site, which stood out in open waters.

13. Gilliland, *Buried Treasure*, 53; Kolianos and Weisman, *Florida Journals*, 23.

14. Kolianos and Weisman, *Lost Florida Manuscript*, 105. According to an expense ledger in Cushing’s hand, two men were paid $1.50 each on June 6, 1895, for their full day’s work at Collier’s, box 2, folder 2/13, Florida Explorations, Penn Museum.

15. Kolianos and Weisman, *Florida Journals*, 23.

16. Kolianos and Weisman, *Lost Florida Manuscript*, 108.

17. Kolianos and Weisman, *Lost Florida Manuscript*, 108.

18. Gilliland, *Buried Treasure*, 53–54; Kolianos and Weisman, *Florida Journals*, 23.

19. Cushing, “Ancient Key Dweller,” 351; Gilliland, *Buried Treasure*, 55.

20. Snapp, “Durnford Collection,” 267, 270.

21. Frank Hamilton Cushing to William Pepper, June 6, 1895, box 2, folder 2/2, Florida Explorations, Penn Museum.

22. Durnford, “Anthropology,” 1034.

23. John Wesley Powell to Frank Hamilton Cushing, October 19, 1895, Manuscript 1848: 17, NAA; Gilliland, *Buried Treasure*, 55.

24. Davis, *Gulf*, 32.

25. Kolianos and Weisman, *Florida Journals*, 48–50.

26. Cushing, “Ancient Key Dweller,” 356.

27. Kolianos and Weisman, *Florida Journals*, 23, 50–58.

28. Gilliland, *Material Culture of Key Marco*, 47–248.

29. Kolianos and Weisman, *Florida Journals*, 50–58.

30. Cushing, “Ancient Key Dweller,” 359.

31. Kolianos and Weisman, *Florida Journals*, 58.

32. Kolianos and Weisman, *Lost Florida Manuscript*, xiii; Kolianos and Weisman, *Florida Journals*, 58.

33. Kolianos and Weisman, *Florida Journals*, xiv.

34. Collier, *Diary*, 3; Kolianos and Weisman, *Florida Journals*, 59.

35. Kolianos and Weisman, *Lost Florida Manuscript*, 162, 259.

36. George Gause, Pepper-Hearst Expedition: Field Note Book of George Gause, chief excavator [March 5, 1896], Wells M. Sawyer Collection, University of Florida, https://ufdc.ufl.edu/AA00021036/00013/27j; Kolianos and Weisman, *Florida Journals*, 59.

37. Cushing, “Ancient Key Dweller,” 387–88, plate XXXV.

38. Gilliland, *Buried Treasure*, 79.

39. Cushing, “Ancient Key Dweller,” 429.

40. Wells M. Sawyer to Weller, March 1896, Wells M. Sawyer Collection, University of Florida, https://ufdc.ufl.edu/AA00021036/00004/35x.

41. Wells M. Sawyer to Kathleen Bailey, March 4, 1896 [postmark], Wells M. Sawyer Collection, University of Florida, https://ufdc.ufl.edu/AA00021036/00004/37x; Wells M. Sawyer to Kathleen Bailey, March 8, 1896 [postmark], Wells M. Sawyer Collection, University of Florida, https://ufdc.ufl.edu/AA00021036/00004/38x.

42. Wells M. Sawyer to Kathleen Bailey, March 17, 1896, Wells M. Sawyer Collection, University of Florida, https://ufdc.ufl.edu/AA00021036/00004/39x.

43. Wells M. Sawyer to Kathleen Bailey, April 12, 1896, Wells M. Sawyer Collection, University of Florida, https://ufdc.ufl.edu/AA00021036/00004/48x.

44. Cushing, "Ancient Key Dweller," 360, 429.

45. Wells M. Sawyer, "The Court of the Pile Dwellers" [ca. 1897], 8, Wells M. Sawyer Collection, University of Florida, https://ufdc.ufl.edu/AA00021036/00014/15j.

46. Cushing, "Ancient Key Dweller," 358.

47. Cushing, "Ancient Key Dweller," 349.

48. Cushing, "Ancient Key Dweller," 422.

49. Kolianos and Weisman, *Florida Journals*, 51; Frank Hamilton Cushing, cartographer, draft of *Plan and Section of the "Court of the Pile Dwellers," at Key Marco, Showing Locations of Excavations and Finds* (Cushing, "Ancient Key Dweller," plate XXXI), Brooklyn Museum Archives, Culin Archival collection: Cushing Collection [6.3.026]: A143.

50. Cushing, "Ancient Key Dweller,"429.

51. Kolianos and Weisman, *Lost Florida Manuscript*, 105.

52. Gilliland, *Buried Treasure*, 60; Kolianos and Weisman, *Florida Journals*, 28, 49.

53. Wells M. Sawyer to Kathleen Bailey, April 12, 1896, Wells M. Sawyer Collection, University of Florida, https://ufdc.ufl.edu/AA00021036/00004/48x.

54. Kolianos and Weisman, *Florida Journals*, 56.

55. Frank Hamilton Cushing to William Pepper, March 1, 1896, box 2, folder 2/3, Florida Explorations, Penn Museum; Gilliland, *Material Culture of Key Marco*, 4–5, 85 [Gilliland dates a different copy of the same letter March 18, 1896].

56. Kolianos and Weisman, *Florida Journals*, 50–57.

57. Cushing, "Ancient Key Dweller," 429; Kolianos and Weisman, *Florida Journals*, 58.

58. Wells M. Sawyer, "Florida Note Book," [March 5, 1896]: 59, Wells M. Sawyer Collection, University of Florida, https://ufdc.ufl.edu/AA00021036/00001/63x.

59. Frank Hamilton Cushing to William Pepper, March 7, 1896, box 2, folder 2/3, Florida Explorations, Penn Museum; Gilliland, *Buried Treasure*, 81.

60. Cushing, "Ancient Key Dweller," 387.

61. Cushing, "Ancient Key Dweller," 429.

62. Wells M. Sawyer, "The Court of the Pile Dwellers" [ca. 1897], 8, Wells M. Sawyer Collection, University of Florida, https://ufdc.ufl.edu/AA00021036/00014/15j.

63. Wells M. Sawyer, Pepper-Hearst Expedition: Notes on the "Shell Hammock" Keys, [ca. 1895–96], Wells M. Sawyer Collection, University of Florida, https://ufdc.ufl.edu/AA00021036/00010/11j; Gilliland, *Buried Treasure*, 71.

64. Wells M. Sawyer, Pepper-Hearst Expedition: Notes on Mound Builder and Expedition Discoveries, [ca. 1895–96], Wells M. Sawyer Collection, University of Florida, https://ufdc.ufl.edu/AA00021036/00009/11j; Gilliland, *Buried Treasure*, 73.

65. Cushing, "Ancient Key Dweller," 360.

66. Frank Hamilton Cushing to William Pepper, March 14, 1896, box 2, folder 2/3, Florida Explorations, Penn Museum; Gilliland, *Buried Treasure*, 83–84.

67. Frank Hamilton Cushing to William Pepper, March 22, 1896, box 2, folder 2/3, Florida Explorations, Penn Museum; Gilliland, *Buried Treasure*, 88.

68. Wells M. Sawyer, n.d., Pepper-Hearst Expedition: Wells Sawyer's Manuscript of Field Note Book Including Lists of Key Settlements and Findings: 125–26, Wells M. Sawyer Collection, University of Florida, https://ufdc.ufl.edu/AA00021036/00011/269j.

69. Collier, *Diary*, 9; Gilliland, *Buried Treasure*, 81.

70. Frank Hamilton Cushing to William Pepper, March 14, 1896, box 2, folder 2/3, Florida Explorations, Penn Museum; Gilliland, *Buried Treasure*, 91.

71. Gilliland, *Buried Treasure*, 91.

72. Wells M. Sawyer to Kathleen Bailey, March 30, 1896, Wells M. Sawyer Collection, University of Florida, https://ufdc.ufl.edu/AA00021036/00004/45x.

73. Frank Hamilton Cushing to William Pepper, April 10, 1896, box 2, folder 2/3, Florida Explorations, Penn Museum; Gilliland, *Buried Treasure*, 92.

74. Gilliland, *Buried Treasure*, 92; Kolianos and Weisman, *Florida Journals*, 60.

75. Collier, *Diary*, 27; Gilliland, *Buried Treasure*, 90–91.

76. Frank Hamilton Cushing to William Pepper, April 10, 1896, box 2, folder 2/3, Florida Explorations, Penn Museum.

77. Carl F. W. Bergmann to Stewart Culin, May 8, 1899, Pepper-Hearst Expedition: Correspondence (1893–1908), Wells M. Sawyer Collection, University of Florida, https://ufdc.ufl.edu/AA00021036/00003/114j; Gilliland, *Buried Treasure*, 106.

78. Gilliland, *Buried Treasure*, 107. Gilliland, likely mixing up last names, writes, "into Mrs. Cushing's parlor."

79. Collier, *Diary*, 30; Gilliland, *Buried Treasure*, 93.

80. George Gause, Pepper-Hearst Expedition: Field Note Book of George Gause, chief excavator [April 19, 1896], Wells M. Sawyer Collection, University of Florida, https://ufdc.ufl.edu/AA00021036/00013/60j.

81. Frank Hamilton Cushing to William Pepper, March 20, 1896, box 2, folder 2/3, Florida Explorations, Penn Museum; Gilliland, *Buried Treasure*, 93. Cushing's letter is dated March 20, but all evidence indicates that the correct date was April 20. Cushing forgot what month it was.

82. George Gause, Pepper-Hearst Expedition: Field Note Book of George Gause, chief excavator [April 27, 1896], Wells M. Sawyer Collection, University of Florida, https://ufdc.ufl.edu/AA00021036/00013/65j; Gilliland, *Buried Treasure*, 93.

83. Frank Hamilton Cushing to William Pepper, May 10, 1896, box 2, folder 2/5, Florida Explorations, Penn Museum; Gilliland, *Buried Treasure*, 94.

84. Frank Hamilton Cushing to William Pepper, May 10, 1896, box 2, folder 2/5, Florida Explorations, Penn Museum; "Through Bill of Lading," May 10, 1896, box 3, folder 3/1, Florida Explorations, Penn Museum.

85. "Dr. William Pepper, Pepper Medical Laboratory," box 2, folder 2/5, Florida Explorations, Penn Museum.

86. "(3) Catalogue of San Marco Specimens," box 3, Florida Explorations, Penn Museum.

87. Frank Hamilton Cushing to William Pepper, May 11, 1896, box 2, folder 2/5, Florida Explorations, Penn Museum.

88. "(3) Catalogue of San Marco Specimens," box 3, Florida Explorations, Penn Museum.

89. Frank Hamilton Cushing to William Pepper, May 10, 1896, box 2, folder 2/5, Florida Explorations, Penn Museum. Cushing wanted to take a Clyde steamship, but they were booked full until the end of the month.

90. Gilliland, *Buried Treasure*, 97.

91. Frank Hamilton Cushing to William Pepper, May 10, 1896, box 2, folder 2/5, Florida Explorations, Penn Museum.

92. Mercer, "West Florida," 692; Free Museum, "Collections and Publications," 16.

93. Gilliland, *Buried Treasure*, 97.

94. Frank Hamilton Cushing to William Pepper, May 13, 1896, box 2, folder 2/5, Florida Explorations, Penn Museum.

95. Frank Hamilton Cushing to William Pepper, May 17, 1896, box 2, folder 2/5, Florida Explorations, Penn Museum.

96. Frank Hamilton Cushing to William Pepper, December 1, 1897, box 2, folder 2/7, Florida Explorations, Penn Museum.

97. Frank Hamilton Cushing to Stewart Culin, August 2, 1896, box 2, folder 2/5, Florida Explorations, Penn Museum.

7. Finding a Forever Home

1. Cushing, "Ancient Key Dweller," 429; Michelle Austin Dennehy, April 12, 2018, Condition Report, Outgoing Loan File, Marco Island Historical Museum, Accession No. 48531, NMNH.

2. "Amid Pots and Skulls: Labors of Washington Scientists in Florida," *Washington Post*, February 3, 1896, 3; "Staff," Department of Anthropology, National Museum of Natural History, accessed February 20, 2020, https://naturalhistory.si.edu/research/anthropology/staff; "Collections Overview," Department of Anthropology, National Museum of Natural History, accessed April 14, 2020, https://naturalhistory.si.edu/research/anthropology/collections-overview.

3. Cushing memorably scolded Margaret Collier, wife of landowner William D. Collier, for smudging the ink on a painted human figure while handling it (see Gilliland, *Buried Treasure*, 106).

4. Gilliland, *Buried Treasure*, 96–114.

5. Cushing, "Mound Builder's Village," 7–10; Cushing, "Ancient Key Dweller," 329–448; "Sea Dwellers and Key Builders of Florida," *Washington Post*, February 25, 1897, 12; "Prehistoric Sea Dwellers: Interesting Lecture by Frank Hamilton Cushing at Congregational Church," *Washington Post*, February 27, 1897, 8; Gilliland, *Material Culture of Key Marco*, 5; Gilliland, *Buried Treasure*, 97.

6. Gilliland, *Buried Treasure*, 109.

7. Frank Hamilton Cushing to William Pepper, December 1, 1897, box 2, folder 2/7, Florida Explorations, Penn Museum; Gilliland, *Buried Treasure*, 109–10.

8. William Pepper to Stewart Culin, February 1898, box 2, folder 2/8, Florida Explorations, Penn Museum.

9. Frank Hamilton Cushing, receipt, February 14, 1898, box 2, folder 2/8, Florida Explorations, Penn Museum.

10. "(2) Catalogue of San Marco Specimens," page 188, box 3, Florida Explorations, Penn Museum.

11. The series were then incorporated into the museums' existing catalog systems, receiving numbers 40126 thru 41172 at the Penn Museum and 240126 thru 241172 at the NMNH. The Cat's museum catalog number became 40915 while in care of the Penn Museum and changed to 240915 when formally transferred to the NMNH years later.

12. Gilliland, *Material Culture of Key Marco*, vi; Carl F. W. Bergmann to Stewart Culin, September 27, 1900, Accession No. 48531, SIA.

13. Cushing to Culin, February 25, 1898, box 2, folder 2/8, Florida Explorations, Penn Museum.

14. Quoted in Gilliland, *Buried Treasure*, 110.

15. Board of Managers Minutes, January 27, 1899, 11, *University of Pennsylvania Museum Board of Managers Minutes (November 1898–May 1902)*, transcription produced July 2013–September 2014, University of Pennsylvania, Penn Museum Archives; "Memorials to Dr. William Pepper: A Statue and a Great Museum," *North American*, December 20, 1899, 5; Gilliland, *Buried Treasure*, 111, 115.

16. Brandes, "Frank Hamilton Cushing," 204.

17. "Famous Ethnologist Dead: Frank H. Cushing's Many Scientific Expeditions and Works," *Washington Post*, April 11, 1900, 11.

18. Gilliland, *Buried Treasure*, 25; Hinsley and Wilcox, *Coming of Age*, 132.

19. U.S. Census Bureau, "Tenth Census of the United States, Schedule No. 1—Population," District of Columbia, Washington, Enumeration District 48, Supervisor's District 17, page 21, 1880, accessed April 15, 2020, Ancestry.com.

20. U.S. Census Bureau, "Twelfth Census of the United States, Schedule No. 1—Population," Pennsylvania, Philadelphia, Enumeration District 1011, page 17, 1900, accessed April 15, 2020, Ancestry.com.

21. Cushing, "Ancient Key Dweller," 352.

22. Frank Hamilton Cushing to William Pepper, November 22, 1895, box 2, folder 2/2, Florida Explorations, Penn Museum.

23. Hinsley and Wilcox, *Coming of Age*, 155, 299.

24. Elise LeCompte and Donna Ruhl, personal communication with the author, 2007–13.

25. Powell, "Report of the Director," 37.

26. Carl F. W. Bergmann to Stewart Culin, June 7, 1901, box 2, folder 2/10, Florida Explorations, Penn Museum.

27. Frank Hamilton Cushing to Stewart Culin, August 2, 1896, box 2, folder 2/5, Florida Explorations, Penn Museum; Frank Hamilton Cushing to William Pepper, December 1, 1897, box 2, folder 2/7, Florida Explorations, Penn Museum.

28. Gilliland, *Buried Treasure*, 99–109; Kolianos and Weisman, *Florida Journals*, 10.

29. Cushing, "Ancient Key Dweller," 359.

30. Frank Hamilton Cushing to William Pepper, March 14, 1896, box 2, folder 2/3, Florida Explorations, Penn Museum; Gilliland, *Buried Treasure*, 91.

31. Wells M. Sawyer, Pepper-Hearst Expedition: Wells Sawyer's Manuscript of Field Note Book Including Lists of Key Settlements and Findings, n.d., 125–26, Wells M. Sawyer Collection, University of Florida, https://ufdc.ufl.edu/AA00021036/00011/269j; Gilliland, *Material Culture of Key Marco*, 20. Cushing frequently refers to his wife as *Emalie*, apparently an affectionate nickname, or *Tennison*, her middle name. For more, see Kolianos and Weisman, *Florida Journals*, 126 n4, 126 n9, or Hinsley and Wilcox, *Coming of Age*, 198–99 n1.

32. Frank Hamilton Cushing to Stewart Culin, July 29, 1896, box 2, folder 2/5, Florida Ex-

plorations, Penn Museum. Cushing retreated to Haven, Maine, for three months after returning from Florida to focus on work and better his ailing health.

33. Frank Hamilton Cushing to Stewart Culin, August 2, 1896, box 2, folder 2/5, Florida Explorations, Penn Museum.

34. Frank Hamilton Cushing to William Pepper, June 29, 1896, box 2, folder 2/5, Florida Explorations, Penn Museum; Frank Hamilton Cushing to William Pepper, July 23, 1896, box 2, folder 2/5, Florida Explorations, Penn Museum; Brandes, "Frank Hamilton Cushing," 184–85.

35. Quoted in Kolianos, "Wood Preservation Dilemmas," 70.

36. Quoted in Gilliland, *Buried Treasure*, 103.

37. Frank Hamilton Cushing to Stewart Culin, December 18, 1896, box 2, folder 2/5, Florida Explorations, Penn Museum.

38. Frank Hamilton Cushing to Stewart Culin, August 7, 1897, box 2, folder 2/7, Florida Explorations, Penn Museum.

39. Frank Hamilton Cushing to Stewart Culin, December 1, 1897, box 2, folder 2/7, Florida Explorations, Penn Museum; Gilliland, *Buried Treasure* 109.

40. Frank Hamilton Cushing to Stewart Culin, February 25, 1898, box 2, folder 2/8, Florida Explorations, Penn Museum.

41. Michelle Austin Dennehy, April 12, 2018, Condition Report, Outgoing Loan File, Marco Island Historical Museum, on file with Accession No. 48531, NMNH.

42. Natalie Firnhaber to Cameran Castiel, July 15, 1991, Outgoing Loan File, National Gallery of Art, on file with Accession No. 48531, NMNH.

43. Gilliland, *Buried Treasure*, 43, 101–2, 108.

44. Kolianos and Weisman, *Florida Journals*, 10; Hinsley and Wilcox, *Coming of Age*, 144.

45. Kolianos and Weisman, *Florida Journals*, 12.

46. Gilliland, *Material Culture of Key Marco*, 27.

47. Quoted in Gilliland, *Material Culture of Key Marco*, 27.

48. Gilliland, *Material Culture of Key Marco*, 3–22; Gilliland, *Buried Treasure*, 55–59, 126.

49. Cushing, "Ancient Key Dweller," 415.

50. Carl Bergmann to Stewart Culin, September 23, 1897, box 2, folder 2/7, Florida Explorations, Penn Museum.

51. Frank Hamilton Cushing to Stewart Culin, August 7, 1897, box 2, folder 2/7, Florida Explorations, Penn Museum.

52. Frank Hamilton Cushing to Stewart Culin, August 22, 1899, box 2, folder 2/9, Florida Explorations, Penn Museum; Gilliland, *Material Culture of Key Marco*, 22.

53. Gilliland, *Material Culture of Key Marco*, 22; Gilliland, "Marco's Buried Treasure," 260.

54. Purdy, *Florida's Wetlands*, 41.

55. MIHS catalog no. 2015–62–1. Gift of Alan Sandlin and Craig Woodward.

56. Cushing, *Genealogy of the Cushing Family*, 504.

57. Measured by the author with permission at the Museum Support Center in Suitland, Maryland, on July 23, 2018, using handheld calipers. These dimensions are approximated because I was not permitted to touch the calipers to the real Cat's surface.

58. NMNH catalog no. A240915A-0.

59. Performed by the author with permission at the Museum Support Center in Suitland, Maryland, on July 23, 2018.

60. Dimmick and Hassler, *American Sculpture*, 520.

61. Traditional Fine Arts Organization, *Resource Library*, Philadelphia Museum of Art, "Thomas Eakins: American Realist," revised June 3, 2011, http://www.tfaoi.com/aa/3aa/3aa94.htm.

62. Eakins and Zilczer, "Eakins Letter," 74.

63. Gilcrease Museum, *Frank Hamilton Cushing*, artist Thomas Eakins, Accession No. 0126.2315, https://collections.gilcrease.org/object/01262315.

64. Philadelphia Museum of Art, *Portrait of Mrs. Frank Hamilton Cushing*, artist Thomas Eakins, Accession No. 1929-184-4, https://philamuseum.org/collection/object/42521; Truettner, "Dressing the Part," 54–55.

65. Gilliland, *Buried Treasure*, 98, 115.

66. Stewart Culin to H. H. Bingham, January 25, 1901, Accession No. 48531, SIA; "The Inflation Calculator," accessed April 16, 2020, https://westegg.com/inflation/.

67. William Henry Holmes to W. J. McGee, August 7, 1900, box 2, folder 2/10, Florida Explorations, Penn Museum; Gilliland, *Buried Treasure*, 116–17. Cushing's claims were supported only by his correspondence with Pepper, which may not have been available to other parties involved, particularly after Pepper's premature death in 1898.

68. Woodbury and Woodbury, "Rise and Fall," 283–96; Culin was the museum's first director from 1892 until 1899, when the position was abolished. He remained a curator at the museum until 1903.

69. John Wesley Powell died the following year on September 23, 1902.

70. Woodbury and Woodbury, "Rise and Fall," 289; Langley was the third secretary of the Smithsonian Institution, from 1887 to 1906.

71. Stevenson was a major figure in the history of the Penn Museum as a curator, board member, and its first female director from 1904 to 1905.

72. Gilliland, *Buried Treasure*, 116.

73. Gilliland, *Buried Treasure*, 117.

74. Bergmann to Culin, September 27, 1900, Accession No. 48531, SIA.

75. Gilliland, *Buried Treasure*, 117–20.

76. S.P. Langley to Robert C.H. Brock, April 5, 1901, Accession No. 48531, SIA.

77. John Wesley Powell to S.P. Langley, April 8, 1901, Accession No. 48531, SIA.

78. S.P. Langley to Robert C.H. Brock, April 11, 1901, Accession No. 48531, SIA.

79. Robert C.H. Brock to S.P. Langley, received April 13, 1901, Accession No. 48531, SIA.

80. S.P. Langley to Robert C.H. Brock, April 5, 1901, Accession No. 48531, SIA.

81. S.P. Langley to Robert C.H. Brock, April 15, 1901, Accession No. 48531, SIA.

82. Robert C.H. Brock to S.P. Langley, received April 17, 1901, Accession No. 48531, SIA.

83. William Henry Holmes to Charles D. Walcott, March 30, 1908, Accession No. 48531, SIA.

84. O. T. Mason, "Memorandum to Registrar," April 1, 1908, Accession No. 48531, SIA. Otis Tufton Mason died only seven months later, on November 5, 1908.

85. H. W. Dorsey to William Henry Holmes, March 17, 1913, Accession No. 48531, SIA.

86. The Cat is housed near staff in a highly secure and environmentally stable environment at the Museum Support Center in Suitland, Maryland. Ironically, this is largely due to the Smithsonian's efforts to fulfill frequent public requests to see the object, a full reversal of the "lock and key" mentality that left it forgotten in a safe more than a century earlier.

87. "Key Marco (Cushing) Collection: Proposed Discards, 1956," box 4, folder 4/17, Florida Explorations, Penn Museum.

88. "History of the Collections," National Museum of the American Indian, accessed May 23, 2020, https://americanindian.si.edu/explore/collections/history.

89. Gilliland, *Material Culture of Key Marco*, 5.

90. Jerald T. Milanich, foreword to *The Calusa and Their Legacy* (Gainesville: University Press of Florida, 2004), xi.

8. Window to the World

1. Thompson and Parezo, "Material Culture," 33, 36; Alexander and Alexander, *Museums in Motion*, 1–19, 74–75.

2. Walcott, "Report" (1918), 11–12; Woodbury and Woodbury, "Rise and Fall," 284–85; Sturtevant, "Anthropological Data Banks," 40–55.

3. Brandes, "Frank Hamilton Cushing," 207–8; Hinsley and Wilcox, "Introduction," 131.

4. Notable later figures who variously became involved in Key Marco research include Frances Densmore, John M. Goggin, J. Alden Mason, Matthew Stirling, William Sturtevant, Harriett Newell Wardle, and Waldo Wedel. More contemporary figures, generally cited throughout this book, include William H. Marquardt, Jerald T. Milanich, Barbara A. Purdy, and Randolph J. Widmer.

5. American Association of Museums, *Excellence and Equity*; Weil, "From Being," 229–58; Stogner, "Media-Enhanced Museum," 385–97.

6. Thompson and Parezo, "Material Culture," 51.

7. Burcaw, *Museum Work*, 102.

8. Cushing, "Ancient Key Dweller," 329–448.

9. Free Museum, "Collections and Publications," 16.

10. Cushing, "Ancient Key Dweller," plate XXXV. The Cat's likeness soon after appeared in an August 22, 1897, article in the *Times* titled "The Origin of the Mound Builders Solved at Last."

11. Fidele Clark, in the absence of Frank Hamilton Cushing, [November 1896], box 2, folder 2/5, Florida Explorations, Penn Museum.

12. Cushing, "Ancient Key Dweller," 438, 445.

13. Cushing, "Ancient Key Dweller," 447.

14. "Sea Dwellers and Key Builders of Florida," *Washington Post*, February 25, 1897, 12.

15. "Prehistoric Sea Dwellers: Interesting Lecture by Frank Hamilton Cushing at Congregational Church," *Washington Post*, February 27, 1897, 8.

16. Cushing, "Ancient Key Dweller," 415.

17. Frank Hamilton Cushing to Stewart Culin, February 25, 1898, box 2, folder 2/8, Florida Explorations, Penn Museum.

18. John Wesley Powell to [Sara Yorke] Stevenson, February 3, 1899, box 2, folder 2/9, Florida Explorations, Penn Museum.

19. Culin, "Archaeological Objects," 200; "Columbian Historical Exposition in Madrid, Spain," Smithsonian Institution Archives, accessed April 20, 2020, https://siarchives.si.edu/collections/siris_sic_12971.

20. Pezzati, "Gold Medals," 19-21; Hinsley and Wilcox, "Introduction," xv; Wilcox, "Analysis," 111–13; Wilcox, "Frank Hamilton Cushing," 153–231.

21. Wilcox, "Frank Hamilton Cushing," 132–36, 149, n13, 155, 224, 231, n9.

22. Jacknis, "Refracting Images," 299, 332, n35.

23. Free Museum, "Exhibit at the Paris Exposition," 169.

24. Free Museum, "Exhibit at the Paris Exposition," 170–71.

25. "A Brief History of NMNH," About the Museum, National Museum of Natural History, Smithsonian Institution, accessed April 20, 2020, https://naturalhistory.si.edu/about/brief-history-nmnh.

26. Walcott, "Report" (1911), 17; Walcott, "Report" (1912), 128.

27. H. W. Dorsey to William Henry Holmes, March 17, 1913, Accession No. 48531, SIA.

28. Rathbun, "Report" (1913), 37, appendix 1.

29. *Hall 21, 22, and 23, Exhibit Photos: Before Renovation*, Registrar's Office, NMNH. Today, the former location of Hall 22 is half "dining area" and half "research wing," accessible only to staff. In 1956, the Key Marco Cat sat in the footprint of the dining area, adjacent to what is now a special exhibition hall that ends at the same "north stairway" described in the 1956 photograph.

30. "Anthropology Hall, National Museum of Natural History," History of the Smithsonian Catalog, Smithsonian Institution Research Information System (SIRIS), accessed December 15, 2020, https://siris-sihistory.si.edu/ipac20/ipac.jsp?&profile=all&source=~!sichronology&uri=full=3100001~!10004~!0#focus.

31. Fundaburk and Foreman, *Sun Circles*, 107.

32. Kellogg, "Report" (1957), 34; Kellogg, "Report" (1959), 45; Kellogg, "Report" (1960), 40–41; Carmichael, "Report" (1953), 4; James Krakker, e-mail message to David Rosenthal, forwarded to author, July 23, 2018.

33. "Hall 22—Case 25," *Hall 21 and Hall 22 Exhibit Photos*, Registrar's Office, NMNH.

34. *Hall 21 and Hall 22 Exhibit Photos*, Registrar's Office, NMNH.

35. Michael Kan to Douglas Ubelaker, February 15, 1983, Outgoing Loan File, Detroit Institute of Arts, on file with Accession No. 48531, NMNH.

36. David W. Penney to Bruce Smith, March 20, 1984, Outgoing Loan File, Detroit Institute of Arts, on file with Accession No. 48531, NMNH.

37. B[ruce Smith] to P., [March 1984], Outgoing Loan File, Detroit Institute of Arts, on file with Accession No. 48531, NMNH.

38. "Visitor Stats," Newsroom of the Smithsonian, Smithsonian Institution, accessed April 20, 2020, https://www.si.edu/newsdesk/about/stats.

39. David W. Penney to Bruce Smith, March 20, 1984, Outgoing Loan File, Detroit Institute of Arts, on file with Accession No. 48531, NMNH.

40. Richard S. Fiske to Bruce Smith, March 26, 1984, Outgoing Loan File, Detroit Institute of Arts, on file with Accession No. 48531, NMNH.

41. Brose, Brown, and Penney, *Ancient Art*, 12; "Ancient Art of the American Woodland Indians," National Gallery of Art, accessed April 21, 2020, https://www.nga.gov/exhibitions/1985/woodland.html.

42. Brose, Brown, and Penney, *Ancient Art*, 79–80, 96–97, 103, 106, 207, plates 71, 208.

43. Brose, Brown, and Penney, *Ancient Art*, 127, 129.

44. Loan Agreement, "Masterworks from the Ancient American Woodlands," completed October 24, 1984, Outgoing Loan File, Detroit Institute of Arts, on file with Accession No. 48531, NMNH.

45. Bruce [Smith], handwritten memorandum, [1984], Outgoing Loan File, Detroit Institute of Arts, on file with Accession No. 48531, NMNH; Jim Rubenstein to Bruce Smith,

Candace Greene, and Adrianne Kaeppler, July 31, 1985, Outgoing Loan File, Detroit Institute of Arts, on file with Accession No. 48531, NMNH.

46. Loan Agreement, "Masterworks from the Ancient American Woodlands," completed October 24, 1984, Outgoing Loan File, Detroit Institute of Arts, on file with Accession No. 48531, NMNH.

47. "Articles Received from the Museum of Fine Arts, 1001 Bissonnet, P.O. Box 6826, Houston, Texas 77005," March 14, 1986, Outgoing Loan File, Detroit Institute of Arts, on file with Accession No. 48531, NMNH; Adrienne L. Kaeppler to Terry L. Segal, April 16, 1986, Outgoing Loan File, Detroit Institute of Arts, on file with Accession No. 48531, NMNH.

48. The Museum Support Center opened in May 1983 after two years of construction and a decade of planning; "Museum Support Center," Media Fact Sheet, August 1, 2018, https://www.si.edu/newsdesk/factsheets/museum-support-center.

49. "Museum Receipt: Outgoing Objects," Detroit Institute of Arts, completed March 25, 1986, Outgoing Loan File, Detroit Institute of Arts, on file with Accession No. 48531, NMNH.

50. Simpson, *Making Representations*, 40–41.

51. "Circa 1492: Art in the Age of Exploration," National Gallery of Art, accessed April 21, 2020, https://www.nga.gov/exhibitions/1991/exploration.html.

52. J. Carter Brown to Frank Talbot, November 1, 1990, Outgoing Loan File, National Gallery of Art, on file with Accession No. 48531, NMNH.

53. J. Carter Brown to Frank Talbot, November 1, 1990, Outgoing Loan File, National Gallery of Art, on file with Accession No. 48531, NMNH.

54. Melinda Zeder to J. Carter Brown, November 28, 1990, Outgoing Loan File, National Gallery of Art, on file with Accession No. 48531, NMNH.

55. Levenson, *Circa 1492*, 9–10; Chuck Twardy, "Brown: Capital Connoisseur," *Orlando Sentinel*, August 4, 1991; "Visits by Foreign Leaders of Spain," Office of the Historian, U.S. Department of State, accessed April 20, 2020, https://history.state.gov/departmenthistory/visits/spain.

56. Levenson, *Circa 1492*, 582–83.

57. "Circa 1492: Art in the Age of Exploration," National Gallery of Art, accessed April 21, 2020, https://www.nga.gov/exhibitions/1991/exploration.html.

58. Kay Larson, "World Views," *New York Magazine*, November 11, 1991, 116–17.

59. Martha Sherill, "The Navigator to '1492,'" *Washington Post*, October 10, 1991.

60. Michael Kimmelman, "'Circa 1492': An Enormous, Magnificent Muddle," *New York Times*, October 21, 1991, https://www.nytimes.com/1991/10/20/arts/art-view-circa-1492-an-enormous-magnificent-muddle.html.

61. Collier County was formed out of Lee County in 1923. The Key Marco objects, when discovered in 1896, were from Lee County, the northern boundary of which now lies north of Naples and Marco island.

62. Lee, "Cat Figurine Star," 309–10.

63. Jennifer Perry, e-mail message to author, March 7, 2017; "From the Archives: Key Marco Cat Draws Thousands, Rain or Shine," *Naples Daily News*, October 8, 2015, originally published on January 8, 1996, http://archive.naplesnews.com/special/from-the-archives/from-the-archives-key-marco-cat-draws-thousands-rain-or-shine-ep-1310279078-340383581.html.

64. Outgoing Loan File, Citizens Community Bank, on file with Accession No. 48531, NMNH; Paula D. Tateo to Susan Crawford, September 23, 1999, Outgoing Loan File, Citizens Community Bank, on file with Accession No. 48531, NMNH; Elizabeth Perdichizzi to Susan

Crawford, November 14, 1999, Outgoing Loan File, Citizens Community Bank, on file with Accession No. 48531, NMNH.

65. John M. Lee to Susan Crawford, September 1, 1998, Outgoing Loan File, Citizens Community Bank, on file with Accession No. 48531, NMNH; the City of Marco Island was incorporated on August 28, 1997; see Bell, "Marco Island" (2018), 92.

66. Elizabeth Perdichizzi to Susan Crawford, August 26, 1998, Outgoing Loan File, Citizens Community Bank, on file with Accession No. 48531, NMNH.

67. "Hero, Hawk, and Open Hand: American Indian Art of the Ancient Midwest and South," Art Institute of Chicago, accessed March 28, 2019, https://archive.artic.edu/herohawk/overview.html; "Outgoing Lease Agreement," June 9, 2005, Art Institute of Chicago, Outgoing Loan File, Art Institute of Chicago, on file with Accession No. 48531, NMNH; "Agreement for Outgoing Loans Requiring Insurance," June 25, 2004, National Museum of Natural History, Outgoing Loan File, Art Institute of Chicago, on file with Accession No. 48531, NMNH; Richard F. Townsend to Bruce Smith, February 4, 2000, Outgoing Loan File, Art Institute of Chicago, on file with Accession No. 48531, NMNH.

68. Townsend, "American Landscapes," 19; Cuno, "Foreword," 7.

69. Cuno, "Foreword," 6; "Hero, Hawk, and Open Hand," Art Institute of Chicago, accessed April 21, 2020, https://www.artic.edu/exhibitions/2840/hero-hawk-and-open-hand; Townsend, "American Landscapes," 16.

70. Townsend, "American Landscapes," 20–22, 26–28.

71. Townsend, "American Landscapes," 28, 30.

72. Richard F. Townsend to Bruce Smith, March 25, 2002, Outgoing Loan File, Art Institute of Chicago, on file with Accession No. 48531, NMNH; Darrell Green to Amy Putnam, July 8, 2004, Outgoing Loan File, Art Institute of Chicago, on file with Accession No. 48531, NMNH; Certificate of Insurance, October 12, 2004, Outgoing Loan File, Art Institute of Chicago, on file with Accession No. 48531, NMNH.

73. Dan L. Monroe to J. Dennis O'Connor, September 9, 2010, Outgoing Loan File, Peabody Essex Museum, on file with Accession No. 48531, NMNH.

74. Dan L. Monroe to J. Dennis O'Connor, September 9, 2010, Outgoing Loan File, Peabody Essex Museum, on file with Accession No. 48531, NMNH.

75. Russell et al., *Shapeshifting*, 113.

76. Russell et al., *Shapeshifting*, 113.

77. Silver Award (Exhibition Budget Over $100K), 2017 Exhibition Competition, Southeastern Museums Conference, New Orleans, LA; Bronze Award (Gallery Installation), 2017 Technology Competition, Southeastern Museums Conference, New Orleans, LA.

9. National Treasure

1. Collier, *Diary*, 13; Gilliland, *Buried Treasure*, 96–114.

2. Falk, *Identity*, 56–58.

3. Purdy, *Florida's Wetlands*, 1.

4. Greenblatt, "Resonance and Wonder," 54; Baxandall, "Exhibiting Intention," 33–41; Falk, *Identity*, 25.

5. Bill McAllister, "Stamps and Coins: Stamping Out Competition," *Washington Post*, September 8, 1989, 58; Dominic Sama, "U.S. Joins in Celebration with New Columbus Issue," *Chicago Tribune*, October 15, 1989, M11.

6. The author has personally observed Key Marco artifact displays at the following institutions in Florida: Collier County Museum (Naples, FL), Crane Point Museum and Nature Center (Marathon, FL), Florida Museum of Natural History (Gainesville, FL), Museum of Florida History (Tallahassee, FL), Museum of the Everglades (Everglades City, FL), Museum of the Islands (Pine Island, FL), Sanibel Historic Museum and Village (Sanibel Island, FL). There are probably many more examples not named here.

7. Rebecca O'Sullivan, e-mail message to author, December 10, 2018.

8. Davis, *Gulf*, 39.

9. Evelyn M. Sivier, "Marco Island Guide: Rotary Club's 1982 Edition," 9, Naples Printing Company. On file at the MIHS, Pub1982–11; Diane Daniel, "Marco Island Welcomes Some Famous (and Very Old) Visitors," *Boston Globe*, February 3, 2019, M2.

10. The sign is presently located on the eastern side of Bald Eagle Drive, just south of its intersection with Old Marco Lane, visible to northbound travelers on Bald Eagle Drive.

11. The sign is presently located on the northeast corner of Collier Boulevard and Bald Eagle Drive, visible to westbound travelers on Collier Boulevard.

12. Quesnell, "Relocating Cushing's Key Marco," 6–7.

13. Susan Crawford to Betsy Perdichizzi, October 7, 1999, Outgoing Loan File, Citizens Community Bank, on file with Accession No. 48531, NMNH; Sturtevant Papers, Box 395, "Reproductions of Key Marco Cat," 1993, NAA; Torben Rick, e-mail message to author, July 6, 2020.

14. "Present Day Marco Island," City of Marco Island, accessed August 13, 2020, https://www.cityofmarcoisland.com/community/page/present-day-marco-island.

15. Jennifer Perry, e-mail message to author, June 6, 2017.

16. "Government Doubles Official Estimate: There Are 35,000 Active Museums in the U.S.," Institute of Museum and Library Services, accessed August 13, 2020, https://www.imls.gov/news/government-doubles-official-estimate-there-are-35000-active-museums-us; Christopher Ingram, "There Are More Museums in the U.S. Than There Are Starbucks and McDonalds—Combined," *Washington Post*, June 13, 2014, https://www.washingtonpost.com/news/wonk/wp/2014/06/13/there-are-more-museums-in-the-us-than-there-are-starbucks-and-mcdonalds-combined/.

17. "Distribution of Museums by Discipline, FY 2014," Institute of Museum and Library Services, accessed August 13, 2020, https://www.imls.gov/assets/1/AssetManager/MUDF_TypeDist_2014q3.pdf.

18. Cushing, "Ancient Key Dweller," 358.

19. A copy of the memorandum of understanding between Collier County Museums and the Marco Island Historical Society is on file with the MIHS at the Marco Island Historical Museum, Marco Island, Florida.

20. "Off . . . Assets: Florida's Islands Are a . . . ," *New York Times*, November 20, 2011, SMA113.

21. Heather Otis, "Cat Statue Restoration," *Pioneering History: The Marco Island Historical Society Newsletter* 27, no. 3 (2020): 12, https://themihs.info/newsletter/.

22. 2015 Museum Excellence Award, Florida Association of Museums Conference, St. Petersburg, FL.

23. Lee, "Key Marco Revisited," 3.

24. Austin J. Bell to Mary Jo Arnoldi, e-mail message, April 21, 2014. The Collier County Board of County Commissioners, at their June 27, 2017, regular meeting, passed a recommendation on the Consent Agenda (Item 16.D.16) to approve loan agreements with the

Smithsonian Institution and the University of Pennsylvania, as well as a memorandum of understanding between Collier County Museums and the MIHS. The meeting's agenda and an executive summary of the project are on file with the Clerk of the County Circuit Court and Comptroller, Collier County, Florida, https://www.collierclerk.com/records-search/bmr-records-search.

25. Harriett H. Heithaus, "The Year of the Cat: Key Marco Cat Returns, This Time to a Home Built for It," *Naples Daily News*, April 21, 2018, https://www.naplesnews.com/story/entertainment/arts/2018/04/21/year-cat-key-marco-cat-returns-time-home-built/523476002/.

26. "Relative Humidity," Florida Climate Center, accessed April 21, 2020, https://climatecenter.fsu.edu/products-services/data/other-normals/relative-humidity; values cited from Fort Myers in September.

27. Emily Garcia, e-mail message to author, January 16, 2020.

28. Brotemarkle, "Cat Came Back," 12–19; Ryan P. Smith, "This Hand-Carved Panther Statuette Embodies a Lost Civilization's Harmony with Nature," *Smithsonian*, January 7, 2019, https://www.smithsonianmag.com/smithsonian-institution/hand-carved-panther-statuette-embodies-lost-civilizations-harmony-nature-180969711/; "Florida Frontiers TV—The Indigenous People of Florida," Florida Historical Society, episode 32, https://myfloridahistory.org/frontiers/television/episode/32.

29. Examples include a presentation by the author, titled "Homeward Bound: The Incredible Journey of Key Marco's Artifacts," to the Southwest Florida Archaeological Society speaker series at the Collier County Museum on November 20, 2019, and an online public presentation by the Florida Public Archaeology Network, titled "Cats Before the Internet: Animal Art in Archaeology," during the coronavirus pandemic on April 23, 2020.

30. 2019 Museum Excellence Award, Florida Association of Museums Conference, Orlando, FL; Honorable Mention (Exhibition Budget Over $100K), 2019 Exhibition Competition, Southeastern Museums Conference, Charlotte, NC.

31. Emily Garcia, e-mail message to author, April 3, 2020.

32. Barker, "Exhibiting the Canon," 127–46.

33. Waitley, *Last Paradise*, 37–79; Bell, *Marco Island* (2018), 9–24; Hrdlička, *Anthropology of Florida*, 14–15, 21; Moore, "Certain Antiquities," 369; Griffin, *Archaeology of the Everglades*, 56–57; Quesnell, "Relocating Cushing's Key Marco," 4; Tebeau, *Florida's Last Frontier*, 29, 140, 144, 146–49, 157–60.

34. Thompson and Worth, "Dwellers by the Sea," 70.

35. I use the term *suggest* rather than *require* here because while Collier County is a certified local government, the City of Marco Island incorporated in 1997 and therefore is not subject to the same ordinances. However, development projects on Marco Island have generally been treated similarly to those in greater Collier County, with archaeological surveys (some large scale) conducted when recommended. The Collier County Historic Archaeological Preservation Board is presently working toward forming an interlocal agreement between Collier County and the City of Marco Island to address potential gaps in the system and to better facilitate the preservation of Marco Island's cultural resources.

36. Gilliland, *Material Culture of Key Marco*, 6, 27; Purdy, *Florida's Wetlands*, 49; Lee, "Key Marco Revisited," 3; Quesnell, "Relocating Cushing's Key Marco," 4–9; Widmer, "Recent Excavations," 10–25.

37. Austin J. Bell, Katie Romey, Rosemarie Fusco, Morgan Andrews, Kristin Conwill, Mara Reynolds, and Casey Wooster, "Rehabilitation of the Marco Island Historical Society's

Archaeological Collections: A National Endowment for the Humanities Project to Curate Recent Collections from Now-Legendary Sites in Southwest Florida" (poster presentation, Florida Anthropological Society Conference, Crystal River, FL, May 11, 2019); Austin J. Bell and Kaitlin Romey, "Too Small to Fail: A National Endowment for the Humanities Project to Curate Archaeological Collections at a Small Southwest Florida Museum" (poster presentation, American Association for State and Local History Conference, Philadelphia, PA, August 30, 2019).

38. "Grant number PG-252747-17," National Endowment for the Humanities, accessed April 21, 2020, https://securegrants.neh.gov/publicquery/main.aspx?f=1&gn=PG-252747-17.

39. Sturtevant, "Anthropological Data Banks," 40–55.

40. MIHS catalog no. 2015-50-1.

41. Ostapkowicz et al., "Pre-Columbian Wood Sculpture," 597–99, 603–5; Ostapkowicz et al., "Black Pitch," 341–58.

42. Kolianos, "Wood Preservation Dilemmas," 69–70.

43. "The Key Marco Cat and the Smithsonian's Cushing Collections: A Digitization Collaboration," University of South Florida Libraries, https://dhhc.lib.usf.edu/project/the-key-marco-cat-and-the-smithsonians-cushing-collections-a-digitization-collaboration/.

44. Stahle and Wolfman, "Tree-Ring Dating," 282–84; Garland et al., "Dendrochronological Dating," 69–78.

45. Garland et al., "Dendrochronological Dating," 71; Stahle and Wolfman, "Tree-Ring Dating," 287.

46. Cushing, "Ancient Key Dweller," 448; Tykot, "Portable X-ray Fluorescence," 46–47.

47. Hale, "Postdepositional Corrosions," 194–220; Tykot, "Portable X-ray Fluorescence," 42–56.

48. Gilliland, *Material Culture of Key Marco*, 224.

49. Hutchinson et al., "Calusa and Prehistoric Subsistence," 64–65; Tykot, "Portable X-ray Fluorescence," 52–53.

50. Torben Rick, e-mail message to author, July 6, 2020.

51. Nash and Colwell, "NAGPRA at 30," 225–39.

52. Sandra Hale Schulman, "Big Win in #NoMoreStolenAncestors Fight," *Indian Country Today*, December 7, 2020, https://indiancountrytoday.com/news/big-win-in-nomorestolenancestors-fight-MQIFoKLGlE-B8gh6h7kASg?fbclid=IwAR1eCedqImcfo5eukcJ5KzRnLRuNpPa9M85lCLJ66X9dUYKVMHKyMk8aoD4.

53. Cushing, "Ancient Key Dweller," 387, 429; Richard S. Fiske to Bruce Smith, March 26, 1984, Outgoing Loan File, Detroit Institute of Arts, on file with Accession No. 48531, NMNH; Gilliland, *Material Culture of Key Marco*, 116; Milanich, *Precolumbian Florida*, 308; Milanich, *Ancient Times*, 126; Marquardt, "Padgett Figurine," 161.

54. Bell, "Cat's Meow."

Bibliography

Archival Collections

Accession No. 48531. Registrar's Office, Department of Anthropology, National Museum of Natural History (NMNH), Smithsonian Institution.

Accession No. 48531. Registrar's Office, Smithsonian Institution Archives (SIA), Washington, D.C.

Manuscript 1848, National Anthropological Archives, Smithsonian Institution.

North America: Florida Explorations, 1894–1903, University of Pennsylvania, Penn Museum Archives.

Sawyer, Wells M. Collection (1893–1908). P. K. Yonge Library of Florida History, Special and Area Studies Collection, George A. Smathers Libraries, University of Florida.

Sturtevant, William C. Papers. Series 5, Smithsonian Accessions, Box 395, National Anthropological Archives (NAA), Smithsonian Institution.

University of Pennsylvania Museum Board of Managers Minutes (November 1898–May 1902). Transcription produced July 2013–September 2014. University of Pennsylvania, Penn Museum Archives.

Publications

Alexander, Edward P., and Mary Alexander. *Museums in Motion: An Introduction to the History and Functions of Museums*. 2nd ed. Plymouth, UK: AltaMira Press, 2008.

Ambrose, Timothy, and Crispin Paine. *Museum Basics*. 2nd ed. New York: Routledge, 2006.

American Association of Museums. *Excellence and Equity: Education and the Public Dimension of Museums*, 1992.

Anderson, David G., and Robert C. Mainfort Jr. "An Introduction to Woodland Archaeology in the Southeast." In *The Woodland Southeast*, edited by David G. Anderson and Robert C. Mainfort, 1–19. Tuscaloosa: University of Alabama Press, 2002.

Appadurai, Arjun. "Introduction: Commodities and the Politics of Value." In *The Social Life of Things: Commodities in Cultural Perspective*, edited by Arjun Appadurai, 3–63. Cambridge: Cambridge University Press, 1986.

Austin, Robert J. "Lithic Acquisition and Use at Pineland." In *The Archaeology of Pineland: A Coastal Southwest Florida Site Complex, A.D. 50–1710*, edited by William H. Marquardt and Karen J. Walker, 657–717. Monograph 4. Gainesville: Institute of Archaeology and Paleoenvironmental Studies, University of Florida, 2013.

Baldwin, James Allen. "Notes and Speculation on the Domestication of the Cat in Egypt." In *Anthropos* 70, no. 3/4 (1975): 428–48.

Barker, Emma. "Exhibiting the Canon: The Blockbuster Show." In *Contemporary Cultures of Display*, edited by Emma Barker, 127–46. New Haven: Yale University Press, 1999.

Baxandall, Michael. "Exhibiting Intention: Some Preconditions of the Visual Display of Culturally Purposeful Objects." In *Exhibiting Cultures: The Poetics and Politics of Museum Display*, edited by Ivan Karp and Steven D. Lavine, 33–41. Washington, D.C.: Smithsonian Books, 1991.

Becker, Kimberly Ann. "The Olmec Were-Jaguar in Transformation: An Examination of the Image of the Jaguar in Olmec Art and Culture." Master's thesis, California State University, Long Beach, 1996.

Bell, Austin J. "The Cat's Meow: The Transformative Power of a Transcendent Artifact." In *Putting Theory and Things Together: Research with Museum Collections*, edited by Joshua A. Bell and Jen Shannon. Washington, D.C.: Smithsonian Institution Scholarly Press, forthcoming.

———. *Marco Island*. Images of America. Charleston: Arcadia Publishing, 2017.

———. *Marco Island*. Images of Modern America. Charleston: Arcadia Publishing, 2018.

Billie, James E. "Introduction." In *Legends of the Seminoles*, 7–9. Sarasota, FL: Pineapple Press, 1994.

Brandes, Raymond S. "Frank Hamilton Cushing: Pioneer Americanist." PhD diss., University of Arizona, 1965.

Brose, Davis S., James A. Brown, and David W. Penney. *Ancient Art of the American Woodland Indians*. New York: Harry N. Abrams, 1985. Published in conjunction with an exhibition of the same title, organized by and presented at the National Gallery of Art, Detroit Institute of Arts, and Houston Museum of Fine Arts, March 17, 1985–March 2, 1986.

Brotemarkle, Ben. "The Cat Came Back." In *Adventures in Florida Archaeology*, 12–19, publication of the Florida Historical Society Archaeological Institute, 2019.

Brown, James A. "The Cahokian Expression: Creating Court and Cult." In *Hero, Hawk, and Open Hand: American Indian Art of the Ancient Midwest and South*, edited by Richard F. Townsend and Robert V. Sharp, 105–23. New Haven and London: Yale University Press, 2004. Published in conjunction with an exhibition of the same title, organized by and presented at the Art Institute of Chicago, November 20, 2004–January 30, 2005.

———. "The Mississippian Period." In *Ancient Art of the American Woodland Indians*, edited by Andrea P. A. Belloli, 93–145. New York: Harry N. Abrams, 1985. Published in conjunction with an exhibition of the same title, organized by and presented at the National Gallery of Art, Detroit Institute of Arts, and Houston Museum of Fine Arts, March 17, 1985–March 2, 1986.

Brown, Robin C. *Florida's First People: 12,000 Years of Human History*. Sarasota, FL: Pineapple Press, 1994.

Burcaw, G. Ellis. *Introduction to Museum Work*. 3rd ed. Plymouth, UK: AltaMira Press, 1997.

Carmichael, Leonard. "Report of the Secretary of the Smithsonian Institution." In *Annual Report of the Board of Regents of the Smithsonian Institution Showing the Operations, Expenditures, and Condition of the Institution for the Year Ending June 30, 1953*. Washington, D.C.: Government Printing Office, 1954.

Carr, Robert S. "Mississippian Influence in the Glades, Belle Glade, and East Okeechobee Areas of South Florida." In *Late Prehistoric Florida: Archaeology at the Edge of the Mississip-*

pian World, edited by Keith Ashley and Nancy Marie White, 62–80. Gainesville: University Press of Florida, 2012.

Carr, Robert S., and John G. Beriault. "Archaeological Monitoring of Utility Trenching North Marco Island Collier County, Florida." Archaeological and Historical Conservancy Inc. AHC Technical Report No. 908. December 2014. AHC Project No. 2013.114. Report on file at the MIHS, Acc. 2014-12.

Chamberlain, Alex F. "In Memoriam: Frank Hamilton Cushing." In *The Journal of American Folklore* 13, no. 49 (April–June 1900): 129–134.

Clark, Merald R. "A Mechanical Waterbird Mask from Pineland and the Calusa Masking Tradition." In *The Archaeology of Pineland: A Coastal Southwest Florida Site Complex, A.D. 50–1710*, edited by William H. Marquardt and Karen J. Walker, 621–56. Monograph 4. Gainesville: Institute of Archaeology and Paleoenvironmental Studies, University of Florida, 2013.

Cockrell, Wilburn A. "Glades I and Pre-Glades Settlement and Subsistence Patterns on Marco Island (Collier County, Florida)." Master's thesis, Florida State University, 1969. Unpublished manuscript on file at Bureau of Archaeological Research, Division of Historical Resources, Florida Department of State.

Coleman, Michael. *Marco Island: Florida's Gulf Playground*. Self-pub.: Marco Island Ink, 2014.

Collier, Margaret M. *The Diary of Margaret McIlvaine Collier, March 5, 1896–April 26, 1896*. Digital facsimile of original handwritten manuscript on file in the Collier Family Archives, MIHS.

Cordell, Ann S. "Technological Investigation of Pottery Variability at the Pineland Site Complex." In *The Archaeology of Pineland: A Coastal Southwest Florida Site Complex, A.D. 50–1710*, edited by William H. Marquardt and Karen J. Walker, 383–543. Monograph 4. Gainesville: Institute of Archaeology and Paleoenvironmental Studies, University of Florida, 2013.

Crane, H. R., and J. B. Griffin. "University of Michigan Radiocarbon Dates XII." In *Radiocarbon* 10, no. 1 (1968): 61–114.

Culin, Stewart. "Archaeological Objects Exhibited by the Department of Archaeology and Palaeontology, University of Pennsylvania, Philadelphia." In *Report of the Madrid Commission, 1892*. Published in conjunction with the exhibition *Commemoration of the Fourth Centenary of the Discovery of America*, organized by and presented at the Columbian Historical Exposition, Madrid, 1892. Washington, D.C.: Government Printing Office, 1895.

Culver, M., W. E. Johnson, J. Pecon-Slattery, and S. J. O'Brien. "Genomic Ancestry of the American Puma (*Puma concolor*)." In *Journal of Heredity* 91, no. 3 (2000): 186–97.

Cuno, James. "Foreword." In *Hero, Hawk, and Open Hand: American Indian Art of the Ancient Midwest and South*, edited by Richard F. Townsend and Robert V. Sharp, 6–7. New Haven and London: Yale University Press, 2004. Published in conjunction with an exhibition of the same title, organized by and presented at the Art Institute of Chicago, November 20, 2004–January 30, 2005.

Cushing, Frank H. "Anthropology: A Preliminary Examination of Aboriginal Remains near Pine Island, Marco, West Florida." In *The American Naturalist* 29, no. 348 (December 1895): 1132–1135.

———. "A Mound Builder's Village." In *The Antiquarian*. Columbus, OH: Landon, 1897.

———. "A Preliminary Report on the Exploration of Ancient Key Dweller Remains on the Gulf

Coast of Florida." In *Proceedings of the American Philosophical Society* 35, no. 153 (1896): 329–448.

———. "Scarred Skulls from Florida." In *American Anthropologist* 10, no. 1 (January 1897): 17–18.

Cushing, James C. *Genealogy of the Cushing Family*. Montreal: Perrault, 1905.

Davenport, Christian. "A Possible Proto-Underwater Panther: Late Archaic/Woodland Carved Bone in the Northern Everglades." In *Florida Anthropologist* 72, no. 2 (June 2019): 54–66.

Davis, Jack E. *The Gulf: The Making of an American Sea*. New York: Liveright, 2017.

Davis, Richard A., Jr. "Geology of the Florida Coast." In *The Geology of Florida*, edited by Anthony F. Randazzo and Douglas S. Jones, 155–68. Gainesville: University Press of Florida, 1997.

deFrance, Susan D., and Karen J. Walker. "The Zooarchaeology of Pineland." In *The Archaeology of Pineland: A Coastal Southwest Florida Site Complex, A.D. 50–1710*, edited by William H. Marquardt and Karen J. Walker, 305–48. Monograph 4. Gainesville: Institute of Archaeology and Paleoenvironmental Studies, University of Florida, 2013.

Diesel, Alleyn. "Felines and Female Divinities: The Association of Cats with Goddesses, Ancient and Contemporary." In *Journal for the Study of Religion* 21, no. 1 (2008): 71–94.

Dietler, John Eric. "Craft Specialization and the Emergence of Political Complexity in Southwest Florida." PhD diss., University of California Los Angeles, 2008.

Dimmick, Lauretta, and Donna J. Hassler. *American Sculpture in the Metropolitan Museum of Art: A Catalogue of Works by Artists Born between 1865 and 1885*. New York: Metropolitan Museum of Art, 1999.

Duggins, Ryan M. "Florida's Paleoindian and Early Archaic: A GIS Approach to Modeling Submerged Landscapes and Site Distribution on the Continental Shelf." PhD diss., Florida State University, 2012.

Durnford, C. D. "Anthropology: The Discovery of Aboriginal Netting Rope and Wood Implements in a Mud Deposit in Western Florida." In *American Naturalist* 29, no. 347 (November 1895): 1032–39.

Eakins, Thomas, and Judith Zilczer. "Eakins Letter Provides More Evidence on the Portrait of Frank Hamilton Cushing." In *American Art Journal* 14, no. 1 (Winter 1982): 74–76.

Ewen, Charles R. "Anhaica: Discovery of Hernando de Soto's 1539–1540 Winter Camp." In *First Encounters: Spanish Explorations in the Caribbean and the United States, 1492–1570*, edited by Jerald T. Milanich and Susan Milbrath, 110–18. Gainesville: University Presses of Florida, 1989.

Fairbanks, Charles H. *Archeology of the Funeral Mound, Ocmulgee National Monument, Georgia*. Tuscaloosa: University of Alabama Press, 2003. First published 1956 by the National Park Service.

Falk, John H. *Identity and the Museum Visitor Experience*. Walnut Creek, CA: Left Coast Press, 2009.

Fewkes, J. Walter. "Aboriginal Wooden Objects from Southern Florida." In *Smithsonian Miscellaneous Collections* 80, no. 9 (1928): 1–5.

Free Museum of Science and Art of University of Pennsylvania. "Collections and Publications: America." In *Bulletin of the Free Museum of Science and Art of University of Pennsylvania* I, no. 1 (May 1897): 16–19.

———. "Exhibit at the Paris Exposition, 1900." In *Bulletin of the Free Museum of Science and Art of University of Pennsylvania* II, no. 3 (January 1900): 169–71.

Fundaburk, Emma Lila, and Mary Douglass Fundaburk Foreman, eds. *Sun Circles and Human Hands: The Southeastern Indians Art and Industries.* Fairhope, AL: Southern Publications, 1957.

Garland, Niki A., Henri D. Grissino-Mayer, Kathleen Deagan, Grant L. Harley, and Gifford Waters. "Dendrochronological Dating of Wood from the Fountain of Youth Park Archaeological Site (8SJ31), St. Augustine, Florida, U.S.A." In *Tree-Ring Research* 68, no. 1 (2012): 69–78.

Gilliland, Marion S. *Key Marco's Buried Treasure: Archaeology and Adventure in the Nineteenth Century.* Gainesville: University Presses of Florida, 1989.

———. "Marco's Buried Treasure: Wetlands Archaeology and Adventure in Nineteenth Century Florida." In *Wet Site Archaeology*, edited by Barbara A. Purdy, 255–61. Caldwell, NJ: Telford Press, 1988.

———. "The Material Culture of Key Marco, Florida." Master's thesis, University of Florida, April 1965.

———. *The Material Culture of Key Marco, Florida.* Gainesville: University Presses of Florida, 1975.

Goggin, John M. "Cultural Traditions in Florida Prehistory." In *The Florida Indian and His Neighbors.* Papers delivered at an anthropological conference held at Rollins College, April 9 and 10, 1949, 13–44.

———. "A Preliminary Definition of Archaeological Areas and Periods in Florida." In *American Antiquity* 13, no. 2 (October 1947): 114–27.

Goggin, John M., and William C. Sturtevant. "The Calusa: A Stratified Nonagricultural Society (with Notes on Sibling Marriage)." In *Explorations in Cultural Anthropology: Essays in Honor of George Peter Murdock*, edited by W. H. Goodenough, 179–219. New York: McGraw-Hill, 1964.

Greenblatt, Stephen. "Resonance and Wonder." In *Exhibiting Cultures: The Poetics and Politics of Museum Display*, edited by Ivan Karp and Steven D. Lavine, 42–56. Washington, D.C.: Smithsonian Books, 1991.

Griffin, John W. *Archaeology of the Everglades.* Gainesville: University Press of Florida, 2002.

———. "Historic Artifacts and the 'Buzzard Cult' in Florida." In *Florida Historical Quarterly* 24, no. 4 (April 1946): 295–301.

Groat, William J. "Wonders of Progress." *Milwaukee Daily Sentinel*, December 27, 1896, 8.

Gross, Liza. "Why Not the Best? How Science Failed the Florida Panther." In *PLoS Biol* 3, no. 9 (September 2005): e333.

Gunnerson, James H. "Mountain Lions and Pueblo Shrines in the American Southwest." In *Icons of Power: Feline Symbolism in the Americas*, edited by Nicholas J. Saunders, 228–57. London and New York: Routledge, 1998.

Hale, Jessica Cook. "Postdepositional Corrosions in Lithic Items Recovered from Submerged Marine Contexts." In *New Directions in the Search for the First Floridians*, edited by David K. Thulman and Ervan G. Garrison, 194–220. Gainesville: University of Florida Press, 2019.

Hamell, George R. "Long-Tail: The Panther in Huron-Wyandot and Seneca Myth, Ritual, and Material Culture." In *Icons of Power: Feline Symbolism in the Americas*, edited by Nicholas J. Saunders, 258–91. London and New York: Routledge, 1998.

Hann, John H., ed. and trans. *Indians of Central and South Florida, 1513–1763.* Gainesville: University Press of Florida, 2003.

———. *Missions to the Calusa.* Gainesville: University Press of Florida, 1991.

Harrington, M. R. "Shell Implement from Florida." In *Indian Notes* 1, no. 4 (October 1924): 218–21.

Herskovits, Melville J. *Man and His Works*. New York: Alfred A. Knopf, 1948.

Hinsley, Curtis M., and David R. Wilcox. "Introduction." In *Coming of Age in Chicago: The 1893 World's Fair and the Coalescence of American Anthropology*, edited by Curtis M. Hinsley and David R. Wilcox, xv–xli. Lincoln: University of Nebraska Press, 2016.

Horse Capture, Joe D. "Time-Honored Expression: The Knowing of Native Objects." In *Shapeshifting: Transformation in Native American Art*, edited by Karen Kramer Russell, 76–85. New Haven and London: Yale University Press, 2012.

Howe, Steve. "Los Cayos De Muspa: A Very Early History." In *Lower Keys Barometer* (Big Pine Key, FL), October 23, 1997, 12–13.

Hrdlička, Aleš. *The Anthropology of Florida*. Tuscaloosa: University of Alabama Press, 2007.

Hutchinson, Dale L. *Bioarchaeology of the Florida Gulf Coast: Adaptation, Conflict, and Change*. With contributions by Lynette Norr and Mark Teaford. Gainesville: University Press of Florida, 2004.

Hutchinson, Dale L., Lynette Norr, Theresa Schober, William H. Marquardt, Karen J. Walker, Lee A. Newsom, and C. Margaret Scarry. "The Calusa and Prehistoric Subsistence in Central and South Gulf Coast Florida." In *Journal of Anthropological Archaeology* 41 (2016): 55–73.

Ingold, Tim. "Materials against Materiality." In *Archaeological Dialogues* 14, no. 1 (2007): 1–16.

Ingold, Tim, and Elizabeth Hallam, eds. *Making and Growing: Anthropological Studies of Organisms and Artefacts*. Farnham: Routledge, 2014.

Jacknis, Ira. "Refracting Images: Anthropological Display at the Chicago World's Fair, 1893." In *Coming of Age in Chicago: The 1893 World's Fair and the Coalescence of American Anthropology*, edited by Curtis M. Hinsley and David R. Wilcox, 261–336. Lincoln: University of Nebraska Press, 2016.

Johnson, Warren E., David P. Onorato, Melody E. Roelke, E. Darrell Land, Mark Cunningham, Robert C. Belden, Roy McBride, Deborah Jansen, Mark Lotz, David Shindle, JoGayle Howard, David E. Wildt, Linda M. Penfold, Jeffrey A. Hostetler, Madan K. Oli, and Stephen J. O'Brien. "Genetic Restoration of the Florida Panther." In *Science* 329, no. 5999 (September 24, 2010): 1641–45.

Karacic, Steven, and Julia B. Duggins. "The Colorful Past of the Hurricane Irma Dugout: Portable X-Ray Fluorescence to Determine Traces of Paint on a Submerged Wooden Artifact." In *Florida Anthropologist* 71, no. 3–4 (December 2019): 151–60.

Kassabaum, Megan C. "Early Platforms, Early Plazas: Exploring the Precursors to Mississippian Mound-and-Plaza Centers." In *Journal of Archaeological Research* 27 (2019): 187–247.

Kavich, Gwénaëlle. "p-XRF Report: Key Marco Cat, A240915-0." Washington, D.C.: Smithsonian Museum Conservation Institute, 2018. MCI request no. 6575.10. Report on file at Department of Anthropology, NMNH.

Kellogg, Remington. "Report on the United States National Museum." *Annual Report of the Board of Regents of the Smithsonian Institution Showing the Operations, Expenditures, and Condition of the Institution for the Year Ending June 30, 1957*. Washington, D.C.: Government Printing Office, 1958.

———. "Report on the United States National Museum." *Annual Report of the Board of Regents of the Smithsonian Institution Showing the Operations, Expenditures, and Condition of the Institution for the Year Ending June 30, 1959*. Washington, D.C.: Government Printing Office, 1960.

———. "Report on the United States National Museum." *Annual Report of the Board of Regents of the Smithsonian Institution Showing the Operations, Expenditures, and Condition of the Institution for the Year Ending June 30, 1960*. Washington, D.C.: Government Printing Office, 1961.

Kind, Claus-Joachim, Nicole Ebinger-Rist, Sibylle Wolf, Thomas Beutelspacher, and Kurt Wehrberger. "The Smile of the Lion Man: Recent Excavations in Stadel Cave (Baden-Württemberg, South-Western Germany) and the Restoration of the Famous Upper Palaeolithic Figurine." In *Quartär* 61 (2014): 129–45.

Knappet, Carl. *Thinking through Material Culture: An Interdisciplinary Perspective*. Philadelphia: University of Pennsylvania Press, 2005.

Kolianos, Phyllis E. "Wood Preservation Dilemmas of Florida's Prehistoric Saltwater Sites: Key Marco and Weedon Island." In *Iconography and Wetsite Archaeology of Florida's Watery Realms*, edited by Ryan Wheeler and Joanna Ostapkowicz, 67–81. Gainesville: University of Florida Press, 2019.

Kolianos, Phyllis E., and Brent R. Weisman, eds. *The Florida Journals of Frank Hamilton Cushing*. Gainesville: University Press of Florida, 2005.

———. *The Lost Florida Manuscript of Frank Hamilton Cushing*. Gainesville: University Press of Florida, 2005.

Kozuch, Laura. *Sharks and Shark Products in Prehistoric South Florida*. Monograph 2. Gainesville: Institute of Archaeology and Paleoenvironmental Studies, University of Florida, 1993.

Lee, Arthur R. "Cushing's Cat Figurine Star of Centennial Exhibit." In *Florida Anthropologist* 48, no. 4 (December 1995): 309–10.

———. "Key Marco Revisited." In *Florida Anthropologist* 49, no. 1 (March 1996): 3.

Levenson, Jay A., ed. *Circa 1492: Art in the Age of Exploration*. New Haven and London: Yale University Press, 1991. Published in conjunction with an exhibition of the same title, organized by and presented at the National Gallery of Art, October 12, 1991–January 12, 1992.

Lord, James. "Zoomorphic Bone Pin from Dade County, Florida." In *Florida Anthropologist* 42, no. 3 (September 1989): 263, 264.

MacMahon, Darcie A., and William H. Marquardt. *The Calusa and Their Legacy: South Florida People and Their Environments*. Gainesville: University Press of Florida, 2004.

Marquardt, William H. "The Calusa Domain: An Introduction." In *Culture and Environment in the Domain of the Calusa,* edited by William H. Marquardt, 1–8. Monograph 1. Gainesville: Institute of Archaeology and Paleoenvironmental Studies, University of Florida, 1992.

———. "Introduction." In *Missions to the Calusa*, edited by John H. Hann, xv–xix. Gainesville: University Press of Florida, 1991.

———. "The Padgett Figurine and Other Pre-Columbian Wooden Statuettes from Florida." In *Iconography and Wetsite Archaeology of Florida's Watery Realms*, edited by Ryan Wheeler and Joanna Ostapkowicz, 152–78. Gainesville: University of Florida Press, 2019.

———. "The Pineland Site Complex: An Environmental and Cultural History." In *The Archaeology of Pineland: A Coastal Southwest Florida Site Complex, A.D. 50–1710*, edited by William H. Marquardt and Karen J. Walker, 793–920. Monograph 4. Gainesville: Institute of Archaeology and Paleoenvironmental Studies, University of Florida, 2013.

———. "Shell Artifacts from the Caloosahatchee Area." In *Culture and Environment in the Domain of the Calusa*, edited by William H. Marquardt, 191–227. Monograph 1. Gainesville: Institute of Archaeology and Paleoenvironmental Studies, University of Florida, 1992.

———. "Shell Mounds in the Southeast: Middens, Monuments, Temple Mounds, Rings, or Works?" In *American Antiquity* 75, no. 3 (July 2010): 551–70.
———. "Tracking the Calusa: A Retrospective." In *Southeastern Archaeology* 33, no. 1 (2014): 1–24.
Marquardt, William H., and Laura Kozuch. "The Lightning Whelk: An Enduring Icon of Southeastern North American Spirituality." In *Journal of Anthropological Archaeology* 42 (2016): 1–26.
Marquardt, William H., Anthony M. Krus, and Victor D. Thompson. "Rethinking the Estero Island Site: A Possible Satellite Village of Mound Key." In *Journal of Anthropological Archaeology* 58 (2020): 1–12.
Marquardt, William H., and Karen J. Walker. "Southwest Florida during the Mississippi Period." In *Late Prehistoric Florida: Archaeology at the Edge of the Mississippian World*, edited by Nancy Marie White, 29–61. Gainesville: University Press of Florida, 2012.
Marquardt, William H., and Karen J. Walker, eds. *The Archaeology of Pineland: A Coastal Southwest Florida Site Complex, A.D. 50–1710*. Monograph 4. Gainesville: Institute of Archaeology and Paleoenvironmental Studies, University of Florida, 2013.
Mason, J. Alden. "H. Newell Wardle, 1875–1964." In *Expedition Magazine* 6.4 (1964): 40.
———. "Primitive Wooden Masks from Key Marco, Florida." In *Archaeology* 4, no. 1 (March 1951): 4–5.
McGoun, William E. "Medals of Conquest in Calusa Florida." Master's thesis, Florida Atlantic University, 1981.
McIver, Stuart B. *Death in the Everglades: The Murder of Guy Bradley, America's First Martyr to Environmentalism*. Gainesville: University Press of Florida, 2003.
Mercer, Henry C. "Anthropology: Exploration by the University of Pennsylvania in West Florida." In *American Naturalist* 30, no. 356 (August 1896): 691–93.
Milanich, Jerald T. *Archaeology of Precolumbian Florida*. Gainesville: University Press of Florida, 1994.
———. "The Devil in the Details." In *Archaeology* 58, no. 3 (May/June 2005): 26–31.
———. *Florida Indians and the Invasion from Europe*. Gainesville: University Press of Florida, 1995.
———. *Florida's Indians from Ancient Times to the Present*. Gainesville: University Press of Florida, 1998.
———. "The Temporal Placement of Cushing's Key Marco Site, Florida." In *American Anthropologist* 80, no. 3 (September 1978): 682.
Mills, John S., and Raymond White. *The Organic Chemistry of Museum Objects*. 2nd ed. New York: Routledge, 2011.
Missall, John, and Mary Lou Missall. *The Seminole Wars: America's Longest Indian Conflict*. Gainesville: University Press of Florida, 2004.
Moore, C. B. "Certain Aboriginal Remains of the Northwest Florida Coast." In *Journal of the Academy of Natural Sciences*, no. 12 (1902): 127–355.
———. "Certain Antiquities of the Florida West Coast." In *Journal of the Academy of Natural Sciences*, no. 11 (1900): 349–94.
Nash, Stephen E., and Chip Colwell. "NAGPRA at 30: The Effects of Repatriation." In *Annual Review of Anthropology*, no. 49 (2020): 225–39.
Newsom, Lee A., Robin C. Brown, and Wendy Natt. "Pineland Cordage and Modified Wood: Material-Technological Aspects of Plant Use." In *The Archaeology of Pineland: A Coastal*

Southwest Florida Site Complex, A.D. 50–1710, edited by William H. Marquardt and Karen J. Walker, 585–620. Monograph 4. Gainesville: Institute of Archaeology and Paleoenvironmental Studies, University of Florida, 2013.

Newsom, Lee A., and Vernon James Knight. "Foreword." In *Iconography and Wetsite Archaeology of Florida's Watery Realms*, edited by Ryan Wheeler and Joanna Ostapkowicz, xiii–xxiv. Gainesville: University of Florida Press, 2019.

Olds, Sally Wendkos. "Article 4—No Title," *New York Times*, April 10, 1988, 225.

Ostapkowicz, Joanna, Rick J. Schulting, Ryan Wheeler, Lee Newsom, Fiona Brock, Ian Bull, and Christophe Snoeck. "East-Central Florida Pre-Columbian Wood Sculpture: Radiocarbon Dating, Wood Identification and Strontium Isotope Studies." In *Journal of Archaeological Science: Reports* 13 (2017): 595–608.

Ostapkowicz, Joanna, Fiona Brock, Alex C. Wiedenhoeft, Christophe Snoeck, John Pouncett, Yasmin Baksh-Comeau, Rick Schulting, Philippe Claeys, Nadine Mattielli, Mike Richards, and Arie Boomert. "Black Pitch, Carved Histories: Radiocarbon Dating, Wood Species Identification and Strontium Isotope Analysis of Prehistoric Wood Carvings From Trinidad's Pitch Lake." In *Journal of Archaeological Science: Reports* 16 (2017): 341–58.

Pané, Fray Ramón. "How They Make and Keep the Zemis Made of Wood or of Stone." In *An Account of the Antiquities of the Indians: A New Edition, with an Introductory Study, Notes, and Appendices*, edited by José Juan Arrom, 25–26. Durham: Duke University Press, 1999.

Patrick, Rembert W. *Florida under Five Flags*. Fifth ed. Gainesville: University Press of Florida, 2013.

Pels, Peter. "The Spirit of Matter: On Fetish, Rarity, Fact, and Fancy." In *Border Fetishisms: Material Objects in Unstable Spaces*, edited by Patricia Spyer, 91–121. New York: Routledge, 1998.

Perdichizzi, Elizabeth, with Katherine S. Kirk. *Island Voices: They Came to Marco Island*. Marco Island, FL: Caxambas Publishing, 2006.

Pezzati, Alessandro. "Gold Medals & Grand Prizes: World's Fairs and the Penn Museum." In *Expedition* 57, no. 1 (2015): 19–21.

Powell, John Wesley. "Report of the Director of the Bureau of American Ethnology for the Year Ending June 30, 1896." In *Annual Report of the Board of Regents of the Smithsonian Institution Showing the Operations, Expenditures, and Condition of the Institution to July 1896*. 32–45. Washington, D.C.: Government Printing Office, 1898.

Purdy, Barbara A. *The Art and Archaeology of Florida's Wetlands*. Boca Raton, FL: CRC Press, 1991.

———. *Indian Art of Ancient Florida*. Gainesville: University Press of Florida, 1996.

———. "The Key Marco, Florida Collection: Experiment and Reflection." In *American Antiquity* 39, no. 1 (January 1974): 105–9.

Quesnell, Quentin. "Relocating Cushing's Key Marco." In *The Florida Anthropologist* 49, no. 1 (March 1996): 4–9.

Rathbun, Richard. "Report on the United States National Museum." *Annual Report of the Board of Regents of the Smithsonian Institution Showing the Operations, Expenditures, and Condition of the Institution for the Year Ending June 30, 1913*. Washington, D.C.: Government Printing Office, 1914.

Read, Charles Hercules. "[Antiquities from Marco, Southwest Florida]." In *Journal of the Anthropological Institute of Great Britain and Ireland* 25 (1896): 406–7.

Reilly, F. Kent, III. "People of Earth, People of Sky: Visualizing the Sacred in Native American

Art of the Mississippian Period." In *Hero, Hawk, and Open Hand: American Indian Art of the Ancient Midwest and South*, edited by Richard F. Townsend and Robert V. Sharp, 125–38. New Haven and London: Yale University Press, 2004. Published in conjunction with an exhibition of the same title, organized by and presented at the Art Institute of Chicago, November 20, 2004–January 30, 2005.

Russell, Karen K., with Janet Catherine Berlo, Bruce Bernstein, Joe D. Horse Capture, Jessica L. Horton, and Paul Chaat Smith and contributions by Kathleen Ash-Milby, Karah English, Aldona Jonaitis, Madeleine M. Kropa, Kate Morris, and Ryan Rice. *Shapeshifting: Transformations in Native American Art*. New Haven and London: Yale University Press, 2012. Published in conjunction with an exhibition of the same title, organized by and presented at the Peabody Essex Museum, Salem, Massachusetts, January 14–April 29, 2012.

Russo, Michael A. "Archaic Sedentism on the Florida Coast: A Case Study from Horr's Island." PhD diss., University of Florida, 1991.

———. *Archaic Shell Rings of the Southeast U.S.* Tallahassee, FL: Southeastern Archaeological Center, National Park Service, 2006.

Saunders, Nicholas J. "Architecture of Symbolism: The Feline Image." In *Icons of Power: Feline Symbolism in the Americas*, edited by Nicholas J. Saunders, 12–52. London and New York: Routledge, 1998.

———. "Introduction: Icons of Power." In *Icons of Power: Feline Symbolism in the Americas*, edited by Nicholas J. Saunders, 1–11. London and New York: Routledge, 1998.

Scarry, C. Margaret, and Lee A. Newsom. "Archaeobotanical Research in the Calusa Heartland." In *Culture and Environment in the Domain of the Calusa*, edited by William H. Marquardt, 375–401. Gainesville: University Press of Florida, 1992.

Schafer, Daniel L. "U.S. Territory and State." In *The History of Florida*, edited by Michael Gannon, 200–22. Gainesville: University Press of Florida, 2013.

Schlereth, Thomas J. "Material Culture Studies in America, 1876–1976." In *Material Culture in America*, edited by Thomas J. Schlereth, 1–78. Nashville: American Association for State and Local History.

Schober, Theresa M. *ArtCalusa: Reflections on Representation*. Naples, FL: Intech Printing & Direct Mail. Published in conjunction with an exhibition of the same title, presented at the Pier Building, City of Fort Myers, November 1–December 11, 2013.

Schwadron, Margo. "Landscapes of Maritime Complexity: Prehistoric Shell Work Sites of the Ten Thousand Islands, Florida." PhD diss., University of Leicester, 2010.

Schwehm, Alice Gates. "The Carved Wood Effigies of Fort Center: A Glimpse of South Florida's Prehistoric Art." Master's thesis, University of Florida, 1983.

Sears, William H. *Fort Center: An Archaeological Site in the Lake Okeechobee Basin*. Gainesville: University Presses of Florida, 1982.

Seeman, Mark F. "Hopewell Art in Hopewell Places." In *Hero, Hawk, and Open Hand: American Indian Art of the Ancient Midwest and South*, edited by Richard F. Townsend and Robert V. Sharp, 57–71. New Haven and London: Yale University Press, 2004. Published in conjunction with an exhibition of the same title, organized by and presented at the Art Institute of Chicago, November 20, 2004–January 30, 2005.

———. "Predatory War and Hopewell Trophies." In *The Taking and Displaying of Human Body Parts as Trophies by Amerindians*, edited by Richard J. Chacon and David H. Dye, 167–89. New York: Springer, 2007.

Simpson, Moira G. *Making Representations: Museums in the Post-Colonial Era*. New York: Routledge, 1996.

Snapp, Annette L. "The Durnford Collection." In *Florida Anthropologist* 49, no. 4 (December 1996): 267–73.

Speck, Frank G. "Some Outlines of Aboriginal Culture in the Southeastern States." In *American Anthropologist* 9, no. 2 (Apr.–Jun. 1907): 287–95.

Spivey-Faulkner, S. Margaret. "Fort Center's Iconographic Bestiary: A Reanalysis of the Site's Carved Wood Assemblage." PhD diss., Washington University in St. Louis, 2018.

Spoehr, Alexander. "Camp, Clan, and Kin among the Cow Creek Seminole of Florida." In *Publications of the Field Museum of Natural History, Anthropological Series* 33, no. 1 (1941): 1–27.

Stahle, David W., and Daniel Wolfman. "The Potential for Archaeological Tree-Ring Dating in Eastern North America." In *Advances in Archaeological Method and Theory* 8 (1985): 279–302.

Stirling, M. W. *Forty-Eighth Annual Report of the Bureau of American Ethnology to the Secretary of the Smithsonian Institution (1930–1931)*. Washington, D.C.: United States Government Printing Office, 1933.

Stogner, Maggie Burnette. "The Media-Enhanced Museum Experience: Debating the Use of Media Technology in Cultural Exhibitions." In *Curator* 52, no. 4 (October 2009): 385–97.

Sturtevant, William C. "Chaikaka and the Spanish Indians: Documentary Sources Compared with Seminole Tradition." In *Tequesta* (1953): 35–73.

———. "Museums as Anthropological Data Banks." In *Anthropology beyond the University*, edited by Alden Redfield, Southern Anthropological Society Proceedings, no. 7, 40–55. Athens: University of Georgia Press, 1973.

———. "Woodsmen and Villagers of the East." In *The World of the American Indian*, 101–49. Washington, D.C.: National Geographic Society, 1974.

Swanton, John R. *The Indians of the Southeastern United States*. Washington, D.C: Smithsonian Institution Press, 1979. First published 1946 by the Smithsonian Institution, Bureau of American Ethnology Bulletin 137.

Sweeney, Alexander Y. "Archaeological Testing and Monitoring of the North Marco Sewerline District along Vernon Place, Marco Island, Collier County, Florida." Brockington & Associates. August 2009. Report on file at the MIHS, Acc. 2014-7.

Tebeau, Charlton W. *Florida's Last Frontier: The History of Collier County*. Rev. ed. Coral Gables: University of Miami Press, 1966.

Thompson, Raymond H., and Nancy J. Parezo. "A Historical Survey of Material Culture Studies in Anthropology." In *Perspectives on Anthropological Collections from the American Southwest*, edited by Lane Hedlund and Margaret W. Conkey with contributions by Department of Anthropology, Arizona State University, and the Heard Museum of Anthropology and Primitive Art, 33–65. Tempe: Arizona State University, 1989.

Thompson, Victor D., William H. Marquardt, Alexander Cherkinsky, Amanda D. Roberts Thompson, Karen J. Walker, and Lee A. Newsom. "From Shell Midden to Midden-Mound: The Geoarchaeology of Mound Key, an Anthropogenic Island in Southwest Florida, USA." In *PLoS ONE* 11, no. 4 (2016): e0154611.

Thompson, Victor D., William H. Marquardt, Michael Savarese, Karen J. Walker, Lee A. Newsom, Isabelle Lulewicz, Nathan R. Lawres, Amanda D. Roberts Thompson, Allan R. Bacon, and Christoph A. Walser. "Ancient Engineering of Fish Capture and Storage in Southwest

Florida." In *Proceedings of the National Academy of Sciences of the United States of America* 117, no. 15 (2020): 8374–81.

Thompson, Victor D., William H. Marquardt, Karen J. Walker, Amanda D. Roberts Thompson, and Lee A. Newsom. "Collective Action, State Building, and the Rise of the Calusa, Southwest Florida, USA." In *Journal of Anthropological Archaeology* 51 (2018): 28–44.

Thompson, Victor D., and John E. Worth. "Dwellers by the Sea: Native American Adaptations along the Southern Coasts of Eastern North America." In *Journal of Anthropological Archaeology* 19 (2011): 51–101.

Townsend, Richard F. "American Landscapes, Seen and Unseen." In *Hero, Hawk, and Open Hand: American Indian Art of the Ancient Midwest and South*, edited by Richard F. Townsend and Robert V. Sharp, 15–35. New Haven and London: Yale University Press, 2004. Published in conjunction with an exhibition of the same title, organized by and presented at the Art Institute of Chicago, November 20, 2004–January 30, 2005.

Truettner, William H. "Dressing the Part: Thomas Eakins's Portrait of Frank Hamilton Cushing." In *American Art Journal* 17, no. 2 (Spring 1985): 48–72.

Tykot, Robert H. "Using Nondestructive Portable X-ray Fluorescence Spectrometers on Stone, Ceramics, Metals, and Other Materials in Museums: Advantages and Limitations." In *Applied Spectroscopy* 70, no. 1 (2016): 42–56.

Van Beck, John C., and Linda M. Van Beck. "The Marco Midden, Marco Island, Florida." In *Florida Anthropologist* 18, no. 1 (March 1965): 1–20.

Vega, Garcilaso de la. *The Florida of the Inca: A History of Adelantado, Hernando De Soto, Governor and Captain General of the Kingdom of Florida, and of Other Heroic Spanish and Indian Cavaliers.* Austin: University of Texas Press, 1996.

Waitley, Douglas. *The Last Paradise: The Building of Marco Island.* Marco Island, FL: Marco Island Eagle, 1999.

Walcott, Charles D. "Report of the Secretary of the Smithsonian Institution." *Annual Report of the Board of Regents of the Smithsonian Institution Showing the Operations, Expenditures, and Condition of the Institution for the Year Ending June 30, 1911.* Washington, D.C.: Government Printing Office, 1912.

———. "Report of the Secretary of the Smithsonian Institution." *Annual Report of the Board of Regents of the Smithsonian Institution Showing the Operations, Expenditures, and Condition of the Institution for the Year Ending June 30, 1912.* Washington, D.C.: Government Printing Office, 1913.

———. "Report of the Secretary of the Smithsonian Institution." *Annual Report of the Board of Regents of the Smithsonian Institution Showing the Operations, Expenditures, and Condition of the Institution for the Year Ending June 30, 1918.* Washington, D.C.: Government Printing Office, 1920.

Walker, Chester P. "Prehistoric Art of the Central Mississippi Valley." In *Hero, Hawk, and Open Hand: American Indian Art of the Ancient Midwest and South*, edited by Richard F. Townsend and Robert V. Sharp, 219–29. New Haven and London: Yale University Press, 2004. Published in conjunction with an exhibition of the same title, organized by and presented at the Art Institute of Chicago, November 20, 2004–January 30, 2005.

Walker, Karen J. "Bone Artifacts from Josslyn Island, Buck Key Shell Midden, and Cash Mound: A Preliminary Assessment for the Caloosahatchee Area." In *Culture and Environment in the Domain of the Calusa*, edited by William H. Marquardt, 229–246. Monograph

1. Gainesville: Institute of Archaeology and Paleoenvironmental Studies, University of Florida, 1992.

———. "The Material Culture of Precolumbian Fishing: Artifacts and Fish Remains from Coastal Southwest Florida." In *Southeastern Archaeology* 19, no. 1 (Summer 2000): 24–45.

———. "The Pineland Site Complex: Environmental Contexts." In *The Archaeology of Pineland: A Coastal Southwest Florida Site Complex, A.D. 50–1710*, edited by William H. Marquardt and Karen J. Walker, 23–52. Monograph 4. Gainesville: Institute of Archaeology and Paleoenvironmental Studies, University of Florida, 2013.

Walker, Karen J., Frank W. Stapor Jr., and William H. Marquardt. "Episodic Sea Levels and Human Occupation at Southwest Florida's Wightman Site." In *Florida Anthropologist* 47, no. 2 (June 1994): 161–79.

Wallis, Neill J., Ann S. Cordell, Erin Harris-Parks, Mark C. Donop, and Kristen Hall. "Provenance of Weeden Island 'Sacred' and 'Prestige' Vessels: Implications for Specialized Ritual Craft Production." In *Southeastern Archaeology* 36 no. 2 (2017): 131–43.

Wallis, Neill J., and Amanda O'Dell. "Swift Creek Paddle Designs from the Florida Gulf Coast." In *Florida Anthropologist* 64, no. 3–4 (September–December 2011): 187–205.

Wardle, H. Newell. "The Pile Dwellers of Key Marco." In *Archaeology* 4, no. 3 (September 1951): 181–86.

Waring, A. J., Jr., and Preston Holder. "A Prehistoric Ceremonial Complex in the Southeastern United States." In *American Anthropologist* 47, no. 1 (January–March 1945): 1–34.

Weil, Stephen E. "From Being about Something to Being for Somebody: The Ongoing Transformation of the American Museum." In *Daedalus* 128, no. 3 (Summer 1999): 229–58.

Weisman, Brent Richards. *Pioneer in Space and Time: John Mann Goggin and the Development of Florida Archaeology*. Gainesville: University Press of Florida, 2002.

Welch, Paul D., and Brian M. Butler. "Borne on a Litter with Much Prestige." In *Leadership and Polity in Mississippian Society*, edited by Brian M. Butler and Paul D. Welch, 1–15. Occasional Paper 33. Carbondale: Center for Archaeological Investigations, Southern Illinois University, 2006.

Wheeler, Ryan J. "On the Trail of the Panther in Ancient Florida." In *Florida Anthropologist* 63, no. 3–4 (September–December 2011): 139–62.

———. *Treasure of the Calusa: The Johnson / Wilcox Collection from Mound Key Florida*. Monographs in Florida Archaeology, Number 1. Tallahassee: Rose Printing, 2000.

Widmer, Randolph J. *The Evolution of the Calusa: A Nonagricultural Chiefdom on the Southwest Florida Coast*. Tuscaloosa: University of Alabama Press, 1988.

———. "The Key Marco Site, A Planned Shell Mound Community on the Southwest Florida Coast." In *Cultural Dynamics of Shell-Matrix Sites*, edited by Mirjana Roksandic, et al., 11–20. Albuquerque: University of New Mexico Press, 2014.

———. "Recent Excavations at the Key Marco Site, 8CR48, Collier County, Florida." In *Florida Anthropologist* 49, no. 1 (March 1996): 10–25.

———. "The Relationship of Ceremonial Artifacts from South Florida with the Southeastern Ceremonial Complex." In *The Southeastern Ceremonial Complex: Artifacts and Analysis*, edited by Patricia Galloway, 166–80. Lincoln and London: University of Nebraska Press, 1989.

———. "Sociopolitical Implications of Off-Shore Fishing in Aboriginal Southeastern Florida." In *Florida Anthropologist* 39, no. 4 (December 1986): 244–52.

———. "The Woodland Archaeology of South Florida." In *The Woodland Southeast*, edited by

David G. Anderson and Robert C. Mainfort, 373–97. Tuscaloosa: University of Alabama Press, 2002.

Wilcox, David R. "Analysis of Registered Members of the International Congress of Anthropology, World's Columbian Exposition, 1893." In *Coming of Age in Chicago: The 1893 World's Fair and the Coalescence of American Anthropology*, edited by Curtis M. Hinsley and David R. Wilcox, 110–19. Lincoln: University of Nebraska Press, 2016.

———. "Anthropology in a Changing America: Interpreting the Chicago 'Triumph' of Frank Hamilton Cushing." In *Coming of Age in Chicago: The 1893 World's Fair and the Coalescence of American Anthropology*, edited by Curtis M. Hinsley and David R. Wilcox, 125–238. Lincoln: University of Nebraska Press, 2016.

Wilder, G. J., and B. J. Roche. "A Floristic Inventory of Marco Island (Collier County), Florida." In *Journal of the Botanical Research Institute of Texas* 3, no. 2 (November 25, 2009): 873–99.

Williams, John L. *The Territory of Florida: Or, Sketches of the Topography, Civil and Natural History, of the Country, Its Climate, and the Indian Tribes, from the First Discovery to Present Time.* New York: A. T. Goodrich, 1837.

Wing, Elizabeth. "Animal Bones Associated with Two Indian Sites on Marco Island, Florida." In *The Florida Anthropologist* 18, no. 1 (March 1965): 21–28.

Woodbury, Richard B., and Nathalie F. S. Woodbury. "The Rise and Fall of the Bureau of American Ethnology." In *Journal of the Southwest* 41, no. 3 (Autumn 1999): 283–96.

Woodward, Sophie. "Object Interviews, Material Imaginings and 'Unsettling' Methods: Interdisciplinary Approaches to Understanding Materials and Material Culture." In *Qualitative Research* 16, no. 4 (2016): 359–74.

Worth, John E. "Creolization in Southwest Florida: Cuban Fishermen and 'Spanish Indians,' ca. 1766–1841." In *Historical Archaeology* 46, no. 1 (2012): 142–60.

———, ed. and trans. *Discovering Florida: First-Contact Narratives from Spanish Expeditions along the Lower Gulf Coast.* Gainesville: University Press of Florida, 2014.

Index

Page numbers in *italics* refer to illustrations.

Agriculture: Calusa and, 18, 67, 69; coconut cultivation, 80; cultural groups and, 67; fertilizer for, 80, 81, 85, 93, 198n26; fruit tree cultivation, 80, 93; Glades culture and, 67; maize cultivation, 67, 68, 69; on Marco Island, 79; pineapple cultivation, 197n14; and soil pH, 198n26; vegetable cultivation, 80, 93; during Woodland Period, 67

American Archaeology, 171, *172*

American Philosophical Society (APS), 101, 113, 135, 136

Ancient Art of the American Woodland Indians, 51, 144–46, 148, 152, 154, 156

Animals: alligators, 193n30; armadillos, 193n30; barracudas, 35; birds, 68, 85, 145, 152, *161;* bobcats, 43, 48; butterflies, 152; cats/felines, 48–51, 56; clams, 70, 99; conchs, 80; cougars, 43, 45, 46; crabs, 45; deer, 18, 120, 129, 148; dolphins, *82;* ducks, 129; eagles, 145; fish, 76, 89, 90, 94, *129,* 145; frogs, 145; images of, *44, 46, 47;* jaguars, 50, 57; lions, 43; mammals, 152; mastodons, 152; Megalodons, 35; mosquitos, 95, 98; mountain lions, 43, 45, 54, 57; Native cultures and, 152; opossums, 48; panthers, 29, 31, 43, 44–48, 54, 55, 56, 154, 190n22; pelicans, 148; pen shells, 70; pumas, 43, 54; rabbits, 110; reptiles, 68, 152; saber-toothed cats, 152; sand flies, 98; sawfish, 35; sea urchins, 70; sharks, 35, 37; shellfish, 76, 90; squirrels, 45; and transfiguration, 152; turtles, 18, 100; whelks, 83; wolves, 140, 148, *161*. *See also* Cats, artistic representations of

Anthropologists and anthropology, 133, 137

Antiquities Act of 1906, 83. *See also* Native American Graves Protection and Repatriation Act (NAGPRA)

Archaeological periods and cultures: Allison/Copena, 51; Archaic, 15, 66, 145; Before Common Era, 186n2; Caloosahatchee, 66–67; Common Era, 186n2; Hopewell Tradition, 57, 66, 67, 68; Mississippian, 56, 66, 67, 145, 148, 154; Ortona, 66; Pleistocene, 15; pre-Columbian, 186n2; Yent, 66. *See also* Calusa; Glades culture

Archaeological techniques and equipment: 3-D mapping and printing, 60, 175; associated context, 59; calipers, 189n6, 205n57; ceramic analysis, 59, 62, 66, 72; dendrochronology, 175–77; destructive analysis, 12–13, 14; digital photography, 60; digital scales, 189n7; electron microscopy, 177; gas chromatography, 175; grid system, 60, 87–*88,* 95, 100; infrared spectrometry, 175; Munsell test, 13; open square tests, 60; radiocarbon dating, 59, 63, 64, 69, 175, 195n14; stratigraphy documentation, 60; strontium-isotope analysis, 175; stylistic analysis, 59; X-ray fluorescence analysis, 66, 175, 177, 178

Archaeology: and anthropology, 54; experimental, 14, 33; and historic preservation, 83; history of, 133; and objects, 1, 2; and wet sites, 85

Archivo General de Indias, 52

Artifacts: adornos, 145; bone, 38, 45, 48, 54, 69,

Artifacts—*continued*
85, 89; bowls, 145; celts, 68; ceramic, 85, 145; chert, 190n39; clay, 3; contamination of, 175; copper, 145; cultural meaning of, 42–43; dating of, 59, 60, 175; decoration on, 68; definition of, 185n1 (introduction); effigies, 145; figurines, 25; galena, 18; human skulls, 54; life cycle of, 179; mica, 145; panther remains, 45, 55; Pensacola Incised, 145; pins, 48; pipes, 68; points, 38; protection of, 178; refuse as, 3; replicas of, 150, 175; sculptures, 39–40; sharks' teeth, 191n71; shell, 3, 15, 30–32, 69, 145, 150; stone, 3, 68, 85, 145, 150; threats to, 178; tools, 15, 18, 30–31; vessels, 15; in waterlogged sites, 87–89; wooden, 11, 25, 39–40, 48, 89, 145, 175. *See also* Ceramics; Key Marco site, artifacts from; Key Marco site, bone artifacts from; Key Marco site, wooden artifacts from; Tools

Art Institute of Chicago (AIC), 151, 152, 153, 157

Bailey, Kathleen, 101

Barfield Bay, 20

Barron River, 71

Barry, John, 125

Beans, Russell, *44*

Bell, Austin J.: on abandonment/destruction of Key Marco site, 75–76; and archaeological surveys in rural Florida, 81; career of, ix–x, 168; and casts of Key Marco artifacts, including the Cat, 125, 158–60; and Key Marco artifacts, ix, 46; and Key Marco Cat, ix, x, 66, 155, 158, 180, 187n24, 205n57; on local feelings about Key Marco Cat, 154–55; on modern Key Marco Cat images and replicas, 161; on "peaty marl" at Key Marco site, 70–71; presentation by, 212n29

Belle Glade, FL, 142

Bergmann, Carl F. W.: and 1896 Key Marco excavation, 108, 109, 116–17; biography of, 116; and casts of Key Marco artifacts, 121, 122, 125–26; and Chicago World's Fair, 137; and Key Marco artifacts, 108, 112, 114, 117, 119, 121, 128, 135; professional background and duties of, 112, 117

Big Marco Pass and Marco River, 21, 95, 200n12

Blue Hill site, 21

Boas, Franz, 134

Brinton, Daniel, 134

British Museum, 2, 49, 83, 96, 175

Brock, Robert C. H., 127, 128, 129

Brooklyn Museum, 102

Brown, John Carter, 147–48

Brown, Robin, 14, 33, 40

Building a Dream: The 25 Year History of the Marco Island Historical Society, 171–73

Bulletin of the Free Museum of Science and Art, 135

Bureau of American Ethnology (BAE). *See under* Smithsonian Institution

Bureau of Engraving and Printing, 161

Busch, Lon, 161

Buzzard Cult, 68

Cahokia site, 67

Caloosahatchee region, 16, *17*

Caloosahatchee River, *17*, 77, 142

Calusa: and agriculture, 18, 67, 69; archaeology of, 11; and body paint, 40; and class, 18; in Cuba, 78; depictions of, 163; diet of, 18, 90; and Europeans, 16–17, 18, 19, 24, 54, 74, 78; and Key Marco Cat, 4, 9, 15, 18, 20–21, 159; and Key Marco site, 154; location of, 15, 16, 20; and mounds, 69; natural environment of, 10; and other Native peoples, 16–17, 18, 75–76, 78; persistence of, 78; population of, 18; and pottery, 16, 69; precursors of, 15; regional impact of, 77; religion and rituals of, 52–54, 56, 75; and slavery, 18; and tools, 30, 31, 32; and weapons, 78; and wood, 11

Cape Canaveral, FL, 18

Cape Romano, FL, *17*, 20

Carr, Robert S., 26, 63

Cats, artistic representations of: bobcats, 47, 48; bone, 48; bronze, 49; cats, 48–51; copper-covered bone, 55; cougars, 46; crouching, 148; dates of, 48, 49, 50, 51; decoration on, 193n30; and divinity, 49, 50; European cave art, 48; felines, spotted, 48; fetishes, 56; Fort Center carvings, 51, 55; Gayer-Anderson Cat, 49–50; images of, *29, 49, 50;* interpretations of, 29, 51; jaguars, 50, 57; lions, 100; *Löwenmensch* figurine, 49; Mahony Figurine, 29, 47–48; mammoth-ivory, 49; masks of, *29*, 47; Millar Figurine, 29; Mississippian, 68–69; mountain lions, 54, 56, 57, 100, 105; naturalistic, 68; Olmec, 57; Padgett Figurine, 29, 47–48; panthers, 29, 47, 48, 50–51, 55, 105, 145, 154; *piasas*/Underwater Panthers, 68–69, 145; pipes, 50; pottery, 48, 54; pre-Columbian Amerindian, 50–51; pumas, 43, 54; religious use of, 56, 57; Rollins Figurine, 29, 47–48; sizes of, 48; steatite, 50; tokens, 56; wooden, 29, 47, 48, 55, 68. *See also* Animals; Key Marco Cat; Key Marco Cat, interpretations and purposes of

"Cats Before the Internet: Animal Art in Archaeology," 212n29

Caxambas Pass, 20, 109

Caxambas site, 21, 174, 191n71

Caxambas village, *17*

Cedar Key, FL, 80

Centennial International Exposition/World's Fair, 80, 85, 93

Ceramics: Caloosahatchee, 16; clays for, 16; dating of, 62, 66, 177; East Florida, 18; Englewood Incised, 188n41; fiber-tempered, 16; Fort Drum Incised, 16; Glades/Glades Plain/Glades Tooled, 16, 62, 63, 188n32, 195n13; Gordon's Pass Incised, 16; Key Largo Incised, 16, *63*, 195n13; Mississippian Period, 68; Northwest Florida, 18; panther-shaped, 48; plain, 16; sand-tempered, 16; Sanibel Incised, 16; shell-tempered, 68, 69; St. Johns series/St. Johns Check Stamped, 62, 188n41; Surfside Incised, 62; vessels, 48, 195n13; Weeden Island, 48; Woodland Period, 67; wood paddled-stamped, 37; Zuni, 125

Charlotte Harbor, *17*, 20

Chatham Bend, FL, 80

Chicago, IL, 137, 157

Chicago World's Fair, 137, 198n17

Choctawhatchee Bay, 145

Circa 1492: Art in the Age of Exploration, 147–49, 156

Citizens Community Bank, 151, 156

City of Marco Island, FL, 163, 168, 171, 209n66, 212n35. *See also* Marco Island, FL

Clark, Merald: on Key Marco artifacts, 57; on Key Marco Cat, 43; map and illustrations by, 17, 22, 29, 39, 53, 71, 82, 107

Clark, Robert, 100

Collier, Barbara, 80

Collier, George, 84

Collier, Margaret "Maggie" Eliza McIlvaine: and 1896 Key Marco excavation, 81, 108–9, 159, 197n14; death and grave of, 84; and F. H. Cushing, 81, 203n3; and Key Marco artifacts, 85, 203n3; marriage of, 80

Collier, Thomas, 84

Collier, William David: and 1896 Key Marco excavation, 108, 109, 179; and agriculture, 80, 81, 198n26; biography and personal characteristics of, 80, 81, 84; businesses owned by, 80, 81, 97, 107; and E. J. Watson, 80; family of, 80, 84, 203n3; and F. H. Cushing, 80, 81–83, 94, 95, 159, 179; and John Gomez, 80; and Key Marco site and artifacts, 80, 81–84, 93, 102; properties owned by, 97, 198n21; and World's Fair, 80, 93

Collier, Wilmer, 84

Collier, W. T., 78, 80, 81

Collier County, FL: creation of, 79, 209n61; displays of Key Marco Cat in, 150, 163, 171; economy of, 150; and Marco Island Historical Museum, 167, 168; Marco Island in, 10, 79; and preservation of cultural resources, 212n35

Collier County Board of County Commissioners, 211n24

Collier County Historical Archaeological Preservation Board, 212n35

Collier County Historical Society, 166

Collier County Museums (CCM): and Key Marco artifacts, 168–70, 210n6; and Key Marco Cat, x, 150–51, 156, 168–70, 211n24; and Marco Island Historical Museum, 167–70, 211n19; and Marco Island Historical Society, 211n19, 211n24; presentation at, 212n29

Collier County Tourist Development Council, 168

Columbian Historical Exposition, 137

Columbus, Christopher, 137, 147, 186n1

Columbus quincentenary, 161

Conwill, Kristin, *169*

Cordell, Ann, 63

Crane Point Museum and Nature Center, 210n6

Culin, Stewart: and C. D. Durnford, 94, 96; and C.F.W. Bergmann, 114, 121, 125; and F. H. Cushing, 94, 96, 114, 117, 118, 119, 120, 121–22, 125, 136, 137; and Key Marco artifacts, 94, 114, 118, 119, 127–28, 134, 137; and Penn Museum, 94, 127, 206n68; and Samuel Murray, 125; and Thomas Eakins, 125; and William Pepper, 114, 137

Cuno, James, 152

Cushing, Emily Tennison Magill, *82*, 96, 100, 107, 118, 125, 204n31

Cushing, Frank Hamilton: and 1876 World's Fair, 80; and 1893 World's Fair, 117, 137; and 1895 Key Marco excavation, 81, 85, 89, 94–96, 102, 200n11; and 1896 Tarpon Springs excavations, 54, 96; career of, 80, 91–92, 120, 134; and C.F.W. Bergmann, 116–17, 137; characteriza-

Cushing, Frank Hamilton—*continued*
tions of, 80, 120; on condition of artifacts, 93; death of, 84, 116, 122, 126, 137, 138, 206n67; drawing and portrait of, *82, 92,* 125; and E. J. Watson, 197n14; family of, *82,* 97, 118, 122, 125, 204n31; finances of, 113; fraud accusations against, 99, 113, 120; health of, 86, 94, 113, 114, 116, 137, 204n32; and J. W. Powell, 94; in Philadelphia, 80, 83, 94, 95, 96; reputation of, 3, 91, 92, 117, 134; and Samuel Murray, 125; and Stewart Culin, 125, 137; and Thomas Eakins, 125; in Washington, DC, 80, 110; and W. D. Collier, 81, 83, 95; and Wells Sawyer, 137; and William Pepper, 94, 96, 110, 137; and Zuni, 56, 120

Cushing, Frank Hamilton, and 1896 Key Marco excavation: on animal carvings from, 45; and artifact deterioration at site, 98–99, 101, 121; on artifact distribution across site, 72, 74; and artifact preservation during, 91, 106–7, 108, 118, 177; artifacts rejected by, 83–84; on canoe paddle from, 65; and concerns about looting, 106; conditions during, 98, 99, 101, 102, 103; correspondence with William Pepper during, 103, 104–5, 108, 109, 110, 118, 202n81; documentation by, 60, 86; on event depositing artifacts into site, 71–72, 73; field journals from, 81, 98, 99, 103; on figurehead/mask pairs at, 47, 57; on fire damage at, 71, 73; funding for, 96, 101, 103, 106, 127; and grid system, 60, *61, 88,* 95, 101; health during, 103; importance of, 92–93; and Maggie Collier, 203n3; on Native engineering at, 71–72; on Natives' original use of site, 21, 74, 89; on number, quality, and variety of artifacts from, 83, 93, 103, 104–5, 106; photos, drawings, paintings, and casts of artifacts made during, 121, 122; recruitment of C.F.W. Bergmann for, 116–17, 137; recruitment of Wells Sawyer for, 121, 137; scholarship on, 160; sections excavated at, 21, *61,* 83, 93; on shark-tooth tools, 37; on site features, 71–72, 89, 90, 101–2; site sketches and maps by, 22, *61;* on site stratigraphy, 86, 87; storage during, 85; techniques used at, 60, 97–98, 99, 106; timbers collected during, 177; and transportation of artifacts from, 91, 93, 106, 107, 109–11, 118, 120; travel to and from, 81, 96–97, 109, 110, 202n89; and visit by J. W. Powell, 107–8; and W. D. Collier, 81–83, 85, 159, 179; on wooden artifacts from, 11, 12, 14, 93, 103

Cushing, Frank Hamilton, and Key Marco artifacts, post-1896 excavation: cataloging and accessioning of, 113–15; colored images of, 120; distribution of, between museums, 114, 116, 126, 127, 128, 131, 206n67; and finances, 113, 114, 116; and health, 114, 116, 137, 138, 204n32; in Maine, 111, 118, 119, 120, 204n32; molds and casts of, 121–22, 125, 126; in Philadelphia, 111, 113, 118, 119, 120, 135; plans for exhibitions of, 136; preservation of, 111, 114, 117, 118–19, 120, 121; scholarship on, 111, 113, 114, 119, 135–36, 177; and Stewart Culin, 118, 119, 136; transportation of, 135; in Washington, DC, 111, 113, 114, 118, 119, 120, 127, 135–36; and William Pepper, 113–14, 116, 118, 119, 206n67

Cushing, Frank Hamilton, and Key Marco Cat: comparison of, to artifacts from other cultures, 50, 55, 105; on condition of, 13; discovery of, 3, 99–101, 102, 103; preservation and storage of, 115, 118, 119–21, 131; on purpose of, 54–55, 56; on quality of, 29, 105, 106; scholarship on, 135; on size and weight of, 13, 29, 105; on style and physical characteristics of, 26, 30, 35, 57, 105; on substances Natives applied to, 13, 38, 40; transportation of, 111, 113, 131, 135, 138, 158; in Washington, DC, 113, 114–15, 138, 158; on wood carved from, 12, 14

Cuthbert, George Elliott, 84–85

Cutler Fossil site, 187n26

Davenport, Christian, 48

Davis, Jack E., 83, 163

De Bry, Theodore, 194n56

Deltona Corporation, 174

Densmore, Frances, 207n4

Detroit Institute of Arts (DIA), 143, 144, 146, 156

Dismal Key site, 21

Disston, Joseph, 96

Dorsett, George, 100

Dorsey, H. W., 139

Durer, Albrecht, 148

Durnford, Charles Day, 83, 93–94, 95, 102, 175

Eakins, Thomas, 125

Ebaugh, Katherine, *165*

Egypt, 49, 50

Enslaved persons, 18

Estero Bay, 17

Ethnography, 54

Etowah site, 68
Everglades, FL, 80
Everglades City, FL, 70–71, 210n6
Exhibitions: *Ancient Art of the American Woodland Indians,* 51, 144–46, 148, 152, 154, 156; *Building a Dream: The 25 Year History of the Marco Island Historical Society,* 171–73; *Circa 1492: Art in the Age of Exploration,* 147–49, 156; *Hall of South Florida People and Environments,* 132; *Hero, Hawk, and Open Hand: American Indian Art of the Ancient Midwest and South,* 51, 151–53, 157; *Key Marco Expedition, The,* 150–51, 156; *North American Archaeology,* 139, *140, 141, 143,* 144, 156; *Paradise Found: 6,000 Year of People on Marco Island,* 157, 168, 171; *Shapeshifting: Transformations in Native American Art,* 153–54, 157
Expedition, 125

Fewkes, Jesse Walter, 6, 134
"First Catalogue of Collections from Muck-beds in the Court of the Pile Dwellers Key Marco S.W. Florida" (Bergmann), 114
Fiske, Richard S., 144
Florida: Archaic Period in, 15; and Confederacy, 79; education about Native peoples in, x; and European contact, 90; and Great Britain, 79; maps of, *19;* Native peoples in, 6, 15, 55, 194n56; Ponce de León in, 77; soil pH in, 199n54; and Spain, 78, 79; and United States, 79, 90
Florida (ship), 200n11
Florida, South and Southwest: agriculture in, 67; archaeology in, 6, *17,* 21; Archaic Period in, 15, 66; artifacts from, 85; Caloosahatchee culture in, 66; Calusa in, 16–17; chert in, 32; climate of, 11, 170; European contact in, 16–17; European diseases in, 78; Florida panther in, 44–45; Glades culture in, 66, 148; hurricanes in, 70; Native peoples in, 9, 10, 17, 78; paint ingredients in, 40; plants in, 9, 10; pottery in, 16, 62; topography of, 10, 20; and trade, 18; wood in, 11
Florida Anthropological Society, 163
Florida Archaeology Month, 163
Florida Association of Museums, 173
Florida Frontiers, 171
Florida Keys, 18, 161
Florida Public Archaeology Network, 212n29
Florida State Museum/Florida Museum of Natural History (FLMNH): Austin Bell and, ix; and casts of Key Marco artifacts, 122, 123; and Key Marco artifacts, ix, 65, 132, 210n6; loan of artifacts from, 150; staff of, 62, 63, 64; and wood identification, 12
Fontaneda, Hernando de Escalante, 19
Forbes, 171
Ford, James A., 64
Fort Center site, 48, 51, 55, 68, 145, 148
Fort Myers, FL, *17*
Fountain of Youth Park, 175
Franklin County, FL, 48

Gainesville, FL, 66, 122, 210n6
Gause, George, 99–100, 109
Gayer-Anderson Cat, 49–50
Geology, 2
Gilliland, Marion S.: on abandonment of Key Marco site, 70, 74; on big cat remains at Key Marco, 45–46; on dating of Key Marco site and artifacts, 61, 65; on deposition of artifacts in Key Marco muck, 73–74; and exhibition of Key Marco artifacts, 150; on human remains at Key Marco, 54, 75; on Key Marco settlement patterns, 74; on lack of European artifacts at Key Marco, 61; on modern development at Key Marco site, 174; on photos, watercolors, and casts of Key Marco artifacts, 122; on use of shark-tooth tools, 35
Glades County, FL, 145
Glades culture: and agriculture, 67; attribution of Key Marco Cat to, 4; and Calusa, 16; ceramic typology of, 62; and Key Marco artifacts, 148; map of, *17;* and Muspa, 20; regional impact of, 77; singularity of, 66–67; and tools, 30, 31, 32, 38; and trade, 18
Goggin, John M., 62, 207n4
Gomez, John, 80
Goodland Point site, *17,* 21
Gretna, PA, 119
Griffin, John, 68
Gulf, The: The Making of an American Sea (Davis), 163
Gulf of Mexico, 10, *17,* 21, 95

Hall of South Florida People and Environments, 132
"Hand-built Island, or Shell City of the Ancient Sea Dwellers of Florida," *22*

Haven, Maine, 111, 118, 204n32
Hearst, Phoebe A., 96
Hearst, William Randolph, 96
Hero, Hawk, and Open Hand: American Indian Art of the Ancient Midwest and South, 51, 151–53, 157
Heye Foundation. *See* National Museum of the American Indian (NMAI)/Museum of the American Indian, Heye Foundation
Hickman, Jane, 125
Hodge, Frederick, 134
Holmes, William Henry, 127, 130–31, 134, 139
"Homeward Bound: The Incredible Journey of Key Marco's Artifacts" (Bell), 212n29
Hontoon Island, FL, 175
Hope Mound site, 96
Hopewell Tradition, 57, 66, 67, 68
Horr's Island sites: Archaic Period at, 15–16; artifacts from, 21, 32, 37, 174, 177, 190n39; topography of, 20
Horse Capture, Joe D., 7
Houston, TX, 144, 146, 156
Houston Museum of Fine Arts, 144, 146, 156
Hovenden, Thomas, 92
Howe, Steve, 20
How to Do Florida, 171
Hrdlička, Aleš, 5, 14, 24, 83, 174
Hudson, Alfred, 100
Hurricanes, 70–71, 168, 170
Hutchinson site, 48

Indians. *See* Native and indigenous peoples
Institute of Museum and Library Services (IMLS), 166

Judd, Neil, 139

Kaeppler, Adrienne L., 146
Kassabaum, Megan, 67–68, 125
Kendall, FL, 48
Key Marco, FL, 4, 79, 199n54. *See also* Marco Island, FL
Key Marco Cat: animals possibly represented by, 43, 45, 47, 51, 100, 105, 114, *115*, 128, 139, 180; appeal and fame of, ix, 3, 6, 9, 25, 79, 159–66, 179, 180, 211n10, 211n11; artifacts similar to, 13, 47–48, 148; authenticity of, 117; cataloging of, 114, *115*, 186n8; C.F.W. Bergmann and, 112, 116, 131; comparison of, to artifacts from other cultures, 50, 55, 105; condition of, 13, 132, 135, 160; dating of, 5, 9, 20–21, 50, 59, 62, 64, 66, 69, 76, 145, 153, 154; depositing of, in muck, 59, 69–70; discovery of, 3, 4, 21, 77, 79, 91, 99–101; historic and cultural events during life of, 5, 90; importance of, 24; insurance value of, 151–52; legacy of, 180; location/provenance of, 95, 101, 102, 151; Marco Island residents and, 154–56; miles traveled by, 4, 160; nickname for, 186n8 (introduction); ownership of, 4; Penn Museum and, 4, 127; in Philadelphia, 111, 135; potential repatriation of, 178, 179; preservation and storage of, 85, 90, 91, 106, 115, 118, 119–21, 131, 155, 160; protection of, 178; quality of, 26, 29, 105, 106, 142, 153; R. S. Fiske on, 144; scholarship on, 135; S. P. Langley and, 128, 130, 131, 139; substances applied to, 13, 38, 40, 66, 119–20; transportation of, 106, 110, 111, 113, 118, 131, 135, 138, 144, 158, 160; uniqueness of, 3; in Washington, DC, 110, 113, 114–15, 119, 138, 158; X-ray fluorescence analysis of, 40, 66. *See also* Cats, artistic representations of
Key Marco Cat, creation of: Calusa and, 4, 9, 15, 18, 20–21, 159; date of, 5; geographic origins, 21, 145; Glades culture and, 4; Muspa and, 20–21; process used for, 9, 10, 25, 26, 30, 33, 38, 40–41, 148; skillfulness of, 30, 40–41; wood carved from, 3, 9, 10, 12–14, 15, 26, 31, 32–33, 163, 187n24
Key Marco Cat, exhibition of: in 1896, at American Philosophical Society, 135; in 1913–50s, 1962–84, at Smithsonian Institution, 4, 5, 139–44, 208n29; in 1985–86, in Detroit Institute of Art traveling exhibition *(Ancient Art),* 51, 144–46, 148, 152, 154, 156; in 1991–92 *(Circa 1492),* 147–50; in 1995–96, at Collier County Museum, 150–51, 156; in 1999–2000, at Citizens Community Bank, 151, 156; in 2004–5, in Art Institute of Chicago traveling exhibition *(Hero, Hawk, and Open Hand),* 151–53, 157; in 2012, by Peabody Essex Museum, 153–54, 157; in 2018–26, at Marco Island Historical Museum, 5, 156, 157, 158, 168–71, 173, 179; misperceptions about, 134, 154–55; unusually long time of, 4, 134, 155–56, 160
Key Marco Cat, images and reproductions of: 3-D model, 175, *176;* in 1896 Key Marco excavation report, 135; drawings, *29, 34, 39,*

44, 104, 163, *165,* 211n10, 211n11; at Florida museums, 132, 161, 168; ice sculpture, *166;* intellectual property rights to, 163, 178; molds and casts, 121, 122–26, 158–60, 205n57; photos, *8,* 26, *27–28, 100, 123, 161, 162,* 163, *164, 172, 173;* statue, 168, *169;* ubiquity of, 161–63
Key Marco Cat, interpretations and purposes of: as abstract representation of a panther, 51; difficulty establishing, 58; as fetish or god of war or hunt, 54–55; as literal depiction of masked performer, 51; and masculinity, 51–52; as *piasa,* 69, 154; possibilities for, 48; and shamanism, 56–57; as shrine furniture, 148; as symbol of clan or kinship, 55–56, 67; as symbol of seasons, 57; as symbol of transformation, 6–7, 51, 152–53; as vehicle for engagement, 159–60; as zoomorphic representation of a panther, 26
Key Marco Cat, style and physical characteristics of: cracks, 122; distinctness of, 154; ears, 26; facial features, 30, 38, 48, 69, 152; feline characteristics, 26, 30, 105; F. H. Cushing on, 26, 30, 35, 57, 105; hardness, 12; head, 105; height and weight, x, 3, 13, 26, 29, 33, 45, 52, 105, 189n6, 205n57; human characteristics, 26–30, 51–52, 105, 152; limbs, 30, 57; paws, 30, 105, 190n22; posture, 26–30, 51, 105; scroll, 69; shoulders, 30; silhouette, 51–52; size, ix; symmetry and asymmetry, 30, 36, 38, 105, 122; tail, 30, 105; tool marks, 35, 105; Wells Sawyer on, 103–4, 105, 106; wood carved from, 3, 9, 10, 12–14, 15, 26, 31, 32–33, 163, 187n24; workmanship quality, 26, 29, 30, 105
Key Marco Expedition, The (exhibition), 150–51, 156
Key Marco site: 1895 excavation of, 81, 94–95, 102, 199n8, 200n14; 20th- and 21st-century excavations of, 62, 63, 66, 68, 174; abandonment or destruction of, 24, 70, 74, 75, 174; archaeological features at, 21, 24, 68, *84,* 89, 101–2, 174; Calusa and, 154; Court of Pile Dwellers at, 21, *23, 61,* 62, 72, 73, 76, 83, 86, 87, *88,* 89–90, 93; dating of, 54, 60–64, 68, 69, 196n44; historical documentation on, 81, 84, 98, 99–100; images and maps of, *17, 22, 23, 61, 71, 84,* 87, *88, 97,* 102, 140; location of, *17,* 21, 92, 93, 163, *165,* 209n61; modern investigation of, 24; owners of, 79–85; as possible location of Muspa, 21; purposes of, 89–90; significance of, 21–24, 59, 61, 85, 92, 99; size of, 93; soil at, 70, 71, 86; and trade, 67; use of grid system at, 60, 95, 100; vegetation at, 102; W. D. Collier and, 96, 102; weather at, 71–72, 73. *See also* Cushing, Frank Hamilton, and 1896 Key Marco excavation; Marco Island, FL; Muspa; Pepper-Hearst Expedition
Key Marco site, artifacts from: absence of canoe remains among, 70, 74, 89; absence of European goods among, 72, 74, 196n44; adzes, *129;* canoe fragments, 70; cataloging of, 113–14, *115;* celts, 68; ceramics, 62–64, 135, 177, 188n32, 195n14; chert, 32; condition of, 70, 177; coral, 177; cordage, 64, 65; cups, 80; dating of, 54, 60–61, 62–64, 65–66, 67–69, 72, 76, 175, 177; decoration on, 67, 68, *129;* depositing of, in muck, 59, 71, 72–73, 75, 76, 77–78; deterioration and destruction of, 98–99, 101, 131, 175; division of, between institutions, 126–31; earbuttons, 55; early anthropologists and, 134; exhibition of, 135–38, 139, 148, 168–70, 210n6; and fire damage, 73–74; flint, 177; floats, 98; geographic origins of, 175, 177; gorgets, 68, *129;* gourd, 63, 85, 93, 98; horn, 93; images and photos of, 139; inventories of, ix; limestone, 177; location/provenance of, 21, 101; Marco Island Historical Society and, 174; netting, 64, 93, 94, 98, *129;* number of, 60, 93, 101, 127; opportunities for further research on, 175–78; ornaments, 93, *129;* painted, 99; pendants, *129;* picks, 98; pipes, *161;* plant-fiber, 21, 64, 65, 74, 80, 93, 94, 98, *129;* "plumett," 100; polished objects, *129;* potential repatriation of, 179; preservation of, 85, 87, 89, 90, 91, 107; processing of, 112, 113–16; redistribution of, between museums, 131–32; rope, 80; saturation of, 87–89; sharkskin, 34; shark-tooth, 93; shell, 68, 80, 93, *129,* 139; significance of, 6, 85, 90, 93, 95, 98, 99, 103; Spanish olive jar, 62; stays, 72; stone, 32, 68, 93, *129,* 139, 177; thatch, 64, 98; tools and tool parts, 83–84, 93, 94, 140–42; transportation of, 106–7, 117–21, 135; wax, 100; weapons, 55, 93; W. D. Cushing and, 80, 81, 83–84
Key Marco site, bone artifacts from: awls, *129;* barracuda jaws, 35; big cat jaws, 45–46, *47;* bodkins, *129;* condition of, 177; daggers, 75; dating of, 177–78; fish jaw, *129;* human, 54, 75, 178, 179; pins, 89, 98; points, 21, 38; tool parts, 35; unspecified, 93; whistle, *129*

Key Marco site, wooden artifacts from: artifacts similar to, 67–68; atlatls, 12, *36,* 93, 110, 119; boards, 64, 85, 100; bowls, 93, 98, 100, 103, *129,* 140, *141;* canoe paddle, 64, 65, 70, 73, 74, 98, *129;* canoes, toy, 33, 93, 100, 119, *129;* carvings, 138; condition of, 65–66, 74, 89, 93, 98–99, 175, 177; cups, 94, *129,* 140, *141;* dating of, 64–66, 148, 175–77; decoration on, 12, 36–37, 64, 68, 110; figureheads, 21, 47, 57, 70, 93, 94, 100, 102, 110, 129, 140, 148, *161;* figurines, 98, 99, 100, 110, 163; fire damage on, 73–74; float pegs, 94, 140, *141;* images and photos of, 99, *100,* 121, 122, 138, 139, *149;* line reels, 98; locations/provenance of, 65, 70, 72, 76; Maggie Collier and, 85; masks, 21, 47, 52, 55, 57, 70, 85, 93, 99, 103, 110, 120, 125, 138, 140, *141;* molds and casts of, 121–22, 125–26, 175; mortars and pestles, 93, 98, 100, *129;* number of, 93; painted, 21, 40, 52, 64, 85, 93, 99, 103, 110, 120, 138; pestles, *129;* photos of, *46, 172;* preservation of, 99, 119; spearshafts, 72, *129;* staves, 55; stools, 93; tablets, 85, 93, 138; tools and tool parts, 36–37, 93, 98; trays, 93, *129;* vases, 103; vessels, 62, 94, 135; W. D. Collier and, 80, 93
Key West, FL, 78, 80
Kice Island, FL, 20
Kozuch, Laura, 37, 191n71

Lake Okeechobee, 13, 18, 47, 48
Langford, Walter, 197n14, 206n70
Langley, Samuel P., 127, 128, 129, 131, 139
LeCompte, Elise, ix
Lee County, FL, 11, 79, 171, 209n61
Le Moyne, Jacques, 194n56
Leonardo da Vinci, 148
Libby, Williard F., 64
Little Ice Age, 16
Little Salt Spring site, 187n26
López de Velasco, Juan, 20
Louvre, 2
Löwenmensch ("lion-human") figurine, 49
Ludlow, Frederick, 197n14

Macomb, Alexander, 79
Madrid, Spain, 137
Mahoney Figurine/Riddle Statue, 29, 47–48
Maine, 111, 116, 118, 120
Marathon, FL, 210n6
Marco Hotel: 1896 Key Marco excavation crew and, 97; in 21st century, 198n21; F. H. Cushing and, 81, 97, 159; images of, 97, 198n21; location of, 198n24; owners of, 80, 81, 97, 198n21; use of, for processing Key Marco artifacts, 81, 107
Marco Island, FL: 19th-century settlement of, 78, 79; 20th- and 21st-century hurricanes in, 70, 170; 20th-century development of, 174, 212n35; and agriculture, 79; Aleš Hrdlička on, 5; archaeology of, 3, 11, 13, 15–16; borders of, 200n12; businesses on, 80, 81, 97; and "Calusa curse," 84; Caxambas site on, 191n71; ceramics from, 188n41; characteristics of, 10; climate of, 10; communication with, 101; and Confederacy, 79; and display of Key Marco Cat, 151, 156; and display of Key Marco site artifacts, 170; economy of, 163; European contact in, 61; figurines from, 13; and fishing, 79; Florida panthers on, 44; and Great Britain, 79; habitats on, 10; Key Marco Cat images on, 163–66; during Little Ice Age, 16; location of, 10, 16; map and images of, *17, 82;* Natives and, 10, 15, 16, 19, 21, 79; as navigational landmark, 79; plants on, 10, 11–12, 14; population of, 92–93, 163; as possible location of Muspa, 19; pottery from, 16, 18; property owners on, 79–85; and Seminole Wars, 79; size of, 10; and Spain, 79; topography of, 20; and trade, 80; transportation to, 94, 95; and United States, 79; and U.S. Civil War, 79. *See also* Key Marco site; Key Marco site, artifacts from; Muspa
Marco Island Cemetery, 198n35
Marco Island Historical Museum (MIHM): Calusa Gallery of, 168; and cast of Key Marco Cat, 175; collections of, 174–75; establishment and evolution of, ix, x, 155, 167–68, 173; exhibitions at, 157, 168, 171–73, 187n24, 198n24; and Key Marco artifacts, 173; and Key Marco Cat, 40, 45, 66, 155, 157, 163, 167–71, 173, 180; location of, ix, 167; photos of, *167, 169;* pre-Columbian ceramics at, 63; staffing of, 167; temporary closing of, 5, 186n10 (introduction)
Marco Island Historical Society (MIHS): and artifact dating, 177; and cast of Key Marco Cat, 122–23, 125, 158; collections of, 174, 177, 188n32, 188n41, 190n39, 191n71, 195n13; and Collier County Museums, 211n19, 211n24; establishment of, 163; and exhibition of Key Marco Cat, 151, 166–67, 168–71; impact of, 163; and Key Marco artifacts, 168–70; and Key Marco Cat,

x, 57; Key Marco Cat ice sculpture at, *166;* staff of, ix–x, 168, *169*
Marco River and Big Marco Pass, 21, 95, 200n12
Marquardt, William H., ix, 31, 56, 69, 207n4
Mason, J. Alden, 207n4
Mason, Otis T., 131, 134, 206n84
Material culture, 2, 42, 185n1 (introduction)
Material Culture of Key Marco, Florida, The (Gilliland), 65
McGee, William J., 127, 134
McGoun, William E., 72–73
McIlvaine, Margaret "Maggie" Eliza. *See* Collier, Margaret "Maggie" Eliza McIlvaine
Memoirs (Fontaneda), 19
Mercer, Henry C., 94, 134
Miami, FL, 18, 48, 187n26
Milanich, Jerald, 65, 66, 68, 72, 207n4
Millar Figurine, 13, 29
Mississippian Period, 56, 66, 67, 145, 148, 154
Mitchell, Henry Laurens, 77
Monroe County, FL, 79
Mooney, James, 134
Moore, Clarence Bloomfield, 72, 83, 84, 94, 199n8
Moore, Katherine, *47*
Morgan Island, FL, 20
Mound Key, FL: as Calusa capital, 17, 52, 54, 75, 90; map of, *17;* and Muspa, 20; Spanish missionaries at, 18, 74
Moundville site, 67, 68
Murray, Samuel, 125, 126
Murray, Samuel (Van Vechten), *126*
Murrays Studio, 119, 121, 125
Museum Excellence Award, 168
Museum of Florida History, 210n6
Museum of the American Indian, Heye Foundation, 84. *See* National Museum of the American Indian (NMAI)/Museum of the American Indian, Heye Foundation
Museum of the Everglades, 210n6
Museum of the Islands, 210n6
Museums: and anthropology, 133; and artifact conservation, 178; and artifact repatriation, 178–79; challenges for, 173; and exhibition development, 152; functions of, 2, 4, 42, 180; history and evolution of, 133, 134, 145, 150, 152, 153, 154, 158; and idiosyncratic/iconic objects, 2–3, 160; increased number of, 166; and objects, 2, 4; and preservation, 180; and provenance, 9; reinterpretations of artifacts in, 179–80; staff of, 112, 113, 117, 136; treatment of artifacts by, 112
Museum Ulm, 49
Muspa, 18–20, *19,* 21, *53,* 75, 78. *See also* Marco Island, FL

Naples, FL, *17,* 94, 150, 156, 161, 210n6
National Anthropological Archives, 95
National Endowment for the Humanities (NEH), 155, 174
National Gallery of Art (NGA), 144, 145, 147, 148, 149, 156
National Geographic Society, 113, 135–36
National Museum of Natural History (NMNH): and casts of Key Marco artifacts, 122; divisions and departments of, 119, 131, 139; in early 2020s, 208n29; F. H. Cushing at, 119; history of, 138–42; and Key Marco artifacts, 119, 127, 131, 136, 140–42, 203n11; location of, 185n7; photos of, 139–42; staff and leaders of, 91, 127, 144, 163. *See also* Smithsonian Institution; Smithsonian Institution, and Key Marco Cat
National Museum of the American Indian (NMAI)/Museum of the American Indian, Heye Foundation, 83, 84, 132, 198n32
Native American Graves Protection and Repatriation Act (NAGPRA), 178–79. *See also* Antiquities Act of 1906
Native and indigenous peoples: and animals, 152; and artifact repatriation, 178–79; archaeology of, 21; Archaic, 15; Aztec, 147; belief systems of, 154; and celebrations of Christopher Columbus, 147; Cherokee, 56; Cochiti, 57; Creek, 20, 55, 56, 78; and crosses, 196n44; ethnographic accounts of, 54; images of, *29,* 194n56; Iroquois, 31; Maya, 25; Mississippian, 56; and museums, 133, 145, 152, 153–54, 178–79; Muspa Indians, 19; and objects, 2, 7; Olmec, 57; oral histories of, 154; Paleoindian, 15, 187n26; and panthers, 54, 55, 56; and religion, 56–57; Seminole, 20, 55, 56, 78, 79; Smithsonian Institution and, 139–40, 179; Spanish Indians, 20; Taíno, 31, 147; Timucuan, 55; Tocobaga, 16; Ucita, 55; US anthropology and, 133; Woodland cultures, 56; Yamasee Indians, 20, 78; Zuni Indians, 55, 91–92, 120, 125
New York Magazine, 149
North American Archaeology, 139, *140, 141, 143,* 144, 156
North Florida, 37

Objects, 1–3, 185n1 (introduction). *See also* Artifacts; Material culture
Ocmulgee site, 46, 55
Okeechobee area, *17*
Olde Marco Historic Village, 163, *165*, 174. *See also* Marco Island, FL

Padgett Figurine, 13, 29, 47–48
Palm Beach County, FL, 48
Pané, Ramón, 31
Panther Key, FL, 80
Paradise Found: 6,000 Year of People on Marco Island, 157, 168, 171
Parezo, Nancy J., 185n1 (introduction)
Paris Exposition, 138, 140
Peabody Essex Museum (PEX), 153–54
Penn Museum: and 1895 Key Marco excavation, 94; American Collections of, 125; C.F.W. Bergmann and, 116, 117; Department of Archaeology and Paleontology of, 116; F. H. Cushing and, 111, 116, 119, 135; founder of, 94; and Key Marco Cat, 4, 105, 127, 128–29, 203n11; staff and leaders of, 62, 67, 125, 136, 206n68, 206n71
Penn Museum, and Key Marco artifacts: big cat jawbones, 46, *47*; cataloging of, 203n11; distribution of, to other museums, 132; division of, with Smithsonian Institution, 114, 116, 127–30; exhibition of, 136; found by C. D. Durnford, 94; loans of, 115–16, 148, 170; molds and casts of, 122, 125; preservation of, 118; storage of, 65
Penny, David W., 145
Pepper, William: and 1895 Key Marco excavation, 137, 199n8; and 1896 Key Marco excavation, 108, 109–10; and C. B. Moore, 94, 199n8; death of, 116; and F. H. Cushing, 94, 96, 103, 104, 106, 107, 113, 114, 117, 118, 119, 127, 136, 137, 206n67; and J. W. Powell, 94, 96; and Key Marco artifacts, 114, 127, 136, 206n67; and Penn Museum, 94; and Stewart Culin, 114, 137; and University of Pennsylvania, 94
Pepper Clinical Laboratory/Pepper Medical Laboratory, 109, 110, 135
Pepper-Hearst Expedition: 100th anniversary of, 166–67; and 1893 World's Fair, 198n17; and conditions at Key Marco, 98, 101; delay in, 96; and discovery of Key Marco Cat, 4; drawings of, *107*; end of, 107, 108–9; funding for, 96, 101, 103, 106, 127; importance of Key Marco Cat to, 106; J. W. Powell and, 134; and Key Marco Cat, 4; members of, 96, 99, 100, 107, 108, 109, 116–17, 121, 137; procedures used during, 97–98; and travel to Key Marco, 96–97; University of Pennsylvania and, 139; Wells Sawyer on, 101, 107. *See also* Cushing, Frank, and 1896 Key Marco excavation
"Pepper-Hearst Expedition, The. The Ancient Shell Settlement of Key Marco Florida Topographic Survey" (Sawyer), *23*
Philadelphia, PA: American Philosophical Society in, 135; antique dealers in, 122; casts of Key Marco artifacts in, 122; C.F.W. Bergmann in, 116; F. H. Cushing in, 94, 95, 96, 113, 114, 118, 119, 120, 135; Independence Hall in, 125; Key Marco artifacts in, 80, 110, 111, 113, 118, 127, 136; Key Marco Cat in, 111; Murrays Studio in, 125; W. D. Collier in, 80; William Pepper in, 109; World's Fair in, 83
Philadelphia Museum of Art, 125
Pine Island, FL, 210n6
Pineland, FL: abandonment of, 76; archaeology in, 11–12, 18, 24; artifacts from, 16, 32; map of, *17*; wood sources at, 11–12, 14
Ponce de León, Juan, 5, 61, 75, 77
Portrait of Frank Hamilton Cushing (Hovenden), *92*
Poverty Point site, 67, 177
Powell, John Wesley: as anthropology pioneer, 134; death of, 206n69; and F. H. Cushing, 94, 96, 107–8, 116, 127, 136; and Key Marco artifacts, 116, 127, 128, 130, 136; at Smithsonian, 94, 127; and visit to 1896 Key Marco excavation, 107–8; and William Pepper, 94, 96
"Preliminary Report on the Exploration of Ancient Key Dweller Remains on the Gulf Coast of Florida, A" (Cushing): on drawings, paintings, and casts of Key Marco artifacts, 121; on exhibition of Key Marco artifacts, 135; on fire damage to Key Marco artifacts, 71–72; on how Key Marco artifacts ended up in muck, 71; on Key Marco Cat, 100, 101, 103, 105; in Marco Island Historical Museum collection, 175; on preliminary excavations, 102; on preservation of Key Marco artifacts, 117, 121
Preservation Assistance Grants, 174
Proceedings of the American Philosophical Society, 135
Punta Gorda, FL, 94, 95

Purdy, Barbara A., 29, 64, 65–66, 122, 160, 207n4
Putnam, Frederick Ward, 134

Randell Research Center, 24
Riddle Statue/Mahoney Figurine, 29, 47–48
Rochester, NY, 94, 96
Rogel, Juan, 18, 52, 56, 74, 75–76
Rollins Figurine/Cat, 29, 47–48
"Rotary Club's 1982 Edition Marco Island Guide," *164*
Russell, Karen Kramer, 153

Safford Mound site, 96
Saint Louis, MO, 153, 157, 161
Saint Louis Art Museum, 153, 157
Salem, MA, 153
Sanibel Historic Museum and Village, 210n6
Sanibel Island, FL, 70, 161, 210n6
San Juan, PR, *161*
Sarasota County, FL, 187n26
Sawyer, Wells Moses: and 1876 World's Fair, 80; and 1893 World's Fair, 137; correspondence of, during 1896 Key Marco excavation, 101, 103, 107; departure of, from 1896 Key Marco excavation, 109; drawings and paintings by, 99, 101, 103, *108*, 121, 122, 140, 150, 151; field documents of, 150; image of, *82;* and Key Marco artifacts, 73, 101; and Key Marco Cat, 12, 35, 101, 103–4, 105, 106, 178; on Key Marco site, 86, 87; maps by, *23*, 87, *88*, 89, 198n21; photos by/attributed to, *28*, *36*, *46*, *84*, 95, 97, 99, *100*, 121, 178; on pre-Columbian tools, 35, 37; and US Geological Survey, 137
Sayford, Irving, 109
Seminole Wars, 79
Seville, Spain, 52
Shapeshifting: Transformations in Native American Art, 153–54, 157
Shen, Chou, 148
Silver Spray (ship), *82*, 96, 97, 101, 108, 109
Smith, Bruce, 144, 153
Smithsonian (publication), 171
Smithsonian Institution: and 1893 Chicago World's Fair, 137; and 1896 Key Marco excavation, 96; and 1900 Paris Exposition, 138; Arts and Industries Building of, 138, 185n7; Bureau of American Ethnology of, 94, 114, 127, 133, 134, 138; C.F.W. Bergmann and, 117; Department of Anthropology of, 112, 146, 148, 158; exhibitions at, 139, *140*, *141*, *143*, 144, 156; history of, 146; and Hope diamond, 3; and Key Marco artifacts, 114, 127–30, 148; Museum Support Center of, 5, 143, 144, 146, 189n6, 205n57, 206n86, 209n48; and repatriation of Native artifacts, 179; staff and leaders of, 80, 94, 127, 131, 136, 139, 144, 146, 148, 163, 206n70
Smithsonian Institution, and Key Marco Cat: accession number of, 186n8 (introduction), 203n11; acquisition and accession of, 4, 128–31, 138, 203n11; casts of, 122; exhibition of, at Smithsonian, 4, 5, 139–44, 155, 156, 157, 208n29; images of, 178; and Key Marco Cat postage stamp, 161; loan of, to other museums, x, 143–46, 147–54, 155–57, 158, 168–70, 173, 211n24; as part of Smithsonian collection, ix, 3, 79; storage of, 5, 112, 131, 139, 146, 160, 206n86; testing of, 40, 175; transportation of, to Smithsonian, 91, 111, 138
South America, 50, 57
Southeast, U.S., 56, 66, 67, 68, 154
Southeastern Ceremonial Complex (SECC), 66, 67, 68
Southeastern Museums Conference, 173
Southern Cult, 68
Southwest, U.S., 56, 57
Southwest Florida Archaeological Society, 212n29
Southwest Florida Regional Planning Council, 163
Spiro site, 68
St. Augustine, FL, 175, 177
Stevenson, Mathilda Coxe, 134
Stevenson, Sara Yorke, 116, 127, 134, 136, 206n71
Stirling, Matthew, 83, 207n4
St. James City, FL, 97
St. Johns County, FL, 79
Storms, 70–71, 73, 168, 170
Sturtevant, William, 163, 207n4
Suitland, MD, 143, 144, 189n6, 205n57, 206n86

Tallahassee, FL, 161, 210n6
Tampa, FL, 80
Tampa Bay, FL, 16, 32, 55
Tarpon Springs, FL, 96, 109, 111
Tarpon Springs site, 54
Tebeau, Charlton, 174
Ten Thousand Islands, FL, 80
Thimmer, Keaton, x
Thompson, Raymond H., 185n1 (introduction)

Tools: adzes, 32, 35; awls, 34, 37, 38; blades, 190n40; blowpipes, 33; bone, 18, 35, 38; celts, 32; ceramic, 18; chert, 32, 35; chisels, 34; choppers, 32; for cutting, 32, 34, 38; daggers, 38; drills, 37; fishing paraphernalia, 38; flint, 35; gouges, 33; hammers, 35; images of, *34, 46;* knives, 35, 38; limestone, 35; planes, 190n47; plant fiber, 18; points, 38; sawfish-tooth, 35, 38; saws, 35; scrapers, 33, 38, 190n47; sharkskin, 33–34; shark-tooth, 11, 14, 30, *34,* 35, 37–38, 190n40; shell, 15, 18, 30–31, 32, 33, 34–35, 190n47; slicers, 38; spokeshaves, 33, 190n47; stone, 18; uses of, 35; wood, 18. *See also* Key Marco site, artifacts from: tools and tool parts; Key Marco site, wooden artifacts from: tools and tool parts
Townsend, Richard F., 152, 153
Toyo, Sesshu, 148
Trees and woody plants: basswood, 14; black gum, 11; brazilwood, 14; buttonwood, 11, 12, 14, 15, 163, 187n24; cypress, 11, 12, 14; driftwood, 14; Florida privet, 11; as fuel, 33; grape, 11, 12; gumbo-limbo, 11, 14; heartwood, 33; hickory, 14; inkwood, 14; ironwood, 11, 12, 13; lignum vitae, 11, 13, 14; mangrove, 11, 12, 13, 14, 72, 86, 98, 102; mayten, 11; oak, 14, 33; palmetto, 11, 98; pine, 11, 13, 175; saffron plum, 11; saltbush, 11, 12; sea grape, 11, 12; spruce, 11, 14; stopper, 11; strangler fig, 40; treatment of, 33, 35; wax myrtle, 11, 12; wild coffee, 11, 12; wild lime, 11, 12
Tucker site, 48
Tykot, Robert, 177

United States, 79, 90, 152
United States National Museum. *See* National Museum of Natural History (NMNH)
University of California Los Angeles, 64
University of Florida, 24, *169*
University of Houston, 65
University of Michigan, 64
University of Pennsylvania: and 1896 Key Marco excavation, 96, 139; and 1900 Paris Exposition, 138; artifact loan agreements with, 211n24; departments of, 96, 137; and F. H. Cushing, 113; and Key Marco artifacts, 96, 110; Pepper Clinical Laboratory of, 96; staff of, 128; Wister Institute at, 125. *See also* Penn Museum
University of South Florida, 175
USA Today, 171
US Geological Survey, 137

Van Beck, John C., 63
Van Beck, Linda M., 63
Van Vechten, Carl, *126*

Wagner, Carl, 168
Walcott, Charles D., 131
Walker, Karen, ix, 69
Walton County, FL, 145
Ward, Henry Augustus, 96
Wardle, Harriet Newell, 62, 72, 207n4
Ward's Natural Science Establishment, 96
Warm Mineral Springs site, 187n26
Washington, D.C.: *Ancient Art of the American Woodland Indians* in, 145; antique dealers in, 122; Bureau of Engraving and Printing in, 161; C.F.W. Bergmann in, 116; F. H. Cushing in, 81, 110, 111, 113, 118, 119, 120, 135–36; J. W. Powell in, 128; Key Marco artifacts in, 117, 118, 119, 127, 135, 136; Key Marco Cat in, 110, 111, 113, 138, 145, 153, 156, 158; National Gallery of Art in, 144; R.C.H. Brock in, 128; Smithsonian Institution in, 111, 138; W. H. Holmes in, 128
Washington Post, 136, 149
Watson, Edgar J., 80, 197n14
Wedel, Waldo, 207n4
Wheeler, Ryan J., 43, 56
Widmer, Randolph J., 24, 65–66, 68, 73, 174, 207n4
Wierzbowski, William, 125
Wightman site, 70
Wilkins, Charles, 94, 95, 102
Winter Park, FL, 47
Wistar, Isaac Jones, 125
"Wood Carvers of Southern Florida," 142
Woodland Period, 56, 66, 67–68, 145, 154
Wooster, Casey, *169*
World's Columbian Exposition, 137
World's Fairs, 80, 85, 93, 117, 133

Yale Peabody Museum of Natural History, 62

Zeder, Melinda, 148
Zemis, 31
Zuni Indians, 55, 91–92, 120, 125

AUSTIN J. BELL is curator of collections for the Marco Island Historical Society and a consulting scholar at the Penn Museum. Austin is a Florida native and lives in Marco Island, where he was named the 2018 Citizen of the Year by the *Naples Daily News*.